Acting On Promise

Reflections of a University President

To

Judy

life companion, constructive critic, and best friend

Acting On Promise
Reflections of a University President

Robert J. Bruce

Polyglot
Press™
Philadelphia

THIS IS A POLYGLOT PRESS ACADEMIC EDITION

Published in the United States by Polyglot Press, Inc.

A member of Polyglot Press Alliance

Philadelphia • Barcelona • Bejing • Rio de Janeiro • Toronto • London •
Sydney • Cairo • Tel Aviv • Mexico DF • Moscow • Trivandrum

Acting On Promise:
Reflections of a University President

by Robert J. Bruce, Trade Cloth

ISBN 10: 1-4115-9983-7

ISBN 13: 978-1-4115-9983-3

Polyglot Press, the portrayal of the parrot on a perch, and the portrayal of a magnifying glass with the words "high legibility typeface" in the lens, and the portrayal of a computer monitor with the words "custom typeset" on the screen are all trademarks of Polygot Press, Inc.

This book is printed on acid-free paper. Designed for readability using Adobe Minion type family.

Library of Congress Cataloging-in-Publication Data

Bruce, Robert J.

Acting on promise : reflections of a university president / Robert J.

Bruce.-- Polyglot Press academic ed.

p. cm.

Includes index.

ISBN-13: 978-1-4115-9983-3 (alk. paper)

1. Universities and colleges--United States--Administration. 2. College presidents--United States. I. Title.

LB2341.B69 2008

378.1'2092--dc22

2008016055

Composition by Polyglot Press, Inc., Philadelphia, PA. www.polyglotpress.com

Printed in the United States of America.

Table of Contents

Preface

When I retired from the presidency of Widener University after 20 years, I told some of my colleagues that I was considering writing a book about my experiences in higher education. The emphasis would be on my years at Widener, two decades of institutional transition that changed the University into a regional and, in the case of several programs, national institution. A confluence of circumstances had made the promise and potential of the University unlimited.

I began writing after months of reviewing personal papers and other materials accumulated during my career. The task proved more difficult than anticipated leading to many iterations of the outline, a dozen or more drafts, and several periods of dormancy.

The content of the book is based on my 40 years of administrative experience in higher education at four institutions, but most particularly, on the years spent as president of Widener University. When offered the Widener presidency, I recall saying to the chairman of the board "I think five years would be a good term." Little did I anticipate that the journey would be one of 20 years; the lengthy tenure the result of leading an institution where dramatic growth and substantive change in both academic mission and physical size were accomplished several times over. Many of my presidential colleagues envied my good fortune at being constantly challenged without relocating.

In several chapters I offer comments and observations about the problematic issues faced by most university presidents: athletics, neighbors, unions, external commitments, faculty interface, life in the "glass house," and rapport with the board.

Although acknowledging the difficulties, I recognized at all times during my tenure that to serve as the president of a university is a most fascinating career thanks to the eclectic nature of the multiple constituencies with whom one does business. I hope that, too, is adequately expressed throughout this volume.

A successful presidency is dependent on both external and internal influences. In 1981, Widener's mission, management strategies and organizational structure were in a state of flux, the result of its transition from a 100-plus-year-old military college (Pennsylvania Military College) to a comprehensive civilian university. Widener was in its infancy; university status had been achieved just two years before and its very name was only nine years old. The sensitivities of PMC supporters were very much an issue. While every effort was made to preserve the history and traditions of PMC, the principal task was to establish a Widener University identity. The pride of the PMC alumni was understandable but the reality was that over the next several decades the future of the University's academic and financial stability would be indelibly linked to the Widener name. It was quite clear that the PMC legacy would survive only if Widener succeeded.

Externally, the unprecedented three decades of growth of higher education brought about by the end of WWII was slowing in 1981, accompanied by predictions of steep declines in traditionally aged undergraduate students. Continuing challenges included civil rights, affirmative action, and the role and status of women in society.

In that environment, the first 18 months of my presidency were crucial to laying the foundation from which an integrated, comprehensive university would emerge. Thus, planning objectives included specific as well as broad themes. The challenge was to provide the leadership that encouraged creative thinking, stimulated growth and effected major change.

Success was achieved by having a vision of what was possible for the University. The enthusiastic and energetic leadership of the trustees and of the academic and administrative staff was critical. The support of the faculty was perhaps unprecedented. The loyalty and commitment of all to the endeavor was extraordinary.

R.J.Bruce

Acknowledgements

A memorable benefit of being involved with an academic institution is the number of extraordinarily gifted individuals with whom one works; each in his or her way contributes to the vitality, success and patina of the enterprise.

Acknowledging everyone who contributed or supported me over the years would be an impossible task. However, I am most grateful to one and all for the part they played in making my years as president meaningful, successful and fun. To the dedicated personnel of the Widener University Maintenance and Safety Departments, the secretarial and support staff, the administrative and senior staff, and to the faculty, a heartfelt thank you!

At the risk of excluding or offending someone there are a number of individuals I hereby acknowledge for their support. The order of appearance is not intended to reflect the level of their contribution!

Pat Brant, assistant to the president, long-time friend and extraordinarily talented professional, my thanks for her dedication to seeing this book become a reality. If it reads well, it is a testimony to her editorial skills, her mastery of the English language and her unique understanding of my thought process.

Mary Anderson, a University Relations editor for many years, who undertook in retirement the task of translating the first two drafts of the text from my nearly indecipherable handwriting and who helped shape the outline of the narrative with her recommendations.

Dorothy Sharrocks, Dee Hernick and Janis Sendek, three superb secretaries who worked with me throughout my years at Widener. They learned to understand and translate my New England accent, worked overtime without compensation (the reward of being a monthly employee), and represented the Office of the President with unusual skill, grace and confidentiality. A special thanks to Janis who served as executive secretary for the last ten years of my tenure. Her intelligence and capacity to listen with sensitivity were highly valued.

Tom Carnwath, my administrative assistant for many years, was a close confidant, counselor and devoted friend. His administrative skills, interaction with faculty and trustees, and his loyalty served me and the entire University community well.

L. Luke Cellini, M.D., the long-time head of the Medical Department at Widener, who as our personal physician could not have been more caring in his response to the needs of my family. From suturing Judy's finger in his kitchen, to making house calls at our home for official guests, and answering my many calls at all times of day or night *grazie tante*!

Clayton Sheldon, whose gentlemanly demeanor and approach to accomplishing any task given to him was legendary.

George Hassel, whose skills and commitment allowed him to ably move from administrative position to administrative position whenever and wherever there was a need for someone to plug the hole in the dike.

Rocco P. Imperatrice III, general counsel to Widener and personal friend, whose stated mission was "to keep Bob out of court" (not an easy task given my proclivity to speak out on most subjects). He successfully achieved that goal for many years.

Larry Buck, one of the most gifted academicians I have ever known. His friendship, understanding of the nuances of faculty concerns and wise counsel on academic matters were major contributors to the success of my administration.

And, to Judy, my children Kim and Scott , their spouses Chris and Gigi and our seven grandchildren, thank you all for making life special and worth living! *Semper familias*!

Introduction
The Development of a Peculiar Enterprise

An entertaining description of the university was offered by Anne Matthews in *Bright College Years: Inside the American Campus Today.* "The American campus is not a democracy. It never has been," she wrote.

> It is hundreds of small intense worlds that touch but do not blend, the realm of carillonneurs and astrophysicists; of midnight roof-climbers and annotators of eighteenth-century sermons and beer-bong savants; of women's ice hockey squads and robotics postdocs and of necrolexicographers, who coax dead tongues like Middle Hittite or Sumerian into convenient dictionary form. Allied, they make a campus; grow enough campuses, and you have the vigorous parallel universe called U.S. higher education: driven, noisy, fecund, the envy of the planet....
>
> The world of academe is strongly territorial, but not very social. Its three tribes – those who learn, those who profess, and those who arrange – carry a great deal of baggage, visible and invisible. All are jealous of traditional boundaries ... but for several centuries, the basic alchemy of the venture has held, learn or leave. Be willing to be changed, or get out. (Matthews 1977, 35-37)

No wonder the general population finds the academic community peculiar. As in all professions, academe has its own language and its own idiosyncratic way of doing things. Its structure and many of its traditions were established over several centuries and have been documented by numerous scholars. A cursory understanding of how the relationships among faculty, students and governing bodies evolved informs our understanding of today's university.

Plato, considered by many to be the *paterfamilias* of formal education, presided over the Athenian academy from 387 BC until his death in 347 BC, thus establishing the alpha point in structured education. However, it was the great medieval institutions of Europe that were the true progenitors of today's university. From the founding of the University of Bologna in 1088 through much of the twelfth century, students paid faculty directly. In effect, the earliest masters were entrepreneurs "selling" their knowledge to students who both hired them and determined their success or failure. An interesting historical aphorism reports that after a lecture the students dropped coins into the teacher's hood, a component of the robes originally designed to provide warmth in the drafty medieval halls. The size of the pupil's offering reflected his approval or repudiation of the material presented by the professor. Perhaps today's student evaluations are successors to this custom, but with less dramatic impact.

Faculty Find a Voice

In the twelfth century with the students effectively controlling the choice of academic content and lecturers, a movement by faculty to organize and assert influence on the academic process led to the adoption of guilds similar to the successful model established by merchants and craftsmen. The individual guilds, known as *universitas*, perhaps could be considered the origin of faculty unions and collective bargaining units.

In the second half of the twelfth century, the University of Paris was founded as *universitas magistrorum et scholarium* (a guild of masters and scholars). The school's structure would be recognized on any contemporary campus; professors were gathered into faculties of arts, law, medicine, and theology. Interestingly, the arts were perceived to be less important than the other four courses of study and functioned as preparatory study for them.

Secular universities with residential colleges emerged in the sixteenth century, Oxford and Cambridge among them. After centuries of church dominance in education and scholarship, the faculty enjoyed relative autonomy for the first time. The 1264 charter of Oxford's Merton College provided faculty with complete authority. They elected the administrators, managed the physical plant, hired and approved the faulty and admitted the students. The only external authority with the right to intervene in the affairs of the college was the Archbishop of Canterbury. Referred to by some as the golden age of faculty, this period ended when both Cambridge and Oxford became stagnant and unproductive leading to a dramatic reform by Parliament in the mid-nineteenth century.

Academic freedom and the forerunner of tenure both entered the scene with the rise of the nineteenth-century German universities that have been heralded as the true beginning of the graduate and research university. Overseen by the equivalent of a ministry of education, the "freedom of teaching" was accomplished under strict government control of finances and administrative authority. Nevertheless, it set a precedent in the establishment of a faculty voice.

From Single Purpose to Pluralistic: the New World

Higher education in the new world began at Harvard in 1636 with a curriculum initially designed to supply learned men to the ministry and to carry on the work of civil government. When institutions expanded their missions to educate the sons of the wealthy and "ambitious poor boys," their curricula were broadened to include science, modern languages, and art.

The concept of universal education had its roots in the 1647 Massachusetts General School Act. It stated that all towns had a duty to establish schools, a duty to be enforced by law. Over time, this belief in universal access to education led to the development of the extraordinary mix of educational opportunities available today in the United States. The Morrill Act (1860) further expanded American education by stipulating that the income from the sale of specified lands would be used to develop agricultural and engineering colleges. These institutions, known as "land-grant colleges," were the precursors to today's major public research universities. In 1876 Johns Hopkins University was founded as a graduate institution. Based on the German university model that emphasized research and the development of separate professional studies, Hopkins was the first of the American universities to deviate from the classic liberal education to curricula that were more comprehensive and utilitarian.

Education as a right rather than a privilege emerged as an accepted fact following World War II (WWII). The Servicemen's Readjustment Act (GI Bill of Rights) enacted in 1944 by Congress in anticipation of the end of the war was an insightful and creative piece of legislation. By providing government funding to veterans to attend college, it changed the face of higher education forever. The number of students who attended college from 1945 to 1975 more than tripled. To meet the demand more college buildings were constructed in that period than in the previous 200 years of higher education. The number of institutions of higher learning grew from fewer than 2,000 in 1960 to over 3,200 by 1980. The students were not just veterans but women and the children of the WWII generation.

The Co-ed

The shift in the role of women in society created another seismic change in the college population. The need for a capable labor pool at home to support the war effort led some 8 million women to enter the workforce during WWII. Once there, they did not wish to return to the restrictive pre-war way of life, but they needed a college education to compete successfully in the marketplace. Between 1950 and 1960 the number of female students increased by 47 percent, between 1960 and 1970 by another 168 percent. In the year 2000, women represented 55 percent of all undergraduate students.

The advent of the comprehensive university such as Widener was also a direct response to WWII when the expectations demanded of higher education changed dramatically. By then, American higher education had become a massive business with tiny colleges and mega universities seemingly teaching everything to everyone.

Speaking at Harvard in 1963, educational reformer and president of the University of California Clark Kerr said: "The university has become the multiuniversity. There are several 'nations' of students, of faculty, of alumni, of trustees, of public groups. Each has its territory, its jurisdiction, its form of government. Each can declare war on the others; some have the power of veto … it is a pluralistic society with multiple cultures. Co-existence is more likely than unity." (Kerr 1966)

Today's universities are complex and sophisticated entities, yet they still exist for the fundamental purpose articulated in Athens centuries ago—to transmit knowledge.

Chapter 1

From V.P. to President

At 3 PM on a gray, rainy November afternoon I stood on a platform flanked by Clarence Moll, outgoing president of Widener University, and Fitz Eugene Dixon, Jr., chairman of its board, listening as Dixon announced to a large gathering of the University community that "at a special meeting of the Board of Trustees less than two hours ago, Robert J. Bruce was unanimously selected as the president of Widener University."

Dixon also thanked President Moll for his years of leadership. The acknowledgement was appropriate and certainly merited: few people knew or truly appreciated the dimensions of the effort Dr. Moll had made during the turbulent 1960s and early 1970s to save an institution on the brink of failure.

The announcement culminated a year-long search and selection process during which I progressed from being a member of the search committee representing the University's vice presidents and administrative staff to becoming a candidate and, on November 24, 1980, president-elect.

Being the inside candidate for the top job of an organization is a difficult and often uncomfortable position. It calls for diplomacy, sensitivity, a thick skin and – as much as is humanly possible – the ability to compartmentalize your desire to successfully compete for the position while doing your job in the most effective way possible. Adding to the discomfort is the fact that the scrutiny of an inside candidate is far more intense than is that of an external applicant. The newcomer is an unknown individual presenting his or her accomplishments without any reference points framed by others. The insider carries impediments perceived by everyone in and outside of the process.

My elevation from search committee member to candidate came midway in the search process. Following a meeting in which candidate credentials had been reviewed, the Hon. John B. Hannum, a judge of the U.S. Eastern District Court of Pennsylvania, and a member of the Widener Board of Trustees, said to me, "son, you are as qualified if not more qualified than most of those we are reviewing for this position. I am going to submit your name for the job."

Search committee colleague and president of the alumni body, James J. Brogan '65BS, who had suggested my nomination independent of Hannum, immediately endorsed his recommendation. Having this vote of confidence was particularly meaningful since the Widener-PMC Alumni Association was managed and served by the department I headed.

Judge Hannum, an old-school gentleman in the most literal sense of the phrase, was courtly in style and speech. In his April 25, 1980 letter to the chairman of the committee, Dr. Norman Auburn, he wrote:

> Dear Norman:
>
> Robert J. Bruce, vice president for Development, Widener University, would, in my judgment, be a worthy successor to our beloved President Clarence R. Moll.
>
> From substantial observation of his character, industry and integrity, he has impressed me and others. I know him as a gentleman of refined manners, punctilious courtesy and the nicest sense of personal honour.
>
> His knowledge of Widener University and awareness of its accomplishments, its goals, and its problems is unique. Mrs. Bruce has the instinctive gentle bearing that the wife of the president of an institution of higher learning should have. If Mr. Bruce is disposed to aspire to the position as President, his ambition, his talent, and power of labour would, in my view, yield for Widener University continuing success for the period of his tenure.
>
> Respectfully submitted,
> John B. Hannum

As I responded to Judge Hannum, I could not think of anyone receiving a more gracious letter of recommendation for any position in the universe. The language was classic John Hannum, especially his comments about my wife.

I resigned as a member of the search committee and submitted my credentials. My departure from the committee necessitated an announcement to the University that I was a candidate, placing me in the unique and awkward position of being the only known candidate; the names of other applicants remained confidential until the final candidates had been selected.

The Widener search had begun with an initial screening by the broad-based committee on which I had served. Its recommendations were given to a Trustee Selection Committee who then interviewed candidates off campus. The final two candidates would be introduced to and interviewed by the University community, after which the Trustee Selection Committee would present its choice to the full board.

In June of 1980, the trustee committee announced that it had selected seven finalists. The final two were to be invited to the University during September and October. I was among the seven.

The Insider

The presidential search process provides the enlightening (if not always pleasant) opportunity to hear what people really think of you and your candidacy, as well as of your vision for higher education. It is not a process for the faint hearted as it generates a great deal of passionate dialogue among the stakeholders. Because university presidents wield an extraordinarily broad range of power, it is only natural that their selection is viewed through the prism of enlightened self-interest. Will the individual's skills strengthen the institution financially and/or academically? Will he or she increase or maintain our prestige in the collegiate or business community? What might this president mean to me personally and to my colleagues in our academic or administrative discipline?

Understandably, most faculty believe that academic experience and academic credentials are of prime importance. To others in academe, the most needed leadership skills are managerial; namely, financial acumen and the ability to raise funds in support of the institution. I would have been seen squarely on the managerial side of the equation. First and foremost, I had served as vice president for development at Widener for five years. Additionally, my previous experience was primarily administrative and, because of family responsibilities and the need to earn a living, I had not completed my doctoral degree. However, I had been a Fulbright Scholar in England, a fact that resonated well with many of the faculty. Additionally, my commitment to the liberal arts and to general education, both instilled during my undergraduate years as a history major at Colby College, as a young teacher, and during my years at Bard College, remained constant throughout my career.

My presidential candidacy coincided with the start of a trend that broke many years of tradition. In the past, college presidents had been vetted primarily on their academic credentials. But in the early eighties a growing number of colleges and universities were hiring non-traditional candidates as collegiate CEOs. Individuals with solid academic credentials (but not considered scholars), business leaders, lawyers, and administrators were being tapped for the position. For example, the newly named president of the University of Tampa had been the vice president of development at Colgate University.

In the final analysis I had strong support among the faculties of the Schools of Business, Engineering, Nursing and Brandywine Junior College, as well as from the senior administrative staff, alumni and students. My support from the School of Law was mixed, as it was among the faculty of the College of Arts and Sciences. The then faculty chairman, a physics professor from Arts and Sciences, told me he could not support my candidacy, saying "while I really like you as an individual and you have done good things for the University, I prefer someone with a more traditional academic background."

Risk and Opportunity

I must confess that, having read many of the candidates' credentials, I felt my administrative experience and academic background made me a very viable candidate. Given encouragement and recognition of my abilities by a member of the board, I was willing to join the fray. Any hesitancy I might have had initially was based on my experience at Bard College.

By 1974 I had served Bard as vice president of the college and acting president. The appointment to the latter position had come with the charge to restructure a number of academic and administrative units and to resolve several areas of financial instability. I had accomplished the tasks, and toward the end of the search process was urged to become an inside candidate for the presidency. Ultimately, although selected as a finalist, I chose to withdraw my candidacy rather than generate further angst among the faculty and staff who had been impacted by the reforms I had instituted.

But the Widener situation was measurably different. During my five prior years at Widener, I had succeeded in my goals and had developed close working relationships with faculty leaders and with members of the Board of Trustees, especially with the chairman.

Among many faculty and staff, I was viewed as a candidate who, because of my limited time at the University, could bring valuable experiences from other institutions. This combination of qualities appealed to those who felt that Widener required a well-considered vision for the future, but just as urgently needed continuity and stability. The transition of the institution from a military college to a civilian college to a multi-college university had meant multiple changes in structure and mission over a single decade.

As a member of the senior staff, I was among those who knew that the components to reshape the University were in place for the right leadership and management team. I was conversant with the organization, issues, problems and opportunities available to the institution. In this case, being the inside candidate provided insights that would normally have taken several years to acquire.

The Inside Candidate: Tough Skin and a Sense of Humor

I am not sure, in retrospect, I would recommend being the inside candidate to anyone, although it did have its moments of comic relief. When the two final candidates were selected for on-campus visits, it was determined that each should be treated exactly the same; interviews with various constituent groups, presentations to the faculty on Widener's two campuses, and a stay in the home of President and Mrs. Moll.

There was something surreal to my wife, Judy, and me about an overnight stay at the president's home, punctuated by interviews on my philosophy of education and thoughts on Widener (about which I knew far too much!) Since our two children, Kim and Scott, were students at St. Lawrence and Colgate Universities respectively, we had to tend to our golden retriever, MacDuff. Rather than put him in a kennel, which he detested, I returned home after dinner to walk and water him. I did the same in the morning before breakfast. I am sure that was a first in presidential searches.

Search Process: a Corporate Model?

For years I have watched the selection of presidents at colleges and universities. I have concluded that the expectation of inclusiveness and consensus that is so fundamental to the academic enterprise works to the detriment of an effective selection process. The university's many constituencies – board, faculty, administrators, students and alumni – must all be involved in the process. Meeting the needs of these various groups often lengthens the search. What otherwise could be efficiently accomplished in four to six months often takes twelve to eighteen. Additionally, if not handled with sensitivity, a search has the potential to create divisiveness rather than opportunity.

I do not know a solution to this problem unless we look to the corporate community. Well-managed businesses have a defined structure for succession in which one or more employees are identified as potential CEO candidates and are then scrutinized for suitability over a period of time. Indeed, individuals are often recruited to the firm specifically to become a member of this pool. In most cases this process provides a smooth transition with continuity to the business plan and a commitment to the organization.

The opposite often occurs when management is forced to institute a search process. In corporate America unscheduled change is usually driven by poor bottom-line performance and shareholder dissatisfaction.

In the academic environment, stakeholders replace shareholders. Each stakeholder group may view the institutional bottom line differently: quantifiable academic prestige, alumni employment, outstanding physical facilities, athletic success, community service, etc. The various goals of the stakeholders define the desirable traits and experiences in the next CEO. Would it be possible for a university to develop consensus about its institutional priorities far enough in advance of the presidential opening to be certain that a pre-established pool of candidates existed? Or is it an intrinsic characteristic of the academy that many faculty and staff feel that a change in leadership calls for new vision from outside the organization? Perhaps the existence of a large cohort of tenured faculty, which has no corporate counterpart, makes it problematic to successfully follow the corporate model of succession planning.

As the process stands, the need for confidentiality is critical because many candidates, often the best candidates, are sitting presidents at other institutions. In the public sector of higher education, sunshine laws open the search process to public inspection, which creates its own set of issues in attracting top candidates. In the private sector, confidentiality is strictly heeded until the final stage, the on-campus interview. Before that point, a candidate must cross the threshold; is he or she sufficiently interested to go public with the candidacy?

The psychology of competing in a presidential search is most interesting. If a candidate goes public, but fails to succeed, he runs the risk of having his faculty and staff wonder why he is unhappy and wants to leave. Additionally, this may raise questions among some in the academic community of his leadership qualities.

A colleague and friend who was president of a fine liberal arts college decided to pursue other challenges, finishing second for the presidency at larger universities on two occasions. I recall his saying: "I'd better get a new position soon because my campus is beginning to ask what's wrong with me!" Soon thereafter, he moved to a larger, more prestigious school but his comment is reflective of an inherent problem in academic searches.

On several occasions during my career at Widener, I was approached for other positions. I considered several campus presidencies as well as CEO of a national organization representing private higher education. In each case, I informed the Widener board chairman, but not the campus. Sharing my views with the chairman was primarily a courtesy, but I can think of no worse scenario than to have a board chair receive an inquiry from another institution without knowing his president was in the job market.

Most colleges and universities have well developed cultures that have been shaped over decades, in some cases over centuries. At these institutions, meaningful change is difficult to achieve and the impact of presidential leadership is subtler and more likely to occur incrementally. As a result, while the presidency may be no less important to the ongoing strength of the school, it may be less appealing as a challenge to potential candidates.

The accepted wisdom allows a new CEO a brief honeymoon in which to re-establish the direction and tone of an organization: six months to understand the culture and operations, another year to implement change. As I reflect back, I realize that my early months were a high wire act of extraordinary highs and lows despite the fact that I knew the organization – or, perhaps, because of it.

Unwanted Diversions

If my first months could be called a "honeymoon," it was one with several unwanted diversions. Just weeks after taking office while I was attending a meeting in Washington, D.C., a shooting on campus resulted in the death of a young minority student. The teenaged girl had been participating in a program to encourage under-privileged and academically disadvantaged students to prepare for possible college admission. Offered only during the summer, the program had been in session just a few days when the tragedy happened. Based on police reports made public after the event, the young woman had been living with an older man who had threatened to shoot her if she left him and enrolled in the program. He was apprehended immediately after the shooting and confessed to the crime.

My first reaction when informed of the incident was to leave the meeting and immediately return to campus. After discussion with the on-site administrators about how they were handling the situation, I decided instead to return that evening as previously scheduled and requested that a meeting be set up with the program's students and those parents who lived nearby. The decision was instinctive and correct. The staff did an admirable job in dealing with the unforeseen tragedy.

A senior administrator later commented that the way the problem was handled clearly indicated that my style as president would be to avoid micro-management, that I clearly trusted those in positions of authority to do their jobs. It was a most unfortunate occurrence but the way it was handled set the tone for decision making during my administration.

A second event in my first year as president occurred when a student told an accounting professor that he had overheard in the dining hall that the final exam for Accounting 205 had been stolen and was being passed around. The professor took the allegation to his dean, who informed the chair of Academic Council. A summer-long investigation revealed that academic fraud among full-time undergraduates was widespread on campus; cheating was considered acceptable, bad only if one got caught.

It was determined that several students hired as student officers by Campus Safety had found a way to access keys to academic offices and were stealing then selling exams. The practice of employing students in Campus Safety was immediately stopped.

As the investigation expanded, insinuations of racial prejudice began to surface, driven by the fact that the two lead perpetrators were African-American, one a star of the football team. Indeed, many of the students involved were members of the football team.

In July, four football players were given Fs in the course and expelled from the University: two were African-American, two Caucasian. Three others, all white, were suspended for one semester and also given

Fs. During the fall semester, another nine students received the grade of F for the course. Students who were expelled or suspended were advised by letter that, among other sanctions, their transcript would permanently show an F for cheating and their GPA would reflect it. The letter continued, "Your participation in this academic fraud has violated the integrity of the University. . . . However, it is not my intention as President, or that of the University to scar you for life as a result of this incident; therefore, you will be eligible to petition for readmission to Widener."

Ironically, the only student who never admitted guilt was the one implicated by all the others. When he claimed racial discrimination as his defense, this Chester resident's father rallied support from the local and state NAACP and several black politicians and activists. A complaint filed with the state Human Rights Commission was later dismissed. There were threats of picketing; the lawyer for the accused later admitted that even he had made threats, specifically of lawsuits to other students if they didn't retract their allegations against his client! The University held firm.

Three observations: First, once facts are determined, make certain that decisions are consistent. Second, do not waver on the principles regardless of threats or inferred retribution. Most important, be sure – in advance of an incident – that policies clearly define penalties for and descriptions of what constitutes academic fraud.

Labor Strike

A third diversion that hovered over the first 18 months of my presidency was a festering labor issue stemming from a collective bargaining unit that had been formed by maintenance and housekeeping personnel with the International Union of Operating Engineers, Local 835 in the last year of my predecessor's tenure. He had consulted me prior to signing a two-year contract with the union. My advice had been to take a strike rather than allow unionization which I felt would have an adverse impact on the institutional culture and operating environment, as well as the potential to spread to other personnel groups. Nevertheless, the contract was signed in January 1981, two months after I was named president-elect. I knew that the matter would have to be readdressed at the conclusion of the two-year contract.

Thus, in the midst of multiple administrative changes, planning sessions to restructure the University and to reconfigure the academic offerings, we engaged legal counsel specializing in labor law to help then Vice President for Administration Ted Locke prepare for negotiations and a probable strike. It was time consuming, energy draining and sensitive given the need to keep students, faculty and other constituents informed and neutral.

When attempts to renegotiate the contract failed the union called a strike on February 3, 1983. Led by several maintenance employees who had become disenchanted with the union and believed the opportunity for change without a union was possible with a new administration, the striking employees returned to work in four days and voted to decertify the union. I am quite sure that two influential factors in their decision were the willingness of the University to accept a strike and the dismal economic climate in the region. (In two days some 500 individuals made application for positions as replacement workers.)

The petition signed by the employees was filed with the National Labor Relations Board. After several months of hearings, the union was decertified. Since that time there has been no effort to unionize at Widener, the result I believe of maintaining open communications and appropriate dialogue with all departments of the University.

Chapter 2

Creating a Leadership Team

In addition to the need for governance and academic restructuring, there were leadership positions to fill. I heartily recommend that new presidents surround themselves with individuals who are as smart as, or smarter than they are, for they will make you look good! Being a type A personality, I also insisted on having a senior staff with high levels of energy, the self-knowledge that they were as good as anyone in their respective fields, and the fortitude to push back – at one another or at me. An example of our give-and-take was a discussion about the merits of introducing a program for students with learning disabilities. Several senior administrators were present, as was Professor Linda Baum who was to head the program. The conversation was wide-ranging and wide open. Following the meeting, Professor Baum said, "I have never been anywhere where people disagreed with the president!" One vice president replied, "That's always been this president's style. But once a decision is made, we are all on the same page."

To provide delineation and accountability between the academic and administrative leadership of Widener University, I formed three top-level organizations. The first was the President's Staff, a senior management cabinet comprised of the five vice presidents: academic affairs/provost, finance/administration, development, admissions/student affairs, and dean of the Law School who carried the title of vice president of the Law Center when the Harrisburg Campus came into being. This group also included the assistant to the president for university relations, the administrative assistant to the president, and the assistant provost for graduate study. Its responsibilities crossed every major academic and administrative function of the University. We met every Monday morning to discuss discrete issues and concerns that crossed jurisdictional lines.

The President's Staff served as my sounding board. Having both the academic and administrative leadership in the same room generated understanding, facilitated problem solving, and lessened the potential for major turf battles, although turf skirmishes are never eliminated when talented people gather.

The second group, the Provost's Council, was chaired by the provost and included the academic deans, faculty chair, registrar and director of the library. Although the deans were aware they could have direct access to the president as needed, the council gave the provost a distinct line of authority and provided the forum in which most academic issues were resolved.

A third management group was the President's Council, which met twice a semester. It was a forum for the President's Staff and the Provost's Council to meet and share information and concerns. [1]

No Surprises

I insisted on a rule with my senior managers that once had guided my work with a board chairman, "no surprises." The tendency to obscure bad news or put a better spin on it is very human. However, without both the positive and negative facts, one cannot solve a problem. My operating philosophy with the senior staff was, "give me the bad news, how you propose to fix the problem, and any suggestion for how I can assist you in turning a negative into a positive."

Over my 20 years as president, there were very few disasters. The board's trust in me and in the judgment of the University's senior administrators enabled us to be creative and to take calculated risks. I jokingly used to ask some of my board colleagues "will you still love us if we screw up?" The response was "you and your group have not done so – why ask?" Fortunately the "what if" was never really tested.

Gathering the President's Staff

I was fortunate that Dr. Norman P. Auburn, who had been in place since my predecessor had announced his intention to retire, agreed to remain as academic vice president and provost for my first year. Dr. Auburn, a consultant from the Academy for Educational Development,

---

[1] R.M. Hutchins, president of the University of Chicago once described the modern university as a series of schools and departments held together by a central heating system. Clark Kerr expanded that thought, writing tongue in cheek, "I have sometimes thought of it as a series of individual entrepreneurs held together by a common grievance over parking." (Kerr 1966, 20)

Inc., had been selected to serve as provost to avoid the perception that there was an heir apparent to the presidency. Norman was the president emeritus of the University of Akron, an institution he had led with distinction for over 20 years. He was also wise and capable of viewing issues through an independent lens.

To my mind, Norman brought complimentary essentials to the table. First, he had become very conversant with Widener and its academic leadership. Second, he would be a steadying influence during the transition of almost eight months, a period when I believed that retiring president Clarence Moll would be uncomfortable with his successor working on campus. Third, Auburn's experience and knowledge of higher education, combined with his knowledge of Widener, meant he would be invaluable to me in quickly setting my strategic plan in place. Finally, I had developed a close working relationship with him over his two years at the University: I trusted him.

Dr. Auburn's agreement to remain in place eliminated the need for an immediate provost search, which would have forestalled the ability to move quickly with academic change. His continuance also enabled me to observe other promising administrators with potential to become Widener leaders or, where none surfaced, to plan and execute national searches.

Development and Finance were two operations where I felt a change in leadership was critical. We would eventually also need a provost, and there was a void where a marketing department should have been.

Chief Development Officer

I had vacated the Development position and therefore knew that an external search would be necessary. Whoever was found for that position would have to be experienced and psychologically unfazed by having a boss with a strong development background, not a situation in which everyone could be comfortable. In addition, it would be obvious to development professionals that Widener was a difficult place to raise money. The traditional university fund-raising pyramid consists of a solid alumni base moving upward to an apex of trustees and friends. During the formative years of Widener, the pyramid was inverted with trustees and friends as the principal supporters. As a result, maintaining a successful development program held numerous challenges for new leadership, especially for someone coming from another college.

My instincts about the position proved correct. It was not until Peter Caputo, who had served as vice president for development at St. Joseph's University, arrived on campus in March 1987 that the Development Office became stabilized and focused. Caputo, with graduate degrees from Duquesne and Pittsburgh Universities, had an interesting background that included seminary studies and a stint as a teacher in Africa with the Peace Corps.

Under Caputo's 13-year leadership, development revenue and alumni participation increased each year. In addition to two capital campaigns that raised over $80 million, the multifaceted program brought in $4 to $5 million annually.

Chief Financial Officer

The area of Finance was critical. I was not comfortable with the incumbent vice president, a long-time and loyal employee of the University. To facilitate change, he was offered a position as a member of the accounting faculty, an appointment intended to recognize his long service to the institution and his ability to contribute in the future. It turned out to be a wise move, providing a comfort level among others that loyalty to the institution was valued.

It was imperative to find someone professionally experienced with the capacity to become an intimate colleague. The relationship between CEO and CFO must be an open and trusting one since the strength of an institution rests on the integrity of its financial foundation.

After screening many candidates, I was about to hire the vice president of finance from a neighboring college when the comptroller of Wilmington Trust Company, a graduate of Pennsylvania Military College, expressed an interest in the position. He was experienced in public accounting, had been employed by the Internal Revenue Service, understood the banking business, and had left the U.S. Army with the rank of captain after serving in Vietnam. Most important, he was an alumnus who was interested in returning to his alma mater, an excellent fit for Widener.

W. David Eckard III '66BS was appointed vice president for finance, and the job was later expanded to include the responsibilities of a VP for administration. It was a fortuitous appointment for Dave provided me with expertise, loyalty, and friendship for eighteen years. He served the University with integrity and great skill.

Academic Vice President and Provost

The position of provost, the chief academic officer of a university, is by definition one of the most important and most difficult in the organization. The CAO is the voice that represents the faculty to the administration while concomitantly presenting the president's policies to the faculty. As the buffer between the two, he or she is always seeking ways to cut the Gordian knot! A president who does not place a strong and respected academician between himself and the faculty may unintentionally encourage unwarranted tension. Regardless of his expertise, a president should no more seek to be his own provost than attempt to be his own development head or financial vice president.

When Dr. Auburn left, as he had always intended, at the end of my first year as president, the successful candidate to replace him was Dr. Clifford T. Stewart who had served as chief academic officer and dean of academic affairs at Adelphi University on Long Island, and as administrator and faculty member at Claremont Graduate University in California. His academic background and reputation as an impressively published psychologist made him a good choice for Widener.[2]

A Provost From Within

Unfortunately, however, in the summer of 1983, just one year after his appointment, Provost Stewart developed a severe case of tinnitus. We agreed that he would step down as provost but continue as a professor of psychology, a position for which he was eminently qualified given his record of teaching, research, and publication.

Dr. Lawrence P. Buck was appointed acting provost for the duration of the work of a search committee. I had become increasingly impressed with Dr. Buck's abilities and the natural political instinct evident in his actions as dean and during his service on the restructuring committee. He had been the successful candidate for dean of the College of Arts and Sciences within the new academic structure and had served as an acting dean in the old organization. I thought he would be a natural as provost and encouraged him to become a candidate for the per-

---

[2] A logical inside choice as Auburn's successor would have been the dean of Widener College, Joel Rodney. However, Rodney had accepted a vice presidency at Salisbury State College in Maryland and had announced his plan to leave Widener on January 1, 1983. His departure led to the appointment of Associate Dean Joseph Arbuckle to acting dean for the spring semester. Filling Professor Arbuckle's term as associate dean of the college was an influential and talented faculty member, Dr. Annette Steigelfest.

manent position. After passing the gauntlet of inquiry and comparative credentialing by his peers, he emerged as the unanimous choice for provost. Larry Buck brought many skills to the position. His colleagues recognized him as a distinguished scholar of medieval history and an outstanding teacher, a *sine qua non* for a chief academic officer. He also had the requisite skills to manage the independent and disparate personalities that comprise a faculty cohort.

One of Larry's greatest values was his willingness to debate issues with me. We had a tacit understanding that if we ever reached the point where after serious debate he could not support a decision of mine he would resign: Never in our 18-year relationship did we ever come close to that point. Indeed, we shared a mutual respect. His good counsel influenced my thinking on academic matters countless times.

Admissions and Administration

Two vice presidents who had served Clarence Moll remained in place. Vincent F. Lindsley continued in Admissions until 1986 when he became V.P. for special projects. Theodore F. Locke, Jr., a retired U.S. Army LTC and 1942 graduate of PMC, served with dedication and talent even after leaving the vice presidency. Like Professor Joseph Arbuckle and Administrator George E. Hassel, Locke became an able utility infielder, serving wherever his skills were most needed.

In April 1986, Michael Mahoney joined the senior staff as director of undergraduate admissions. Mahoney came to Widener with 25 years of experience in the administration of student programs. Following a reorganization, he became vice president for admissions and student services in 1995, responsible for undergraduate admissions, financial aid, and all aspects of student life, including athletics.

Many years later in a taped interview, Michael recalled his first months at Widener, which he joined after five years at the College of Notre Dame, a small Catholic women's college. "It was culture shock," he said. "The biggest difference was, at Notre Dame when all else failed they prayed for a miracle. With Bob Bruce, it was considered part of the strategic plan that you would create miracles!" [3]

---

[3] From an interview with P. Brant taped 5/14/99. Brant interviewed some thirty administrators and faculty, recording their observations and memories of the Bruce administration. These are now in the archives of the Wolfgram Memorial Library, Widener University.

New Appointment, New Department: Assistant to the President for University Relations

An administrative change that became effective within a year of my appointment was in the area of institutional marketing. Patricia G. Brant, a former CBS-TV publicist with a writing and event-coordination background, was given the responsibility for all activities related to the external world including marketing plans, publications, public relations, advertising and photography/artwork. Mrs. Brant's office was also charged with coordinating all special events. In order to provide her with the influence needed to pull this important area together, Pat was named assistant to the president for university relations and reported directly to me.

This marked the founding of a formal University Relations Department, an important step because the foregoing lack of centrality had created an environment without any fixed accountability and had led to confusion among the public.

The Hiring Process: Pitfalls and Pleasures

I learned a valuable lesson during the process of hiring the provost. One of the candidates, a dean from nearby Villanova University, seemed a perfect fit and clearly impressed the Widener interviewers. Because the question of relocation was moot, we shared only a cursory discussion about family. In all the time we spent together there was never an indication that his wife, also an academic, was anything but supportive of what was to be an excellent career step. When we met to clarify the final details before the position was offered, he informed me that regrettably he was unable to proceed because of his wife's concerns. Somewhat incredulous, I suggested his decision was comparable to a bridegroom bowing out at the altar. He sheepishly confided that his wife said she would find it inconvenient to her career if he were unavailable in the late afternoons or weekends to watch the children. When I asked the obvious question: "Didn't you know her objections before you entered the process?" His response was "No, it never dawned on me she wouldn't find the position acceptable." He also confided that because his wife had not wanted to discourage him, she had not shared her concern until she saw that he was a serious contender. I can only surmise that she let it progress hoping he would not get the offer and she could avoid a confrontation. Lesson learned. Always interview the spouse as a part of the process.

On several later occasions, candidates asked me why I wanted to meet their spouse since I was not hiring them. My response: "I may not be hiring them, but I sure want to know if they are supportive of my hiring you."

In contraposition to the candidates who have not cleared the decks for their candidacy are those seeking to end a spousal relationship by relocating. One candidate for the top Development position arrived with his wife for the final step in the interview process, a dinner with Judy and me at our home. The wife was supportive of his candidacy but mentioned she would not be able to move until the end of their children's school year. In fact, she never moved; they separated soon after he was hired. Judy and I laughed at how well they did as a couple during the evening they spent with us. It must have been an agreed upon performance to get him resettled professionally and assist her out of an unhappy relationship.

The Global View

A thought shared with me by University Board Chairman Fitz Eugene Dixon, Jr. when I became president remained with me throughout my career. He told me to "remember that you are the only one in this organization paid to think globally." It was a simple but insightful bit of wisdom for a CEO. Everyone else has a function in, or responsibility for, a piece of the organization. Their judgments are often colored by what is best for their area of responsibility. The CEO must make decisions against a benchmark of the goals of the organization.

My interest in becoming president of Widener was based on my belief in its potential for increased stature and academic excellence. At the time of my retirement in the year 2001, I felt that the transformation had been successful; Widener University had attained a new level of academic excellence and a commensurate reputation. It was most gratifying on the day of the inauguration of my successor, James T. Harris III, to have Jim personally thank me for leaving him such a financially stable and academically vibrant institution.

Chapter 3

Restructuring the University and Academic Governance

In 1981 Widener was still in its formative years as a comprehensive university. I had begun organizing a personal vision for its maturation on the very day I was named president-elect. However, Dr. Moll was in charge for eight more months, a transition period that was far too long with the incoming CEO already on campus.[1]

The changes from military school to civilian university between 1972 and 1981, accompanied by four name changes in such a brief span of time, had resulted in confusion within the public perception and uncertainty as to the core values and culture of the institution.

A restructuring of the institution into an integrated academic and administrative organization would provide the foundation upon which the framework for academic program expansion could be built. Dr. Auburn's agreement to remain as provost meant that he would oversee the faculty debates that would provide the details of change for the University governance structure.

After assuming the presidency on July 1, 1981, one of my first memoranda sent to the University community dealt with the rationale for introducing an integrated institutional structure. The memo also announced the formation of a planning task force. The major points were:

- the University must be able to develop new academic opportunities and make adjustments to existing programs;
- the relationship among academic units had become clouded and was being further strained by duplication

---

[1] Fortunately, Clarence Moll and I were in agreement on this sensitive issue: I was respectful that he was still president and refrained from offering opinions to many who sought to discuss internal matters; he was sensitive about implementing policy changes that could have a tail long enough to restrict my options.

and unclear lines of administrative responsibilities; and
* the move toward an integrated university was a correct and logical goal at this point in Widener's history.

The Task Force on University Structure

The establishment of a broad-based forum to debate the issues of change would be critical to any restructuring. Discussions would have to be frank and invite input from as many campus constituencies as possible. Effective and knowledgeable leadership of the discussions would be necessary.

Under the chairmanship of Provost Auburn, the Task Force on University Structure was constituted on August 14, 1981. It was to complete its work by February 1, 1982. By necessity, the membership was heavily weighted with academic administrators and key administrative officers. The Assistant to the Provost and Dean of Brandywine Junior College Dr. Andrew A. Bushko served as vice chair. The secretary was Joseph Arbuckle, associate dean of Widener College.

From 1972 to 1981, the college had seized every chance to introduce academic programs that might broaden its appeal, but the organizational structure was still that of a single-purpose, single-campus institution; the enterprise had become unwieldy and increasingly difficult to manage. The law school, the junior college and the college for part-time and evening studies each had its faculty and staff hierarchy headed by a dean. However, Widener College was comprised of four academic centers – Management & Applied Economics, Nursing, Engineering and Arts & Sciences – led by the equivalent of a department head functioning under the title of dean. As an historian, I could not resist comparing Widener of 1981 to the states under the Articles of Confederation of 1781. Each of the academic colleges and centers of the University was operating much as the states had under Article Two, that is with varying degrees of the "sovereignty, freedom and independence . . . not expressly delegated to Congress." Substitute university for congress and college or center for state, and one can sense the confusion of the organizational structure.

Following the 1972 transition of Pennsylvania Military College and Penn Morton College (together known as PMC Colleges) to Widener College, the Board of Trustees had engaged the Academy for Educational Development (AED) to analyze the institution's status and opportunities for development. One of its recommendations suggested that Widener was "at a point where sharpening its objectives must become a high priority" (AED 1975, 4). It was with this observation in mind that I undertook my initial planning as president.

During my faculty address on September 8, 1981, I shared my belief that "a basic philosophical issue is the question of what organizational structure is best suited to carry out the educational mission of the University in the years ahead." The task force was to commence its work under the premise that Widener "should move toward becoming an integrated university." In other words, the task force had been asked to recommend an organizational model to allow the existing centers of Widener College to become free-standing schools of a university. The faculty within each of the colleges, schools and centers, working through the respective deans, would be expected to participate in sending recommendations to the task force.

While the overarching organizational model was easy to design, there were certain issues of concern. Who would oversee the curricular philosophy and distribution requirements for the baccalaureate programs? How would the professional and discipline-specific requirements be incorporated into interdisciplinary programs? To whom would the libraries report? A major discussion point with far-reaching impact was how the graduate programs should be organized and administered.

To clearly establish the parameters for discussion, a presidential memorandum stated that no existing academic policies would be changed or eliminated until deliberated by the new governing body. This directive, which preempted attempts by deans to more favorably position their programs prior to restructuring, was extremely important in assuring that the transition to a university structure and governance model would be accomplished in an orderly fashion.

Organizational Structure *Before* Academic Governance

One of the more sensitive issues confronting the Task Force on University Structure was the issue of academic governance. Many deans and the faculty chair argued that any structural changes recommended by the task force would be potentially unworkable if the issue of academic governance were not debated in parallel.

After careful thought, I disagreed. The university structure would be the platform from which all other changes were launched, and it needed to be in place quickly. I had always intended to move immediately into deliberations on governance once the recommendations on structure were completed. The decision to address structure first was based on the need to give focus to an institution that called itself a university, but organizationally existed as a series of freestanding schools and programs. The relationships among the various academic disciplines were important, but of greater importance was the synergistic impact that would come from each academic unit being made a part of an integrated whole. Moreover, I firmly believed that to study the issues of academic governance while debating the objectives of organizational structure would lead to protracted discussions. Instead, I expressed my confidence that a subsequent task force comprised largely of faculty could successfully design the academic governance appropriate to the University's organizational model. [2]

In the end, the task force included within the appendices to the final report a working document entitled "Suggested Guidelines for the Development of a University Governance Organization." It was a subtle approach by those who wanted to link structure and governance to begin to define the conversation.

Grass Roots Involvement

The task force was instructed to use subcommittees for special areas such as financial and admission procedures, distribution requirements among the various schools, and other cross-college issues. The deans of Widener College, working with faculty committees and subcommittees as needed, were charged with transforming their academic centers into potential schools or colleges. The task force would serve as arbitrator of the recommendations from the centers and would be responsible for facilitating a plan of action at the conclusion of the study.

In addition, the provost asked each of the deans to establish subcommittees as needed in his or her academic unit. This approach accomplished two things: It provided faculty engagement in the process, and synthesized discussion points for the task force, thus eliminating debate on details and enabling the process to move ahead more expeditiously.

The task force completed its deliberations on December 9, 1981 with a heated discussion as to whether the full University faculty should

---

[2] Some years later, an academic dean commented that the Task Force on University Structure provided a glimpse at my management style: "identify the issue, focus on it, resolve it, and move on."

be given the opportunity to review the recommendations before their submission to the president. The dean of Arts & Sciences and the faculty chair argued together that the early review would provide input and generate broad-based support for the document. Furthermore, they believed that failure to do so would be perceived by some faculty as an act of bad faith. Others on the committee felt it would delay the process too long. A compromise resolution suggested that the president be given the final draft of the document in the form of an appendix to the minutes of the task force dated December 9. Simultaneously, the faculty would be provided the opportunity to review the document. The task force would then reconvene on January 6, 1982 to discuss any faculty input. This was a classic academic approach that all parties accepted.

At any university, inclusion of faculty as often as possible in academic governance matters is the preferable *modus operandi*. It is not always possible to achieve because debate on issues can drag decision making beyond practical limits. But in this instance, allowing faculty time to reflect over the holiday on what was to be a momentous change for the University, while also providing the president with the opportunity to begin work on the restructure was a win/win.

The Final Recommendations on Structure

On January 6, 1982, Chairman Auburn submitted the final task force report with two minority reports attached. As expected, the major recommendation was to reconstitute the existing centers of Widener College into four schools and colleges, College of Arts and Sciences, School of Nursing, School of Engineering, and School of Management, with equal standing to the School of Law, Brandywine Junior College, and University College.

An integral part of the task force's final report was a document titled "Recommendations Regarding Intra University Relationships and Functions." It stated 26 points detailing the jurisdiction for academic control that contributed to the operation of an integrated university.

For example, recommendation number three provided a thoughtful policy for managing graduate programs by placing responsibility for each within the founding school or college. The curriculum, it noted, should be the responsibility of the school's faculty; the dean should oversee its administration; the existing degree requirements should remain in place; and major programmatic changes should be referred to a University Governance Organization (UGO). It further recommended that the UGO's Curriculum Committee establish a subcommittee to deal with all concerns relating to the form and substance of all graduate programs. A critical recommendation stated that there would be no designated graduate faculty, no dean of graduate studies. It was a good, clear, defined policy for graduate programs.

This recommendation is illustrative of the wisdom of the task force in recognizing key underlying issues. First, had it attempted to centralize administrative control of graduate studies, there would have been vigorous opposition since the graduate programs provided the host schools with both prestige and revenue. (The revenue in turn provided leverage during budget discussions and consideration of disbursement of excess revenues.) Second, it recognized that the University was not yet equipped to finance a traditional graduate studies model complete with a designated graduate faculty. Indeed, the well-considered recommendation was practical and sensitive.

Leveling the Playing Field for CAS

While the restructuring dramatically changed the entire University, it was nowhere more evident than in the soon-to-be named College of Arts and Sciences (CAS). One particular provision set the tone for equality among units; namely, no school should expect to employ its own faculty in academic areas that could be provided by the Arts and Sciences faculty. For example, the School of Nursing could not hire its own chemistry faculty, nor the School of Engineering its own humanities professors. I was committed to the premise that a core of liberal arts courses was a necessity if a Widener education were to prepare undergraduates for employment or graduate studies, and that CAS faculty would teach those general education requirements and all other arts or science service courses.

This decision elevated CAS to equal partnership with the professional schools. It also shaped the academic structure of what would become the College of Arts and Sciences. Prior to reorganization, Arts and Sciences existed without a defined relationship to the other academic units of the University other than as a provider of service courses. The impact of the restructuring was immediate and, over time, monumental as CAS developed a wide array of academic majors and cross discipline offerings.

As a result of an abundant market of Ph.D.s and the restructuring of the role of CAS, the quality of faculty hires became comparable to those at highly selective liberal arts colleges. Candidates realized the opportunity not only to teach baccalaureate and general education courses, but also to develop majors in their academic disciplines. In addition, majors with limited numbers of students continued to be offered because of the large number of non-liberal-arts undergraduates being taught by the faculty. Having four physics teachers with only three physics majors is a luxury not found at most institutions!

At times, multi-level discussions were enjoined between the College of Arts and Sciences and another academic unit, often about course content, sometimes about selection of faculty. For example, the content of the "Anatomy and Physiology" courses for prospective nurses differed from that presented to science majors. No one benefited if large numbers of nursing students failed to grasp the relevance of this required course so it was imperative that the CAS faculty supply professors who could teach "A&P" with skill and sensitivity to the needs of the students. Over the years, and throughout the curriculum, the right teacher always seemed to be found, a tribute to the flexibility and cooperative spirit within the College of Arts and Sciences.

Academic Governance Task Force Formed

The Task Force on University Structure took the first major step toward how Widener University would be perceived both internally and externally, and how it could grow academically. The next logical question was "how do we manage it?" In preparation for a discussion on academic governance, I had read several position papers including one prepared in house in 1979, shortly after the attainment of university status. Despite the passion of the document's authors, the report had never gained traction. I asked several who had served on that committee why the recommendations were ignored. The consensus answer was twofold: the committee was attempting to impose a university governance structure while still maintaining a loose collegiate federation, so the result lacked cohesion; second, the majority of the 1979 committee members had worked exclusively at Widener so few had first-hand experience of a university model, or the knowledge to establish one.

As we turned our attention to academic governance, we began with the first task force's report appendix, "Suggested Guidelines for the Development of a University Governance Organization."

I had been very pleased with the restructuring document itself, but most uncomfortable with the choice of University Governance Organization (UGO) as the name for the controlling body of academic governance. Thus, my memo establishing the second study toward the University's reorganization convened the Task Force for *University Academic Governance* (UAG), again under the able leadership of Provost Norman Auburn. At the first weekly Provost's Council meeting after distribution of the memo, several deans asked for an explanation of the significance of the name change.

As had been written in my charge to the committee, the UAG name was meant to emphasize that the focus of this task force would be academic. I further conveyed my belief that University Governance Organization was inappropriate for use below the trustee level. The task force held its initial meeting on February 10, 1982, just one month after the submission of the restructuring document.

Many of the members of the UAG task force had participated in the structure discussions and therefore understood the complexities of the issues. However, to establish the appropriate environment for the discussions, I attended the organizational meeting and spent considerable time responding to questions and defining my vision for a university academic model.

A Model Defined

Foremost, I believed that a university had to be dynamic, with an operational style that encouraged creative thinking as a guiding principle of academic governance. Second, the envisioned university would depend upon goodwill, cooperation and commitment to a common cause by all faculty and academic leaders. To achieve this universal commitment to collegiality, each dean should understand the objectives of other collegiate units. New programs had to be implemented within a context that all academic units understood. Furthermore, the academic and financial well-being of the University had to transcend the parochial concerns of any individual college or school; new programs would be evaluated against the dual criteria of academic soundness and financial feasibility.

A few committee members were stunned when I asked that UAG not be seen as a traditional faculty senate, but rather as a governing body that was representative of both faculty and academic administrators. A traditional faculty senate by its very name signals a division between faculty and those colleagues charged with providing administrative leadership to the academic enterprise. To separate the two is counter to a meaningful, collegial, governance organization.

To curb faculty uneasiness about the locus of control of academic governance, it was stressed that collegiate academic policies and practices correctly belonged within the purview of the faculty of the individual schools and colleges, as did the creation of new school-specific academic programs and procedures. The committee was urged to design a vertical rather than horizontal matrix for University-wide governance procedures, suggesting that representation in an over-arching governance structure would be most effective if it were unicameral. The how of the process to elect members was left to the task force.

In short, the charge to the task force was to design a structure to coordinate University-wide academic policies, enhance academic decision making and program development, preserve the integrity of the separate schools, and allow for timely action on academic issues. It was, perhaps, a deceptively simple charge for it was an ambitious undertaking. Individuals were being asked to put aside the human instinct to protect one's turf.

Recommendations were to be completed by June 15, 1982, another fast track effort. It came as no surprise that the faculty chair challenged the deadline. In my experience, no matter what deadline is set for the end of collegiate deliberations, there is always concern that the time is insufficient! However, without tight deadlines decision making at a university can become paralyzed. I asked for a good-faith effort and promised to revisit the deadline if the task simply could not be completed in sufficient detail.

Some immediate questions were asked and answered. What limits were attached to the term academic governance? The committee was instructed to make recommendations on this issue. Were there appropriate external models? No; the need to construct a unique, functional model for Widener was the goal.

Framing the Deliberations

In order to focus the discussions and avoid unproductive digression, Provost Auburn asked for a series of working papers. Two of the most fundamental were to respond to the questions: (1) What constitutes a faculty member? (2) What method of apportionment should be used? (While proportional representation among faculty was not mandated it was suggested that it might be the most appropriate and equitable model to consider.) Two committees were established: the

Subcommittee on Membership Arrangements, chaired by Dean Andrew Bushko and the Subcommittee on Structure and Function, chaired by Dean Joseph Arbuckle. One of the rationales for the formation of these two groups was to protect Dr. Auburn from criticism. His role as advisor to the president and his leadership of the restructuring effort opened him to the possibility of being seen as the originator of the academic task force's final recommendations. Committees very obviously put a faculty opinion into the mix and firmly established the provost as facilitator of the task force. It was a decision that generated goodwill with the deans and faculty members serving on the task force.

Illustrative of the dynamics that challenged a task force trying to weld independent units into one with universal objectives was the stand taken by the Law School. Principally because of tension over revenue sharing and the limited opportunity for faculty interaction due to distance, the law faculty believed itself to be looked upon as a lesser partner within the University. As is common among professional schools that do not share the campus of the parent university, the substantial benefits of affiliation were largely overlooked, including the economy of scale in purchasing; access to capital markets, investment and accounting services; marketing support; and avoidance of duplication in certain administrative areas, notably technological.

From the beginning of deliberations, the Law School attempted to promote a position of greater independence. This was unsurprising since the dean had previously sent a memo suggesting the Villanova University governance structure as a model for the relationship of Widener Law to Widener University. At that time, Villanova's law school operated as an autonomous unit of its university with the freedom to make decisions without regard to other units. While its income and expenses belonged exclusively to the law school, it shared in the capital funds of the university – a great deal for any law dean! When it was also suggested that the law dean be designated a vice president and report directly to the president, not the provost, it was obvious that Widener Law was attempting to protect its turf. Since the goal was to create an integrated university while allowing for the differences in academic units, the Villanova model was antithetical to the objective. Its rejection enabled the development of a multi-campus University Faculty and University Council.

The Final Recommendations

The final task force report included recommendations that provided an academic operating platform for Widener. A summary of the key elements follows.

1. The faculty of each college or school would handle internal academic policies and practices. Presided over by the dean, each would determine its own composition, committee structure and method of operation, all approved by the provost and within the framework of selected guidelines from the Association of American University Professors (AAUP).

2. An overarching University Faculty, comprised of all voting members of each collegiate faculty plus those University personnel holding faculty status, would convene at the pleasure of the president, of 15 percent of its members, or of its legislative arm.

3. A University Council would be established as the legislative arm of University Faculty, in accordance with the recommendations of the Task Force on University Structure. (When first proposed, that recommendation had been met with consternation by some faculty, especially those proponents of strict adherence to AAUP policies, and those who were unhappy with the inclusion of academic administrators in the structure.)[3] Specifically, the UAG Committee recommended that University Council be comprised of the college deans, the provost, and full-time faculty representatives elected by their peers from each school except University College (which had no full-time faculty).[4]

4. University Council would deal only with issues of university-wide impact, serving the collegiate units on the two campuses as they related to the University. Additionally, it would address only the development of *major new* policies and procedures that would affect University operations; existing policies and practices would remain until

---

[3] The faculty member who headed the Widener College branch of the American Association of University Professors was intent on seeing as many AAUP positions adhered to as possible and forwarded AAUP policies to the task force for information. By the group's choice, selected AAUP policies were included in the final recommendations, specifically, only policies relating to academic freedom and tenure were reaffirmed.

[4] The definition of a full-time faculty member was one teaching at least half time at the rank of instructor or above. The option was left open for individual schools and colleges to offer franchise to lecturers.

modified. Perhaps the most challenging issue was to define what constituted a major change in policy or practice, a nicety that went directly to the issue of control.

5. Several committees should be established within University Council, among them Budget/ Long Range Planning, Promotion, Tenure/Academic Freedom, Academic Affairs, and Faculty Affairs.

The Academic Affairs Committee would "consider new programs and majors, or termination of existing programs or majors with university-wide impact." The wording constituted a major step toward an integrated University since it established the authority of council over individual schools.[5]

The Faculty Affairs Committee would provide policy recommendations on contracts, compensation, fringe benefits, and merit increments. It would also be the committee of informal inquiry on dismissal for cause, in accordance with AAUP procedures. During my tenure as president, this committee opined on several difficult faculty cases and proved to be an essential part of Widener's academic administration.

Deliberations on the Role of the President and Deans

The inclusion, or not, of Widener's president as a voting member of University Council generated a great deal of heated discussion. Provost Auburn recommended that the president be the presiding officer of the council, a proposal that drew opposition from several members of the task force.

The larger issue was whether or not the president should even be a member of council. The representative of the School of Law, Professor William Connor, was joined by others in making the case that the president should not be a member of council because in his role as CEO he is the final arbitrator on all recommendations made by council. The task force attempted to compromise on the issue, finally writing that the president "should be an ex-officio member with the right to attend and participate in any of the activities and meetings without the right

---

[5] In practice, since academic changes and additional programs originated in the individual schools and colleges, rarely did the Academic Affairs Committee contradict recommendations. However, it did force any academic plans for program additions into a careful, well-thought-out process that included an awareness of the impact of new programs upon the University's resources and its academic fit within the University.

to vote." The provost responded in an elegantly stated position paper dated May 18, 1982 that "to have the president as an ex-officio member of the Council without the power to vote flies in the face of the spirit of collegiality we have been striving to establish and maintain at Widener University. I fail to understand why the faculty members serving on the University Council would feel threatened by the presence of the President at Council meetings. The President should be considered a colleague who is striving to achieve the same ends as the faculty. His participation in meetings should be welcomed, not deplored."

When the final report recommended that the deans not serve on standing committees of council, Provost Auburn wrote in a minority report (joined by the deans of Engineering and Nursing), "By curbing the power of the deans, the task force seems to be recommending the creation of a body with the characteristics of a Faculty Senate rather than a faculty-administrative University Council. "Further," he opined, "while the presence of deans on most standing committees would be helpful, I fail to see how the Committee on Budget and Long Term Planning can function effectively without decanal representation."

I suspect that some faculty agreed with Dr. Auburn's point that in order to create a new ethos, all University factions should be considered colleagues and equals. The UAG had provided the platform to break down the traditional "us vs. them" mentality.

My Response

The positions taken regarding the roles of the deans and president in academic governance reflect a dynamic that has persisted since the evolution of the modern university. Each institution resolves the argument based upon its traditions and culture. I had not shared my personal convictions on the issues with the task force. However, I believed that for a university to operate effectively, all members of the university's academic community had to function in a collegial and integrated manner. To that end, I rejected the task force's recommendations on the role of the deans and president. The implementation language read: "... The president of the university will be a member of the University Council with the right to vote.... The academic deans will be eligible to serve as voting members of University Council but may not serve as chairpersons of committees."

The Provost's Role

There were numerous opinions about who should chair the new University Council, an appointment that to many sent a clear statement as to the context and philosophy of the entire governance structure.

Since the council was to be the representative "House" of the faculty, some professors felt strongly that no academic administrative officer should be in a position of leadership. However, the exclusion of the chief academic officer would have created a de facto, though modified, faculty senate. The task force, recognizing the significance of the issue, recommended that the provost should serve as the presiding officer of University Council but vote only in the case of a tie. The precedent for this role is, of course, the Vice President of the United States in the U.S. Senate.

The key element of the deliberations was not who would preside at council meetings, largely a symbolic function, but rather who would control the mechanism of appointing committee chairs and setting the council agenda. The task force recommended that a steering committee comprised of one representative of each school or college selected from the elected members of the council, set the council's agenda in consultation with the faculty chair. It further called for the chair of the Steering Committee to be the presiding officer of University Council. This was significant for it made the provost the gatekeeper of the agenda.

Additionally the task force felt that the presiding officer should appoint the chairs of the standing committees from the non-decanal representatives to council. It logically followed that under the new structure, the provost would have considerable influence in the composition of the Steering Committee. The willingness of the task force to invest in the provost a leading role in the academic governance organization was collegiality at its best.

Reflecting back, however, I am not sure the task force envisioned how pervasive the authority could be in the hands of a strong provost. When Dr. Lawrence P. Buck became provost in 1984 he, as one of the architects of the governance structure, understood the nuances of the document and used them to the University's advantage to guide and shape University Council business.

The UAG Committee did an extraordinary job in designing a pragmatic working model for intracampus and intercollegiate cooperation on academic policies while allowing the issues of principal concern to faculty to remain within the separate schools and colleges. For example, decisions regarding promotion, tenure and academic freedom were guided by universal procedures but all final recommendations were made within the separate schools and colleges. University Council was the body that kept all of the component parts in academic alignment.

Implementation of the Restructuring and Governance Recommendations

The recommendations of the Task Forces on University Structure and on Academic Governance were both presented at the September 1982 faculty meeting. It was reported that the Board of Trustees had adopted the report of the Task Force on University Structure, thus the academic centers of Widener College had ceased to exist on July 1. In addition to University College, the Main Campus now housed the School of Engineering, School of Management, School of Nursing, and the College of Arts and Sciences, each operating under its former, frozen bylaws.[6] Widener College, although now without programs, faculty or students, was authorized to continue as the constituted body for governance issues; its procedures would be operative in all academic matters bridging the first and second semesters. The continuance of Widener College, now overseen by its last faculty chair, was important for tenure and promotion matters since the review and evaluation process began in the fall and concluded in the spring semester.

The Academic Committee of the Board of Trustees was then reviewing the governance report and was expected to approve it that month. However, the next order of business was to address the myriad details attendant to the process of implementing the new University governance structure while insuring that the transition was as efficient and seamless as possible. While Widener College continued to handle tenure and promotion issues, University Council – although not yet formally approved by the Board of Trustees – was charged with resolving any jurisdictional issues among the academic units that surfaced during the first semester of operating under the new organizational structure.

Concomitantly, a University-wide committee of faculty chaired by

---

[6] See Chapter 4 for information about the establishment of the other two schools of the Main Campus, Hotel and Restaurant Management and Human Service Professions.

Professor Marion Fox of the College of Arts and Sciences was tasked with drafting bylaws for University Council. Comprised of the faculty chair and one other dean-appointed professor from each college or school, the committee was to have its recommendations ready for council's consideration at its first meeting in January 1983.

In the midst of the voluminous changes that were transforming the University, we had to begin preparation for the accreditation visit by the Middle States Association of Colleges and Schools. Preparation for a Middle States visit is enormously time consuming. However, the required review provides an opportunity to engage large numbers of the campus community in a self-study process. Given the major structural changes and academic challenges that were occurring the timing of this MSA review was fortuitous: it gave us a chance to benchmark the major transformations and to outline in a comprehensive way how the changes would guide the University in the future.

At the same time, faculty committees were engaged in the monumental task of writing a new faculty handbook. Dr. Thomas Emmitt, a senior advisor to the American Council on Education and a recognized expert on higher education faculty governance, was engaged to assist the Faculty Affairs Committee of University Council in drafting the handbook. In actuality, the work of the Handbook Committee meshed well with the preparation for accreditation since we were very aware that the Middle States report had to have a coherent set of faculty policies and rules in place to reflect the new governance structure.

This was an extraordinary time at Widener University. We were frantically busy with committees and projects, establishing new schools and administrative departments, as well as drafting policies and procedures to make it all work – while still doing our primary jobs, serving and teaching students.

Maturity Brings Improvements

The final task force report on structure provided a fine academic operating platform for the establishment of a young university. But as the governance structure matured, the substantive differences between Law School and the schools on the Main Campus demanded recognition. For example, several years of experience proved that the *de jure* application of University governance limited the Law School participation to three committees: Academic Affairs, Budget, and Faculty Affairs.

In recognition of this reality, the law faculty obtained part of its initial wish for independence; the University Council that emerged was comprised of faculty representatives from only the Main Campus schools in Chester. Initially Council met as a separate body. Subsequently, the Chester campus faculty and University Council held joint meetings with specific discussion items open to faculty comment following Council business. Unless the agenda included a topic that had evoked some passion in one faculty group or another, the open sessions were not well attended.

Chapter 4

Planning and Strategic Thinking

After the task forces on structure and governance concluded their work, the vision for Widener was formulated by a planning group of senior administrators and academic deans, expanded as needed with other faculty and staff. The group's image of Widener's future was designed with broad strokes and constantly rethought as objectives were reached. We also regularly tested and recalibrated assumptions to reflect changing demographics and other shifting external factors that influenced our decision making. "What if" scenarios were the *modus operandi*. The confluence of many needs created an interesting dynamic for planning. Since it had to occur while we also maintained operational effectiveness, the multi-year process was fascinating and kinetic.

Throughout, the principal goals were to improve the quality of our academic programs, create an integrated organization, expand graduate program offerings, reshape the public perception of the institution, and upgrade and expand the physical facilities. A durable tenet was to weigh the impact and cost benefit of all decisions against the value brought to students.

Our planning process utilized an approach different from the strategic planning model that was the passion of corporate America. To me, traditional strategic planning took too long, was overly complicated by the volume of analytical data produced, and sometimes was paralyzed by the creation of a decision-making process. We also ignored the models often used in higher education that produce a highly detailed strategy that subsequently resides on a shelf until requested by an accreditation team.

My preferred planning nomenclature was *strategic thinking*. Strategic thinking relied on many of the analytical processes of strategic planning but factored in a heavy influence of intuitive reasoning and deductive thought. The process encouraged creativity derived only in part from quantitative analysis. It required understanding the environment in which the University operated and competed. Goals and objectives were benchmarked against realistic budget figures and financial projections, although we tended to weigh toward optimistic rather than negative outcomes. Any plan had to be dynamic enough to integrate shifting external influences or unexpected opportunities that needed resources. The operating ethos in our decision making was to stretch, never to be risk adverse.

Strategic thinking was enormously successful for Widener, largely because it was incremental in application, allowing for open-ended dialogue about core objectives and institutional values as they were collectively understood by the group. Significantly, the team was comprised of capable professionals who understood the University's objectives and were type A personalities who challenged one another, and me. They also understood that strategic thinking is a more disciplined process than it appears. While it encourages flexibility and creativity during the discussion phase, after the data is gathered and the numbers are crunched, you must decide to proceed or retrench. Once the "go" has been attached to a plan, there can be no second-guessing.

The approach did on occasion elicit comment and some concerns by accreditation team members who were uncomfortable with the absence of a traditional comprehensive strategic plan. These concerns disappeared with the sharing of detailed written strategies for specific programmatic decisions. The critical factor was that the strategically thought-out decisions were invariably successful.

Sharing the Vision

It was important to provide the faculty each year with an understanding of the strategic thinking of the University as well as of the external factors influencing decision making. It was crucial that they be aware of the potential consequences to Widener of demographic trends, and of economic change brought about by state and federal government policies. Thus, the sharing of a global overview of the world in which we were competing became a theme of the annual opening faculty meeting each September. This approach proved invaluable, especially when proposals for additional or expanded academic initiatives at Widener seemed counterposed to regional and national trends.

It was gratifying when, near the end of my tenure at Widener, several senior faculty members shared with me how much they had enjoyed the annual opening faculty address, saying it had provided them with the macro information needed to understand the context of our planning.

Planning Against Predicted Declines

The data for the initial planning effort in 1981 were the United States demographic projections. These data showed a steady decline in the numbers of traditional college-age students until the early twenty-first century. Figures, as reported in the January 29, 1980 *Chronicle Of Higher Education*, predicted a national decline of college-age students by 25 percent, with the northeast region projected to be down 22 percent. The decline was further projected to be 38 percent by 1995.

Given the stark demographic trends, the planning group weighed the viability of each existing academic program and possible areas of program expansion against short- and long-term financial projections. Key to the deliberations was a conscious effort to think in terms of growth opportunities rather than adopt the retrenchment strategy that many colleges and universities were publicly espousing. Retrenchment is not a viable long-run strategy for a tuition driven institution. Status quo, without the support of a large endowment, is a move backward.

The planning document produced in academic year 1982-83 creatively utilized three planning benchmarks: retrenchment, maintenance of status quo, and expansion including the introduction of new academic initiatives. Each of the models was based on a careful analysis of the positive and negative ramifications: cost effectiveness, ability to generate revenue, space utilization, and – less quantifiable but of equal importance – the impact upon the University's external image and internal morale.

Engineering, nursing and business enrollments were then very strong at Widener and elsewhere while the traditional arts and sciences and two-year programs were static or in decline. However, as we analyzed the market environment in increments of three and five years, the regional studies suggested that, with more focused University branding, the undergraduate catchment area could be expanded. In addition, we believed that the new, free-standing College of Arts & Sciences would enhance the reputation of our liberal arts offerings. Finally, a continued emphasis on pre-professional undergraduate programs and applied graduate programs would increase enrollment numbers. These planning assumptions were not wishful leaps of faith but well-considered assessments of available data. Thus, the dismal national and regional demographic projections presented what we believed to be sur-mountable challenges.

The School of Law, the Hotel and Restaurant Management pro-gram, University College and selected graduate programs were all tar-geted as academic areas with growth potential. The School of Law, as one of only 175 programs accredited by the American Bar Association, was endorsed by the planning group as having the greatest potential not only for enrollment growth but also for broadening and establish-ing Widener's reputation as a graduate institution.

Planning the Future of the Delaware Campus

In support of the decision to use law as one of the lead academic programs, a first priority was to increase space for the School of Law. The only way to expand the Law School on the existing acreage would be to close Brandywine College. Brandywine had been very successful during the Vietnam War era when college attendance assured male stu-dents of a draft deferment. The prospects for its future were clouded by the end of the Vietnam conflict and the demographic projections for the 1980s and 1990s. However, a financial analysis completed with the first planning study refuted the logic of closing Brandywine at that time as it was still in a very positive cash flow position. Long-range projec-tions suggested that the option of closing the college should be revisited in the future.

In a memo dated July 26, 1982, the planning group was tasked to study and develop an analysis of the following items:

- potential program development on the Delaware Campus if the Law School were to relocate to a third campus site;
- a financial plan, including the potential for floating a $900,000 bond issue, for the purchase of property or land;
- development plans for a $1 million-plus capital campaign for renovation and additions to existing buildings if the Law School remained on the campus;
- provision of the necessary square footage to attain accreditation by the American Association of Law Schools (AALS) and for future expansion;
- the impact on the Law School faculty and students if the school were to be relocated to another site;
- the impact on the public image of the University if it were to open a third campus located in Delaware; and

• the fiscal impact of a third campus as to administrative, personnel and operating costs.

During the ongoing planning process, periodic reports were given to the Long Range Planning Committee of the Board of Trustees. They initially agreed that the most attractive option was expansion onto the property of the Brandywine Country Club (BCC) contiguous to the Delaware Campus. A private club with approximately 100 acres, BCC was giving serious consideration in the 1980s to selling its property and merging with another country club. Following six months of discussion and a near agreement of sale at $3.5 million, we abandoned our purchase effort when a real estate developer offered the club $7 million.

Simultaneously, conversations were being held with the City of Wilmington. As part of its revitalization effort, the city was anxious to attract people downtown in the evenings, and was therefore willing to provide a financial subsidy with the potential to reduce our development costs up to 50 percent as compared to a standard real estate venture. However, no suitable locations were found. The most attractive option was a vacant school four miles from the Delaware Campus that came very close to meeting the School of Law requirements. It had good access to Interstate-95, thirteen acres, and a purchase price under $9 a square foot. The estimate for conversion and renovation was $1.5 to $2 million, placing the project cost under the $3.5 million approved by the board for the Brandywine Country Club offer. The downside to the site was the absence of contiguous property for future expansion. Moving the School of Law there, while resolving immediate needs in a cost effective manner, would have left the question of future growth unresolved.

While searching for a relocation site for the Law School, we remained aware of the question of Brandywine's viability. The decline in the school's enrollments seemed likely to continue for several reasons, notably the high tuition being charged at private junior colleges, the competition from an increasing number of public community colleges, and the recruitment of the traditional two-year student by four-year institutions attempting to fill their classrooms in a depressed market.

Once we determined that the demographic shifts of the late 1970s and early 1980s signaled the shrinking market for private-sector, two-year education, we faced a conundrum; if we moved the Law School and then Brandywine ceased to exist, could the remaining academic units financially carry the Delaware Campus?

Widener had engaged the services of a Wilmington architectural and planning firm to assist with the evaluation of both off-campus sites and the potential for Law School expansion on the existing campus. With its help, the decision was made not to open a third campus but, instead, to reconfigure the Delaware Campus.

Planning began immediately for the expansion of the Law School and for expanded accommodations for students studying in a second program initially identified as having growth potential: the Hotel and Restaurant Management (HRM) program.[1]

To house both law and HRM students, twelve townhouses were constructed on campus. Expanded library and classroom space was built at a cost of approximately $3.5 million. The resulting 34,000 sq. ft. of new study and living space was operational for academic year 1984-85.

1985 Planning Task Force

The inability to increase the land holdings of the Delaware Campus led to two very consequential administrative decisions. The first was to consolidate all full-time baccalaureate programs on the Main Campus in Chester, an integral part of which was the commitment to develop new and expanded programs and physical facilities. The second was to expand the Law School on the Delaware Campus into a regional Law Center offering masters' programs as well as paralegal and other undergraduate law-related programs.

These decisions were based on planning that had begun in the summer of 1982 when the collegiate deans had been given two months to prepare a three-year plan for their individual college or school. The documents included enrollment projections, projected faculty increases, new program development with implementation plans, operating and capital expenditures needed to support programmatic changes and personnel increases. Each dean submitted a draft plan in late 1982 which, after a year of continued planning, resulted in the decisions to consolidate the undergraduate programs and expand the School of Law.

In 1985, a third major task force was created to develop recom-

---

[1] The Hotel and Restaurant Management program, introduced as a two-year associate degree program within Brandywine College, had grown dramatically to 510 students in 1982. It soon offered both associate and baccalaureate degree programs and was known after the restructuring as the School of Hotel and Restaurant Management.

mendations based on these two resolutions. During its deliberations, the task force engaged in constant dialogue with the deans. Their input was creative, directive about what was needed to strengthen the academic quality and viability of the programs in each school, and in most cases, reality based. The exercise meshed well with the earlier announced plans to expand into graduate education. The list of proposed program expansions, especially new graduate offerings, was extensive. Reflecting back on the process, it was clear that the deans felt empowered to take responsibility for the future of their academic disciplines, a direct result of the restructuring of the University into discrete academic units.

Of equal importance was the mandate to seek accreditation by specialized academic associations for it raised the academic standards across the University. Written into the institutional mission, the goal signaled that Widener was serious about becoming a regional force in offering high quality graduate programs. The outcome of the 1985 planning discussions set the strategic direction of the University over the next two decades. During the three years 1986 to 1989 the possibility of establishing a third campus in the state capitol of Harrisburg became a reality when the law school opened a new campus in August 1989.[2]

Over 20 years, numerous planning documents were written in addition to those required by Middle States and the American Bar Association. The first two dealt with University reorganization and academic governance, the third on graduate program expansion. Subsequent three-year comprehensive plans periodically developed by all academic and administrative units became the foundation for individual operational plans.

---

[2] Development of the Harrisburg Campus is discussed in chapter 8.

Chapter 5

Managing the Enterprise

Today, a university must manage real estate, investments, pensions, medical care, human resources, legal issues, technology, etc. As far back as 1938, A.J. Carlson wrote in the *Bulletin of the American Association of University Professors,* "The legal aspect of the American university is that of a business corporation, to be sure not-for-profit but modeled essentially on the corporation for profit in the business world rather than on the traditions of the Old World universities as a free republic of scholars. The president of the university is virtually the general manager of the corporation." (Carlson 1938)

During my years as Widener's president, I made the point to corporate acquaintances that I was the CEO of a business that had over $100 million in revenues, 1,300 employees and close to 10,000 customers. On occasion, I would then be asked why the university followed the time consuming process of attempting to build consensus on issues when the hierarchical vertical structure of the corporate world was very efficient. University trustees puzzled by a faculty position on a policy matter were apt to ask, "Why don't you just tell them to do it?" The answer is that, while universities look like corporations, they do not function like corporations. For instance, corporations do not have an equivalent to academic tenure.

Although some, both in and outside academia, fail even to observe the corporate similarities, outsiders occasionally argue that the university should adopt more than just industry's structure and procedures; that is should replicate a for-profit business. There are, however, inherent differences. First, if a university exists as a place where the primary purpose is the search for truth, a testing of beliefs, the give and take of knowledge and the exchange of ideas, it logically follows that this purpose is best achieved in an atmosphere of collegiality and in an environment that is not overly proscribed or structured. Second, very few businesses would tolerate a product line that annually loses money, but this occurs regularly on a campus. Chemistry and physics programs exist at a loss on many campuses yet are important to the reputation and academic strength of the institution. Additionally, universities deliver some services that are economically marginal or that actually produce debt, yet increased productivity is not desirable, or not feasible. Class sizes can be increased but will eventually reach the point of being educationally unsound; a student in a lecture of 300 is less likely to have the same experience as one in a seminar of 10 or a class of 16. The number of nursing students participating in a clinical rotation is limited by the supervisory capacity of the instructor, the occupancy of an operating theater or treatment room.

Carlson's description of the university president as corporate general manager was quite accurate and still holds some seventy years later. Yet, unlike corporate managers, the effective academic leader should make decisions by fiat only when all other means are exhausted. One essential for successful academic governance is the provision of a forum for debate. Faculties must be given a voice, even if, like the rest of us, they sometimes speak *ex cathedra* in areas beyond their expertise; a sociologist opining on the fiscal policies of the university is not different than an electrician expressing an opinion on law enforcement. It is an opinion, sometimes founded in knowledge, sometimes not, but usually delivered with passion!

A second essential for successful academic governance is the rapport between a college president and the board of trustees, particularly the board chair. Without a trusting and candid working relationship, the implementation of tactical and strategic plans can be an arduous process and the daily management of the university logistically uncomfortable.

Clark Kerr succinctly defined the role of an institutional chief executive when he wrote in *The Uses of the University*: "The President becomes the central mediator among the values of the past, the prospects of the future, and the realities of the present." (Kerr 1966, 37)

Revamping the Budget Process

The budgeting process inherited by my administration was inadequate and bordered on chaotic. Reform was crucial, not only for future growth but to eliminate deficit budgeting in the present. In fact, the then-existing method of budget building most clearly illustrates the inadequacies in the critical area of financial management.

Prior to my presidency the budget for the next fiscal year, which began on July 1, was approved by the Board of Trustees in its December meeting, seven months before the start of the new fiscal year. At that same meeting, tuitions and salaries were approved, also seven months before the budget was implemented. Worse, the compilation of the operating budget and recommendations for salary and tuition increases were originated during the late autumn, nearly a full year before the enrollment would be known.

The deans, vice presidents and others who prepared the budget projections that were submitted to the Budget Office, and ultimately to the trustees, were not only doing so too early, they were basing their projections for a year hence on numbers from the current fiscal year plus hoped-for additions. It was an incremental budget with no standards for justifying increases. Each cost center submitted a budget to the Budget Office, which compiled the total revenue projections and expenditure requests. Not surprisingly, there was usually a large deficit, but the proprietary nature of each cost center's budget impeded any attempt by the financial staff to reallocate funds or make dramatic cuts.

A shortfall from the projected enrollment in a tuition-driven institution is always a calamity. It is a catastrophe if budgets and salaries have been announced. Budget adjustments in September or October when the student cohort is finally known create a negative environment at the outset of the academic year, and since salaries are in place beginning in July, any shifts in budget allocations cannot include personnel costs. The negatives of such a budget model become even more critical in times of high inflation, such as during the Carter era. It was obvious that something had to change.

In the midst of the budget deliberations during my first year, Dave Eckard came to me in frustration over the lack of controls saying "Boss, you have a problem; we are not going to have a budget!" In short order, I agreed with his suggestion to freeze the budget at the fiscal year 1981-82 level. Interestingly, the response to the freeze was overwhelmingly positive, indicating that the cost center managers supported a more rational approach.

Once the budget was baselined on an already known fiscal year's performance, enhancements in control and support systems could be implemented and conversations begun on new approaches to budgeting. I recommended to David that we implement a zero-based budget model. He and the then budget director George Hassel were familiar with the concept which was at the time the financial mode of operation in the corporate community. They proceeded to develop an adaptation for use at the University.

Zero-based budgeting called for an annual justification of all expenses, an exercise that seemed unrealistic since a university has so many fixed costs (i.e. tenured faculty), thus David and George coined the term "modified zero-based budget" (MZBB). The intent was to focus cost centers on those areas of expenditure where savings could have a real financial impact. A salutary benefit was the dramatic change in the University's culture as the Budget Office began reviewing and allocating resources across schools and colleges. A composite picture of the University emerged and the budget was balanced with shared input. Each cost center manager understood the financial fundamentals of other cost centers, which proved to be advantageous for decision making.

The balanced budget, the most severe of fiscal disciplines, became a guiding principal in the operating philosophy of the University. Indeed, a decisive policy was set one evening when Board Chairman Fitz Dixon presented the University with a check for $1,206,000 from the Estate of George D. Widener with the caveat: "Do not ever run a deficit in the future; this will pay off the current debt." An additional restriction was set after the discharge of the debt. The board recommended that one percent of revenue be placed into a contingency fund as a reserve against possible operating deficits. Eckard suggested that it be raised to two percent to ensure sufficient funds for an annual transfer to the endowment, a sound suggestion that was endorsed by the board as policy.

The MZBB system was introduced in academic year 1983-84 with outstanding success. The discipline imposed on cost center managers to review all major budget items and justify both existing and new requests led to increasingly sophisticated levels of data made available for fiscal decisions. An example of one that touched the students was the Widener Payment Plan, a pioneering effort to give families some relief from the burden of making twice annual, substantial tuition payments. Parents were offered installment plan options for a nominal annual fee of $50. Unlike the plans managed by financial firms and banks then used by most colleges and universities, the plan was administered internally. It was an instant success, resulting in many students remaining at the University who might have left for financial reasons. The plan also assisted us in managing cash flow more efficiently.

To better manage the budget, the board supported the administration's recommendation that a preliminary budget be approved in the spring with final budget adoption in the fall after the enrollment figures, and actual expenditures from the previous fiscal year, were known. The change made realistic budget building an actuality.

Budgeting and resource allocation at a university are uniquely complex because of the nature of the enterprise. Decisions made to expand in one area usually have significant financial impact in another. At Widener a good illustration was the decision to pursue accreditation for the School of Management by the American Assembly of Collegiate Schools of Business (AACSB). To achieve accreditation, faculty ratios and teaching loads had to be lowered and changed, additional facilities were needed, and University College's part-time business offerings fell under new regulations. The ripple effect was enormous but accreditation was deemed necessary to enhance Widener's reputation for quality. Without a cost-based budget and control system, the 1987 decision to pursue AACSB accreditation could not have been implemented.

Schools with large endowments need to guard against relying on the knowledge that they have the capacity to absorb deficit budgeting. Such reliance can circumvent the difficult choices in spending priorities (and there is never a surfeit of worthy initiatives).

The push and pull between academic demands and administrative controls, and the issue of accountability in managing resources, create a constant yin and yang at all universities. The most dramatic example at Widener was the budget latitude afforded the law dean. As the largest single financial contributor to the revenue of the University, the Law School was granted financial incentives. Specifically, after supplying a contribution of eleven percent of revenue (later, twelve percent) to the University, and paying its share for services rendered by the University administration, additional surplus could be kept by the School of Law, though it was not to be used for enriching salaries. The result was the creation of a Law School endowment within the University endowment, and the direct funding of certain physical plant and scholarship enhancements for the School of Law.

Although the incentive served us well, I understood that the lack of total control of all revenue became an irritant to the financial staff. Inevitably, Vice President David Eckard and Law Dean Anthony Santoro clashed on fiscal management. Whenever issues arose relating to turf or policy among senior staff members, I instructed them to stop trading emails and sit down to resolve the issues, an approach that effectively stopped schisms from forming because both parties had to be part of the resolution. However, at one juncture, when the interaction between Eckard and Santoro was on the verge of becoming counterproductive, I told them that, though fond and appreciative of both, "unless you find a way to resolve your issues, one of you is not going to be here next year." I'm told they met one evening at the Sheraton Brandywine Inn, a corporation owned by Widener, and had a "spirited" conversation until the early hours of the morning. They agreed to disagree in certain areas while providing a united front once decisions related to Law School financing were formulated. I had anticipated that result since each member of the senior staff had enormous professional respect for the others.

Although the MZBB was successful, the shift in the demographics for college age students in the late 1990s, led me to conclude it was time to rethink the budget process; we needed more flexibility to shift resources among schools and colleges. To accomplish this, personnel costs would have to become a part of the operational budget. (Under the MZBB approach only new staff or faculty positions were included.)

We named the new system Managing to Budget. It provided budget targets determined by a University-wide senior administrative and academic group. Naturally, the change was met with concern for it was more centrally controlled. However, in a time of tightening resources and increased competition for students, it was a logical progression.

Managing to Budget facilitated the transfer of resources among disciplines with greater ease and allowed cost center managers the option of shifting personnel costs to operations by not filling or eliminating positions. In short, it gave them greater management flexibility. The safety valve in this process was the ability of the cost center managers to appeal the target financial figures and goals. If the appeal were considered valid, the request was added to a priority list of revised targets that would be funded subject to available resources after final revenue figures were determined. The overall impact of the change was positive, reflecting the reality that environment determines the management tools.

The change in budget procedures coincided with Dave Eckard's decision to accept a position at another institution. He had given eighteen years of extraordinary service to Widener and, despite my best efforts to convince him otherwise, felt he had contributed what he could to his alma mater and that it was time to move on.

Joseph J. Baker succeeded Eckard as the vice president for administration and finance. With his years of experience as a senior financial manager in the insurance industry, Joe brought a different set of skills to the position. During David's tenure and after Joe's arrival, in keeping with the ethos of Widener as a dynamic, creative institution, changes and innovations in financial management occurred regularly.

Endowment Building

A majority of private colleges are tuition driven, relying on student revenue supplemented by fund-raising to enhance income. A number of venerable private institutions share the advantage of large endowments – a billion dollars and up, with Harvard University in the lead with an endowment over $30 billion.

In recent years, an interesting phenomenon has been the shift of public institutions and systems to operating models similar to those in the private sector. Among the many reasons for this trend is the decrease in taxpayer support for public education; the original concept of the land grant institutions, to provide education to the common man, has become an artifact of history. Combined with tax restructuring, the huge shift in government spending during the decades of the 1960s and 1990s to priorities such as social welfare, medical support and domestic security has diluted the government's ability to support areas such as higher education. As a result, one now finds public institutions such as the University of Texas, Texas A&M, Ohio State, and Virginia boasting endowments of over a billion dollars, the result of aggressive fundraising.

The size of the endowment is a critical factor to the long-term stability of any institution. Boards and presidents who do not make endowment building a major priority place limits on the ability of the institution to maintain or increase quality. In the worst case, they place the institution at risk when demographics shift and enrollment downturns occur. Building an endowment is a long-term project, particularly difficult for younger institutions without the alumni or financial base to provide support. A university that is committed to producing graduates in the human service areas such as teaching, social work, and nursing will find it more difficult to attract substantial endowment support than institutions that graduate large numbers of businessmen, engineers and technocrats.

In 1981, Widener's endowment was $1.6 million. We joked that it provided us with two weeks of reserves! The challenge from the onset was to build the endowment while finding the resources to fund the academic program development and physical plant investment necessary to support our admittedly ambitious plans. A series of decisions were made to contain risk while moving forward. The first was to fund infrastructure and physical plant additions (over $100 million in 20 years) without running up large debt-to-equity ratios. To do so, we made judicious use of bond issues to supplement the internal funding. The second, as mentioned earlier, was to build the endowment through stringent internal financial controls and creative fund-raising.

The creativity was a necessity because traditional approaches to raising endowment monies were largely unavailable to Widener in the 1980s and 90s. The alumni base was small and comprised principally of military school graduates. Many supported Widener. Others, while intellectually accepting of the decision to transform the institution, had no emotional attachment to the new school. Furthermore, many of the PMC graduates were in professions that prohibited them from contributing at major levels. Those who had obtained wealth were identified and approached; fortunately, a majority became supporters over a number of years. Since the first alumni holding a Widener degree had graduated less than a decade earlier, it was clear the long-term future of the University would be financially bright. But the need was in the present.

Dave Eckard and his staff employed their management skills and the new budget system to begin to increase the endowment. Each year, all unspent funds from restricted accounts and from the board-mandated contingency reserve were transferred into the endowment. In addition, during the 1990s we established a position dedicated to deferred and planned giving within the Development Office: Donald Boyd '83BS, '94JD was employed to establish a program to attract gifts from life-income, annuities and estate planning that began to show results, and should continue to produce resources in the years ahead.

In the early 1990s, we found that vesting investment authority with an external professional can avoid conflicts, particularly if the board of trustees includes one or more individuals with the knowledge and skill to dominate internal investment strategies. At Widener, that very situation led the board to mandate that a majority of investments be in very conservative fixed income securities while the equities market was blazing. While the reinvestment of our gains was good, we missed a major opportunity. As a result, we engaged PNC Bank, a major step forward in setting parameters and investment guidelines for the University. It was agreed that the role of the Finance and Endowment Committee of the Board of Trustees would be to set investment policy and review performance, not to manage investments.

In fiscal year 2000, the endowment passed the $40 million mark. While still much too small for the size of an institution like Widener, it provided a margin of safety unavailable in earlier years.

Innovative Financial Aid Management

In fall 1997 Brian Mitchell, then the president of the Association of Independent Colleges and Universities of Pennsylvania (AICUP), telephoned me to say that Walter Cathie, an expert in financial aid with a national reputation as an innovative manager, was seeking a position in eastern Pennsylvania. The call was fortuitous as it coincided with my decision to review and revise Widener's financial aid programs. Walt was invited to campus and impressed me as both imaginative and aggressive, in short, an excellent fit for Widener.

Walt Cathie had spent twenty years at Carnegie Mellon University before accepting the position as dean of enrollment management at Wabash College in Indiana. A recent marriage to a woman who had once been his college sweetheart was bringing him to Pennsylvania. His new wife lived in Doylestown and had taught for many years at a Friends School. He was seeking a position that would allow him to join her.

Hired as dean of enrollment management for the Main Campus, Walt's obvious value was in financial aid. When he assumed responsibility for the School of Law's aid programs two years after joining Widener, the transition was not without resistance; law schools are protective of their autonomous operations in administrative areas. However, the decision to give Cathie responsibility for the total University financial aid area proved to be cost effective when he developed and marketed a unique form of aid packaging.

Two actions Cathie initiated were particularly successful. The first was working closely with consultant Brian Zucker to develop a matrix for the awarding of undergraduate aid. The result was an extraordinarily effective and sophisticated design still in place at Widener. Based on a mathematical platform that uses regression analysis to place applicants into categories of academic ability, financial need, geographic location and quality of high school, the matrix quite accurately predicts what level of aid would maximize the acceptance rate for the various student cells.

Cathie's second activity with long-term benefits was to move Widener into the loan business. A member of the advisory board of the Sallie Mae Corporation, he was well versed on the way loans were packaged nationally. He believed he had the appropriate contacts and knowledge to make Widener an originator of Federal Stafford loans, long the exclusive and profitable purview of commercial banks and large corporations such as Sallie Mae. He knew that there were no prohibitions to a university's being the originator of student loans, therefore cutting out the commercial lenders from profiting from the origination fee. If a program could be devised that saved the student money while being profitable for the institution it would be a win-win situation.

The marketing environment in which Walter promoted his idea of becoming a lender institution was one in which maximizing the use of financial aid was imperative for survival. The traditional need based model for financial aid had been abandoned by higher education, and parents and students were shopping aid packages during the admissions process. Institutions that could offer grants and scholarships rather than loans and work-study were winning the admissions sweepstakes.

At the same time, however, the introduction of merit grants and scholarships to increase the admissions numbers had led to an increased practice of discounting, whereby scholarship aid is funded from a college's operating budget. Properly administrated discounting is an effective tool; however during these years many institutions found themselves in the trap of discounting in order to matriculate sufficient numbers of students. I well recall a conversation with a fellow president in which he commented: "We have the largest entering class in our history, but no more revenue." This was discounting at its worst!

Ironically, the use of discounting escalated in part as a result of the increase in college ratings by the media, notably *U.S. News and World Report*. Poorly researched data led editors to publish subjective dictums about the value of a college or professional school. Initiated simply to boost circulation, these rankings were taken as entirely credible by potential students and changed the culture of educational marketing. If the magazine ranked you lower than your competition, discounting helped level the playing field.

The trend toward discounting continues to put some institutions in jeopardy. Colleges that are at the 45 to 60 percent level will be unable to sustain that level without facing financial self-destruction. During my years at Widener we kept the discount rate at about 30 percent and focused our attention on maximizing net tuition income (the gross tuition less the University-provided financial aid).

When Walt Cathie proposed his lender model, the discounting and financial aid packaging wars were becoming entrenched as a way of doing business. We were looking for new approaches, but the program as proposed would be a first nationally for an under-endowed institution such as Widener. Thus, it presented some unknown and inherent concerns. CFO David Eckard was greatly concerned that the exposure to financial risk was beyond Widener's capacity to handle. The major issues were the exposure as a lending agency and the concomitant responsibility for the outstanding debt of the loans.

After Cathie's concept was refined I determined that the potential rewards of lower rates to students and additional revenues to support Widener's financial aid program outweighed the potential risks. With board approval, we made the decision to put the program in place.

The critical elements of the plan called for Widener to establish a line of credit to finance student loans and to negotiate a sales contract that would enable us to sell the loan portfolio at a profit. Walt worked his way through all the barriers and over all the obstacles. By the spring of 1999 Citibank was selected to partner with Widener. From the outset, I determined that we had to offer the Widener Stafford Loans for less than the students would pay in the commercial market. Without that benefit the University would be profiting at the expense of its students. Students were also given the option of three lenders, including the Widener Stafford Loan.

While the federal government set the interest on the loans, originators could make loans more attractive to students by lowering the rate. Walt proposed that the University not pass along the three percent origination fee that we were charged for each student borrower. To accomplish that we had to increase the market share, making up in volume what was lost in our lower rate.

In the first year $6 million in Widener Stafford Loans were originated among the graduate student population with a net profit to the University of $233,000. By academic year 2000-01 over 80 percent of our students were using the lender program. The annual volume was $23 million and escalating each year. The net earnings over the first seven years of the program were over $6,886,000, generating new funds for program development University-wide, as well as for the endowment of the Law School, which generated the largest percentage of loans.

Marketing and Public Relations

Before the University Relations Department was established in 1981 (and depending on what one read) Widener either had 2,500 or, if part-time students were added in, 6,000-plus students. The perspective changed from college to college and from department to department, each of which publicized whatever information best suited its needs. While name changes and mergers had muddied the University's image, more damaging were the "mixed messages" and the disproportionately large sums being spent to advertise non-traditional, part-time programs in University College.

Market researchers hired in 1982 provided eye opening community perceptions of Widener. Residents closest to campus were most familiar with part-time evening programs and thought that the master's in business was part of University College. Those at the outer geographic limits of the research barely knew the name Widener; PMC, by then closed for a decade, drew better name recognition. Although obvious, the need for centralized marketing met with resistance from several deans. It not only relieved them of the opportunity to promote their schools however they saw fit, or to divert their promotional budgets to other priorities, it also relieved them of those budgets. As the founder of University Relations, Mrs. Brant designed market plans for the entire University that combined and redirected funds that had formerly been the purview of selected programs. Primarily for that reason, the decision to have University Relations report directly to the president was crucial to its success. Without that imprimatur, University Relations would not have been able to accomplish all it did between 1981 and the end of the decade.

After establishing basic tracking systems, universal themes, coordinated broadcast and print advertising, a family of publications, a pro-active public relations effort, and both a new logo and new slogan, a second market research project was undertaken in 1987 by Professional Research Consultants (PRC, Inc.) The gratifying results showed that the public perception of Widener's identity was beginning to be established, and the sense of institutional quality had risen dramatically since 1981.

The staff of copywriters, graphic designers and a photographer agreed in 1991 to submit a large packet of its work to professional ad agencies across the country for evaluation and comment. A daring and unprecedented experiment, it could easily have backfired. It did not. Praise poured in for the consistent quality and ingenuity of the materials. Amusingly, an applicant for a design position subsequently submitted several of our brochures as evidence of his capabilities!

Pat Brant was exacting, with high expectations for her staff and colleagues, and excellent rapport with her internal and external contacts. She introduced Widener to professional marketing. Following her retirement in 1998, she made the following retrospective comments in material sent to me:

> The marketing of a university as complex and dynamic as Widener was both exhilarating and exhausting. We started from nothing, just a few Xeroxed flyers and press releases about accepted students, many of whom attended elsewhere. When I first began there in 1972, the slogan, "Widen Your World with Widener" was, sadly, intended primarily to tell people how to pronounce the name.

> Clarence Moll had saved the college from self-immolation, but the pride was gone, and so was much of whatever talent had been there. The brand-spanking-new Widener College was operating in systems and traditions that were decades old.

> The miasma and self-doubt were probably the biggest challenges to face the new president in 1981. In the very first year of his administration, Bob Bruce began to promote a new sense of purpose; a gathering of individuals and new ideas that generated an upbeat, can-do atmosphere. From the grounds keepers to the vice presidents, he laid out expectations for performance that required no less than maximum effort.

> Throughout his presidency, Bob Bruce walked the beat. He knew which light bulbs were burned out, which accounts were overdrawn, and who, even midway down the ladder, was malingering. If you measured up, you stayed. If not, the slot was refilled. Because it was all done from a base of first-hand knowledge, without prejudices, and with the drumbeat of pride ever in the background, Bruce succeeded in exacting performances that turned Widener into a university that could recruit both faculty and students on a national basis. He restored the pride, and kept upping the ante.

The Impact of Technology

The application of updated technology as a management tool created a seismic shift in operational style and attitude at Widener University. Over a two-year period, Dave Eckard and his staff selected and installed an administrative computer system that provided managers with enhanced, timely data. All of the University's financial transactions were consolidated on the system, as were student financial aid, class registration, alumni data, development records, and personnel information. The primary database grew to over 80,000 names. Perhaps the most important benefit was the introduction of a single University-wide chart of accounts that integrated Business Office functions between the two campuses.

Driven first by engineering, science and management, the demand for computer applications as a teaching tool spread rapidly across all academic disciplines. Over the next twenty years, the growth in technology for academic use was as extraordinary at Widener as it was elsewhere; early concerns about student computer literacy quickly became worry about keeping up with the demand.

Following extensive study by both academic and administrative committees, microcomputers in the form of IBM personal computers were introduced across both campuses in the mid eighties and the University's mainframe operating system, the Burroughs's 6900 was dismantled. (The once-ultra-important languages supported by the 6900 – COBAL, FORTRAN and Pascal – became antiquities within the blink of an eye.) An advantageous contract with IBM provided substantial discounts, not just to the University, but also to individual staff, faculty and students.

The introduction of PCs increased productivity through applications that became available at the desktop. Email became the communication mode of choice. Spreadsheet applications replaced their typewritten progenitors and adding machines. Reports created on computer networks changed the University's way of doing business.

The Administrative Computing Services Department and the Academic Support Services Committee of the faculty were in separate, continuous planning mode, and not without tension. The clash between advocates for a central computing model and the preference of the academics to control their specific academic applications was a dynamic that continued for a number of years. Although it was clear that the debate over "academic computing" vs. "other computing" was counterproductive and not cost effective, the tensions were in some aspects a positive force because they later generated creative thinking on how to resolve computer management at the University.

In academic year 1996-97 a campus-wide asynchronous transfer mode (ATM) network was installed on the Main Campus. When coupled with the extensive fiber optic network that was introduced over several years at a cost of some $5 million, this technology signaled that the time had come to combine all of the University's computing delivery systems under one office.

A Joint Technology Advisory Committee of the major academic and administrative users was formed to study the management and organization of technology, specifically computing, at Widener. I chaired the committee, a learning experience. Being surrounded by technology experts reaffirmed my belief that a manager doesn't really have to be expert in the use of the systems; he just needs to understand what they can do if fully utilized. After months of study, the committee's consensus was to appoint a chief officer for information technology, serving at the vice presidential level. The title stated unequivocally to the University community that the debate over academic vs. administrative computing control was over.

It was clear at the outset of the search for the new vice president that the position was administrative, one in which communication and diplomacy would outweigh hands-on technology skills. After an extensive search, my long-time administrative assistant, Thomas H. Carnwath was chosen. Tom had developed excellent rapport with both faculty and administrators but particularly important to his selection and his success was the approbation of the leading faculty computing experts.

In 1997, with the completion of the ATM and fiber optic network, Widener's technological infrastructure was recognized nationally as a model for cutting edge technology when appropriately applied in higher education. Several members of the computing staff subsequently served as consultants with 3Com Network Technology, an industry leader located in Silicon Valley. This relationship proved to be mutually supportive, with Widener becoming a beta test site for 3Com and a visitation site for techies from colleges and universities across the country.

What a transformation! Within two decades Widener had progressed from a rudimentary computing system to an integrated, interactive system that was a source of great pride for all the staff and faculty who worked so diligently to see it happen. From FORTRAN to the World Wide Web, wired residence halls and classrooms, Widener's 20-year journey into sophisticated technology applications mirrored the changes occurring in society.

The future will require careful selection and management of technology. Each college and university must have the vision to adapt advances to its own environment and mission. It is clear that progress in some fields comes more slowly than in others. For example, libraries have not divested themselves of hard copy. Distance learning has not replaced the human interaction that occurs on campus among students and faculty. The traditional residential campus has not begun to disappear. But knowledge in the sciences, economics, health sciences and mathematics has exploded with the capability of the computer to produce permutations for research that were impossible in the past. The potential for technology in the future is limited only by human imagination.

Getting the Job Done

Warren Bennis, an authority on leadership, writes in *The Unconscious Conspiracy* that inadvertent circumstances prevent presidents from leading. His so-called First Law of Academic Pseudodynamics states that "routine work drives out non-routine work or: how to smother to death all creative planning." He postulates that much of the conspiracy comes from the involvement of presidents in so much daily minutia that there is little time to think strategically about broader issues. His challenge to presidents is to create organizational space that will enable them to exercise leadership. (Bennis 1976, 19-20)

The administrative structure introduced at Widener placed the responsibility for major administrative functions in the hands of specialists who had the authority to get the job done within the framework of University policy. It was notably successful for me. However, the process only works if the president is comfortable with his people, has enough self-confidence to avoid the need to micro-manage, and has the capacity to hear and absorb a great deal of information without getting bogged down in detail.

Chapter 6

Expanding the Academic Framework

Institutions without substantial endowments (e.g. many privates) are limited in their options to remain financially sound. They can be more efficiently managed, increase financial support, or engage in managed growth. The latter is usually achieved by expanding existing programs or introducing new ones; less commonly growth is achieved through acquisition or merger with other institutions. It is a source of pride that during my presidency, Widener University successfully pursued all of these options.

From the outset of my administration, we believed that a thorough knowledge of the demographics offered an opportunity for Widener to engineer strategic growth. Our reorganization into an integrated University had provided the necessary platform for such growth, in part by engaging the deans and faculty in the concept of the University's collective strength as an entity rather than as an umbrella for competing departments and disciplines.

Establishing an environment in which Widener's academic community understood the value of creative growth was critical. Equally important was the recognition that all things are cyclical, including enrollment trends and the popularity of academic majors. At some point most programs morph from a big-enrollment attraction into an established offering with a smaller revenue return. The infrastructure of support for any program had to be seen internally in such a way that a reallocation of resources could be accomplished with a minimum of angst.

Thanks to the genuine partnership between academics and administrators, good data analysis, and strategic thinking, Widener seized opportunities to be aggressive and creative as it redesigned itself into a better institution. Indeed, within the context of the mission as a comprehensive university, we became known as an institution that was very agile at anticipating academic needs and moving swiftly to fill them.

Accommodating Working Adults

Illustrative of this need-based programming were two marketing approaches introduced by University College, the unit offering programs for non-traditional students. To accommodate the market of working adults, particularly women, University College developed a Weekend College format and several off-campus sites. This approach exemplified the "new thinking" among our academic units; in this case, go where the students are, and schedule courses to suit their availability.

At its apex, University College enrolled over 2,000 students in associate, baccalaureate and certificate programs on and off campus. It was a substantial revenue producer for more than fifteen years until the market for non-traditional students became saturated with too many institutions pursuing the same student population. The part-time nature of its programs negated the need for a standing faculty, thereby avoiding long-term commitments to tenured individuals and the attendant cost of benefits. The use of faculty from the other schools and colleges of the University, coupled with extensive employment of adjunct faculty, made the college very cost effective.

Widener was fortunate to have Dr. Arlene DeCosmo as dean of University College. She had extensive knowledge of the adult-student universe, was aggressive in pursuing new academic opportunities in a changing marketplace, and was an effective administrator. She also fully appreciated the demands of Widener's integrated structure. Thus, when the decision to pursue specialized academic accreditation for all major programs became a constraint on University College, Dean DeCosmo was both pragmatic and gracious. For example, the accreditation for the School of Management imposed very strict regulations on all business course offerings and the faculty who taught them. Bowing to Management's accreditation requirements was a tradeoff the dean understood; to support another academic unit, and for the long-term benefit of the University, University College ended its control of evening business courses and thereby suffered the loss of enrollment.

Accreditation of the Disciplines

The decision to adopt specialized accreditation of all major disciplines as an operating standard was based on the belief that to do so would enhance the long-term academic reputation of Widener. Whatever short-term adjustments to resource allocation were needed to achieve this goal would be worth the effort. Goal VI, No. 4 in the faculty handbook stated that the intention was "to present each academic program in the University in such a way that, where appropriate and possible, it will meet or exceed the standards for accreditation by the relevant national accrediting agency for that discipline." (Widener 1987)

This objective was not only demanding but significant: it set the expectation for a combination of creative growth with academic quality. The process of self-study and the external validation that specialized accreditation brought to the University were enormously positive forces. The impact on faculty then and in the future was also universally positive.

The School of Engineering was the first to respond to the challenge. The initial step toward accreditation was taken in the mid-80s under the leadership of Dean Thomas McWilliams when the school introduced discipline-specific majors in electrical, mechanical, civil, and chemical engineering. These majors replaced a single multi-disciplinary program that had been in place since the early 1970s, but was a program that burdened graduates seeking employment with a non-specific diploma when recruiters were hiring specialists.

The process to achieve full accreditation by the Accreditation Board for Engineering and Technology (ABET) was strenuous and required a substantial commitment of human and financial resources. Over a five-year period, faculty were hired across all engineering disciplines, curricula were developed, and laboratory facilities were renovated and added. The commitment of resources to achieve accreditation was costly but appropriate, especially so since engineering students were traditionally among the brightest of the undergraduate population. The result was ABET approval of the four engineering disciplines as majors by 1990. The multi-disciplinary program was kept as an option but drew little student interest.

The business school was the next to ask approval to seek accreditation. Because the School of Management anticipated increased competition from local institutions, an independent consultant was engaged in 1987 to review the academic and financial issues that would influence a decision to pursue accreditation by AACSB (then known as the American Assembly of Collegiate Schools of Business, now as the Association to Advance Collegiate Schools of Business – International). The consultant's report provided a clear understanding of the extent of the substantial incremental costs that would be incurred by the University. Nevertheless, the administration recommended, and the Board of Trustees approved, initiation of the process to gain accreditation. The challenges were major in magnitude, but it was considered significant to achieve inclusion among the select membership of AACSB for the imprimatur carried an implied program quality that would be necessary in an increasingly competitive market for business faculty and students. Among the incremental expenses was the need to change from faculty with an M.B.A./CPA to those with a Ph.D. in accounting. Accounting doctoral holders, because they were so scarce, were for a time among the most difficult and costly faculty to recruit, creating financial strain not only for Widener but for all AACSB schools.

There were times during the multi-year odyssey to obtain AACSB status that the pursuit looked problematic. In 1992, for example, undergraduate applications for Widener business programs declined by 38 percent, reflecting predicted national and regional trends. Yet, the commitment to seek specialized accreditation for business, which was achieved in the fall of 1997, and other programs did not waiver.

Expansion of Graduate Programs on the Main Campus

In the last decades of the twentieth century, a growing number of Americans were baccalaureate educated. As the degree became the entry level qualification in the workplace, it was apparent that advanced degrees would increase an individual's marketability. Widener's response was to encourage faculty in all disciplines to work with their deans in developing appropriate graduate programs.

In the 1980s, the College of Arts & Sciences began to explore the possibility of a Master of Liberal Studies and a doctoral program in education. The Schools of Engineering and Management both expanded their graduate programs, and opened off-site courses. The M.B.A. curriculum was redesigned to make it more sensitive to the impact of technology on business applications and to recognize the internationalization of corporate America. The business school opened a Master of Public Administration, a master's in Long-Term Care Administration and a Master of Health and Medical Services Administration, a program that achieved national status and was one of the few H.M.S.A. graduate programs in the nation accredited for part-time study. Certificates in other health-related fields were added for those who held an M.B.A. and wished to transition to a specialization in the ever-growing health care industry. A small, but excellent program that attracted public attention was an M.D./M.B.A. offered jointly with Jefferson Medical College, a prestigious medical school in Philadelphia. The program, designed for physicians who wished to be medical management specialists, offered concentrations in medical services administration and in health administration. Additionally, a dual M.E./M.B.A. degree attracted corporate engineers.

The School of Nursing was also active in generating graduate offerings. Master's level programs (M.S.N.) were introduced in the areas of Burn, Emergency and Trauma, Nursing Service Administration, Oncology, and Nurse Practitioner. The last of these programs grew from my service on the boards of Crozer Chester Medical Center and the Crozer Keystone Health System which heightened my awareness of the shifting trends and demands on the health care industry.

I knew that the tightened reimbursement for health providers combined with skyrocketing costs of malpractice insurance was leading physicians to rethink the way they managed their practice. Many family doctors and those in internal medicine had begun to employ nurse practitioners rather than add physicians; the synergism among these professionals worked well in promoting quality medical care at lower costs. I was convinced that a Family Nurse Practitioner program was a natural fit for the School of Nursing. After some months of persuasion, the dean of nursing agreed to conduct a feasibility study, which led in turn to a highly successful program offered both on the Main Campus and in central Pennsylvania.[1]

In the mid 1990s, a feasibility study for a master's level program in physical therapy was developed by the newest of the University's schools, Human Service Profession, that included an undergraduate track designed to retain outstanding Widener baccalaureate students following their graduation. The funding for the study, and for the subsequent start-up of the program, was made possible by the Strawbridge Foundation.[2]

---

[1] Internally, I encouraged L. Luke Cellini, M.D., the University's director of Health Services, to consider the addition of nurse practitioners to assist him. With some reluctance, he did so. Within months I recall him commenting that hiring nurse practitioners was among the best decisions he had made!

[2] Dr. George Strawbridge, Jr. a member of the Board of Trustees, had an interest in providing seed capital to explore and implement new academic programs. Two of the University's major programs, University College and Physical Therapy resulted from his support. Having someone like Dr. Strawbridge on the board was an extraordinary asset to the University — a savvy businessman and creative thinker.

Physical Therapy was a perfect fit to the University's mandate that the graduate programs were to be applied, clinical or professional in content. As a profession, physical therapy had grown dramatically from 48 accredited programs in 1970 to 119 programs in 1991. Projections for future expansion of the profession postulated the need for physical therapists to continue to grow until well into the twenty-first century.

Assured of funding from the Strawbridge Foundation, Widener had the unique opportunity of being able to hire a director and provide him or her with time to develop curriculum, hire faculty, and work with University Relations on marketing. The strongest candidate for the position was Ms. Bonnie Teschendorf, the director of the Physical Therapy Program at Columbia University. I recall making the final approach to her at the University Club in New York City for several hours one afternoon. A condition of Professor Teschendorf's acceptance of the position was a commitment to a new facility to house the program. This agreement led in 1992 to the construction of Cottee Hall. As a colleague from an Ivy League institution, Teschendorf's employment generated enthusiasm for the project among faculty.

The master's in Physical Therapy was an immediate success. In 2000, it was redesigned into a doctoral degree to reflect the shifts in the health care industry and to remain competitive in the allied health field.

The University's first doctoral program (D.N.S.) was designed to prepare nurse educators for faculty teaching positions at the university level. The National League for Nursing, the accreditation body for nursing education, had moved toward mandating that nursing faculty should be doctorally prepared. Until the introduction of D.N.S. programs the only options open to nursing faculty were Ed.D. or traditional Ph.D. programs. The D.N.S. was a directed doctoral degree that filled a need for nursing faculty who wished to meet the new credentialing standards for their profession.

Centralizing Graduate Program Administration

In the fall of 1987 graduate student enrollment at Widener reached 1,700 in thirty masters and three doctoral programs. The rapid expansion of the number of graduate programs in the 1980s necessitated a review of how the programs could share a common administrative infrastructure given that the decision had been made earlier to keep the locus of graduate programs within the province of the individual college or schools.

Widener was not ready to move to a separate graduate school headed by a graduate dean, but the appointment of an assistant provost for graduate studies was appropriate, though controversial with some deans who feared a potential loss of control. It was accomplished after a Middle States site visitation team recommended the need for better coordination of the increasing number of graduate programs.

Dr. Joseph DiAngelo filled the position first, followed by Dr. Stephen Wilhite. Aggressive and creative, DiAngelo established University-wide policies and procedures to ensure the quality of graduate programs, including the development of demographic statistics and a system for evaluating new graduate program proposals. The needs of the growing numbers of graduate students were addressed with efforts to better provide support services. He also introduced a coordinated registration and scheduling matrix, and a Graduate Student Handbook.

Task Force on Graduate Programs

Wilhite, a member of the College of Arts and Sciences faculty with a doctorate from Oxford University, was appointed to the position of assistant provost for graduate studies when DiAngelo accepted the position of dean of the School of Management. Working with a Graduate Council and the provost, Wilhite formed the University's fourth major task force, The Task Force on Graduate Programs, to study (a) the impact, if any, of graduate programs on the University's image and enrollment and (b) to make recommendations for the future administration and structure of graduate studies at Widener.

In response to the first part of the study, the task force encouraged the continued growth of graduate programs, acknowledging that over the decade of 1981-1991 their existence had begun to enhance the perception of the University, and positively influence full-time-enrollment statistics. In 1983 there had been 1,099 students enrolled in graduate studies, of whom only 44 were full-time. Within five years, the number had grown to 1,970 students, with 264 full-time. The trend was evident and expanded exponentially in the 1990s.

To frame the discussion for the second part of its charge, the task force set three ground rules. First, all graduate programs at Widener would be applied, clinical or professional, not research-based. Second, the University would continue to recognize the need to hire faculty who were qualified to teach both graduate and undergraduate students, eschewing the notion of a traditional graduate faculty. Finally, no graduate assistants would teach in undergraduate classrooms, although they would be permitted to assist in laboratory sections.

With the parameters for expansion set, the Task Force on Graduate Programs next asked each college and school to perform a self-assessment of the strengths and weaknesses of existing graduate programs.

It also developed a methodology to promote understanding of the impact of new offerings in terms of the increased costs to the University for support services, space, and human resources. Its use would enable the academic leadership to compare the revenue enhancement of, for example, an entirely new graduate program targeted to small numbers of part-time students against the introduction of new concentrations. A master's in clinical social work, offered as both full- and part-time courses of study in fall 1991 by the faculty of the Graduate Program in Social Work, exemplified the use and success of the methodology.

Graduate Studies Create a "New Widener"

The dramatic expansion of graduate studies on the Chester campus created a major realignment of the perception of Widener, bringing recognition of its comprehensive nature after many years of being known as an undergraduate campus. The University Relations staff developed successful marketing and media strategies to reflect the reality, but it was a challenge to encourage the acceptance of the "new Widener" by Main Campus senior faculty. Because Chester had a long history as an undergraduate campus, many considered graduate studies an add-on rather than an integral part of the whole, creating the necessity to constantly remind deans and administrators that not all decisions would be made based upon the needs of undergraduate students.

The shift in income from undergraduate to graduate programs exceeded our projections. As with any variation in a paradigm, internal issues relating to support services, fees and tuition and, of course, faculty teaching loads had to be reexamined. Constant discussions and ongoing adjustments to old habits helped modernize the institution. Finally, the acceptance of an integrated institution became a reality.

Faculty assignments and course loads were adjusted several times over the years as it became necessary to allow some professors, because of the nature of their academic specialization, to teach only graduate students. Their loads were lower (nine hours) than for those faculty exclusively teaching undergraduates (twelve hours) in recognition of the work involved in overseeing dissertations and the increased expectation for publication. Despite these exceptions, the basic Widener philosophy held: there was neither a separate graduate dean nor a separate graduate faculty; everyone hired to teach was considered sufficiently credentialed to prepare both graduate and undergraduate students.

The decision to restrict graduate programs to applied, rather than research-focused, was significant for it allowed Widener to find a niche in the marketplace without duplicating, at enormous cost, traditional research programs already in place at many area institutions. Applied programs also helped to define, and continued to strengthen, Widener's mission as a comprehensive university. Their introduction clearly changed the reputation and mission of Widener for all time.

Mergers and Acquisitions

A corollary strategy for the growth and shaping of academic quality is to pursue acquisition or merger opportunities. The rationale for an acquisition must be based on the potential for enhancing the profile of the institution and/or increasing the market share; either will in turn result in increased revenues and greater academic opportunity. The strategy worked so well for Widener that I was asked to present a paper at the 1987 Conference at Wingspread to representatives of education associations and private institutions. (Bruce 1987)

An acquisition in private higher education is substantially different from one in the corporate community, principally because the financial techniques needed to emulate the corporate model are unavailable. Increased market share may be the objective of an academic acquisition, but without the capacity to issue stock or easily liquidate assets, academic acquisitions can be financially difficult to effectuate.

In considering an acquisition, each of the parties must enter the transaction with the belief that consolidation will be beneficial to both entities. In reality, one institution in every merger will be financially stronger and have greater growth potential, a fact that will dramatically enhance its leverage during negotiations. But shared values and a clear understanding of expectations by each institution are paramount.

The decision to expand by acquisition cannot be justified simply on cost savings because colleges are so labor intensive. For example, the 1992 opening of Widener's third campus in Harrisburg, Pennsylvania, while producing some economy of scale by being an integrated part of the Law School, still made it necessary to duplicate services to students and to hire faculty (some of whom we had hoped to supply from Wilmington).[3]

As Widener looked at merger possibilities, benchmarks were developed for evaluating the opportunities. Among them were:

- a clear understanding of what each institution wanted from the merger,
- benefits outside the existing Widener structure that had the potential to expand the totality of the University, and
- confidence that significant financial gain or academic enhancement would result from the merger.

The success of a merger lies with the CEO and other principals participating in the negotiations. Some ill will is inevitable during the process, but it is critical that the universities' leadership be prepared to assuage the fears of their respective constituents. If not well managed, the skepticism of faculty and administrators can be detrimental to the assimilation process. Sharing goals and information about the merger to as wide a group as possible must be a priority for both institutions.

The acquisition of the Delaware Law School and merger with Brandywine College, reflected the above criteria and began the transformation of Widener into a university. Together they provided new academic dimensions and, from Brandywine, a second campus.

Law School Acquisition

Although the Delaware Law School had a checkered past when acquired, was unaccredited, and under enrolled, there had been two distinct pluses to the merger: it was located in Delaware, and was the only law school in the state. These facts drove a number of decisions pertinent to the future of the school that began in 1971 as Delaware Law School, became the Delaware Law School of Widener University in 1977 and Widener School of Law in 1988. For example, since the state of Delaware was the seat of a great many business incorporations, a curricular emphasis on corporate law was a logical choice. Also, it offered a unique opportunity to build a special relationship with the highly regarded Delaware judiciary and legal community.

This last was not an easy task given the animosity that had existed

---

[3] See further discussion of the Harrisburg Campus, Chapter 8

between the school's founding dean, Alfred Avins, and the state's bench and bar. Avins, who opened the school in a downtown Wilmington YMCA, was a very conservative individual whose special mission in life seemed to be to tweak the ABA over the control of accreditation policies and the legal community over bar exams. Having been with him on several occasions, I can personally say he was a brilliant but eccentric individual with few social graces.

Brandywine College Affiliation

The affiliation between Widener University and Brandywine College in 1976 was a good business stratagem by both parties. Brandywine found a partner to share the costs of its underutilized campus; Widener gained a property on which to house the law school it had acquired a year before. Additionally, affiliation with the much larger Widener University ensured Brandywine's financial stability in the immediate and short-term future.

There were, however, two issues that threatened Brandywine's long-term existence. First was a pedagogic dilemma: How does a college offering associate degree programs in Fashion Merchandising, Food Management, Business and Secretarial Sciences fit within a university that is staking its future on expanding professional and graduate programs?

Second, the external projections for a diminishing market for private two-year colleges in the last decade of the twentieth century provided a subtext for all planning efforts. Nevertheless, a good-faith effort was made to integrate Brandywine into the Widener universe. Brandywine was academically reorganized to offer majors that were more closely aligned with Widener's bachelor's offerings, thus providing A.A. and A.S. candidates with a curricular path into the baccalaureate programs on the Main Campus.

Doctor of Clinical Psychology: A Discreet Approach for Merger

In the summer of 1988, Wilmington College President Dr. Audrey Doberstein, a graduate of the doctoral program in clinical psychology (Psy.D.) then located at Hahnemann University in Philadelphia, advised me in confidence that the founder and dean of the program, Dr. Jules Abrams, and his faculty were discussing a possible departure from Hahnemann if an appropriate university setting could be found. Dr. Doberstein thought Widener might be a good fit for the program.

I was intrigued, for that particular Psy.D. program was nationally recognized as being among the country's academic best. After querying her about why its principals were considering a move from a parent institution with a reputation in medicine and allied health to a comprehensive university, Dr. Doberstein shared enough information to justify in my mind that a further conversation might be productive. I agreed to speak with Dr. Abrams under the condition that he must make the first contact. If things proceeded, I did not want Widener to be perceived as initiating a conversation to pirate a program from another institution.

I came away from that initial meeting with Jules Abrams impressed with his sincerity, his intellectual acumen, and his commitment to both his students and faculty. It was intriguing to meet an academic dean who had the confidence and emotional dedication to his program to actively seek an option to a deteriorating situation.

Abrams and his faculty shared concerns stemming from both organizational and philosophical priorities. After operating for many years with relative autonomy at Hahnemann, the Psy.D. program had been moved to the School of Medicine and was reporting to the chairman of the Department of Mental Health Sciences, a psychiatrist by training. In that era, a philosophical divide existed between clinical psychologists and most medical practitioners, including many psychiatrists, on how best to treat patients with psychological and behavioral problems. As physicians, psychiatrists often believed the best patient treatment included appropriate drug therapy. However, as a result of their training clinical psychologists were more inclined to follow a combination of modalities including psychotherapy and other behavioral modification techniques. Therefore, being housed in the School of Medicine made the clinical psychology faculty feel marginalized. Further, they did not respond well to the chairman's management style.

Serendipitously, I had the opportunity to observe their chairman during Widener's on-going discussions with the Hahnemann clinical psychologists. He and I were serving on a search committee seeking a new chief of psychiatry for the Crozer Medical Center, I as a Crozer board member and he representing Hahnemann's medical school, which provided psychiatric residents to Crozer. After observing his very assertive manner, I understood Dr. Abram's issues.

When the decision to proceed with discussions was made, I thought that I first should tell the president of Hahnemann that we had been approached by Abrams. However, I learned that unless the discussions were held in the strictest confidence, Abrams would not move forward; he was greatly concerned about retribution by the chairman against the faculty. He further felt that it was his responsibility to speak with the Hahnemann administration at the appropriate time.

I selected Provost Larry Buck to be the point person for Widener, a task he did most ably. While I was involved on a daily basis in setting the conditions under which negotiations were being held, it was more appropriate to have the fine points negotiated between Dean Abrams and the provost, thus building understanding and trust between the two. It also provided me with the necessary space to be objective, and allowed the provost's grasp of academic detail to hone the talking points.

After six months of conversation, an agreement in principle was reached, and then approved by Widener's Board of Trustees on February 9, 1989. At that time Dean Abrams and the Psy.D. faculty, accompanied by Widener's Assistant Provost Stephen Wilhite and CAS Dean Annette Steigelfest met with the program's students to discuss the impact of the transition. It was a very sensitive conversation since student concerns were multiple, including change of location, library resources, housing and, most serious, financial aid and scholarships.

Provost Buck then went to Hahnemann to represent Widener's position to his counterpart, the dean of the School of Medicine and vice president of academic affairs, and to negotiate the details of the program transfer. Following that meeting, I met with the president of Hahnemann. The conversation was strained but we agreed that the institutions would cooperate to facilitate the transfer with minimal disruption to the students. Although the tenor of the talks was professional, to say there were no ill feelings on the part of Hahnemann would be a colossal misstatement.

In July 1989, after several months of negotiations with Hahnemann, Widener announced that in September it would introduce a Doctor of Clinical Psychology program headed by the nationally known clinical psychologist and educator Dr. Jules C. Abrams. His title would be associate dean for the Institute for Graduate Clinical Psychology in the College of Arts and Sciences. No mention was made of Hahnemann in the announcement although what had transpired was widely known in the region and profession.

A tribute to the reputation of the program and of Jules Abrams was the fact that all fifteen of the faculty and ninety of the students moved to Widener. Only the few students enrolled in the heavily scientific research track of the program remained at Hahnemann. Moreover, accreditation by the American Psychological Association was allowed to move with the program, an unheard of event in higher education. It quickly became apparent that two very similar academic cultures had melded into one; the comprehensive and humanistic philosophy of Widener matched the professional and humanistic philosophy of the program. It was a textbook acquisition.

The Remarkable Silence

Two things about the Psy.D. negotiations were remarkable. First was the universal commitment within Widener to seeking new academic opportunities. The second, and most extraordinary, was the commitment of trustees, administration and faculty to confidentiality. In order to gain acceptance of the program into the College of Arts and Sciences, the entire plan and academic organization had to be presented to over 130 CAS faculty who discussed and approved the program in complete confidentiality. No word of the discussions or negotiations ever leaked, nor was any confidence ever broken.

I attributed this to the work of the provost, the Dean of Arts and Sciences Annette Steigelfest, and to the fact that the faculty – used to being consulted and treated as partners in the educational enterprise – appreciated both their inclusion and the sensitivity of the situation. They were also well aware of the tremendous professional risk their soon-to-be new colleagues were taking.

The introduction of the Psy.D. students and faculty to campus galvanized the acceptance of cultural change within the institution. More significant, the source of University revenues began to change dramatically over several years with close to 50 percent of revenue ultimately coming from graduate and professional programs, including the School of Law.

A humorous vignette relating to the merger was shared by Dave Eckard with Pat Brant during a 1998 taped interview.

> In July of 1989, the Philadelphia-area colleges and universities hosted the annual meeting of the National Association of College and University Business Officers .... The pre-meeting event called the President's Dinner ... [was] hosted by Aramark Corporation....
> We were standing on the veranda ... [when] Joe

Neubauer, chairman and CEO of Aramark ... walked over particularly to introduce his wife to me and my wife. His wife [commented], "I don't know that much about Widener University." I said, "We are known as a rather aggressive, and somewhat entrepreneurial institution. For example, we publicly announced a couple of days ago that the Doctor of Clinical Psychology program from Hahnemann University was moving en masse to Widener University." At that point, Mr. Neubauer says "yes, I'm familiar with that. I'm on the board at Hahnemann. Honey, it's about time we go greet some other people!"

The postscript is that his daughter Melissa graduated from the Widener Psy.D. program, as did his son-in-law who met her while they were students in the program. Indeed, Mr. Neubauer was the commencement speaker at his daughter's 1995 graduation and the family subsequently established a generous scholarship in support of Clinical Psychology graduate students.

A strategy of acquisition and merger has been reaffirmed over the years by the fact that Widener's School of Law and Doctor of Clinical Psychology programs are among the University's most profitable and publicly recognized academic programs. The strategy requires a great deal of work and the emotional toughness to back off if the due diligence or the negotiations seem problematic, but it can be well worth it in the end.

Human Service Professions Becomes Eighth School

In academic year 1992-93, the Center for Education, the Center for Social Work Education and the Doctor of Clinical Psychology program were combined into the eighth school of the University, the School of Human Service Professions (SHSP). Most of the units of the School of Human Service Professions had been initially housed in the College of Arts and Sciences (CAS) but were not a good fit there, nor in any of the other existing schools. Eventually the complexity of administering CAS precipitated the need for a discrete academic unit for programs in the human services. An important by-product of the formation of SHSP was that it allowed the College of Arts & Sciences to refocus its mission on the more traditional liberal arts and sciences, and on providing general education.

Dr. Wilhite, who had been instrumental in the formation of several of the programs that comprised the new school, was appointed dean while retaining his appointment as assistant provost for graduate studies. Each of the academic units within the new school was headed by an associate dean who reported to Wilhite. The master's program in Physical Therapy, discussed earlier, was the first program developed by SHSP.

Growth by Spin-off: from Brandywine, A School of Hospitality

Under the creative leadership of Brandywine Dean Andrew A. Bushko, Brandywine soldiered on for several years, redefining itself as needed. For example, an associate degree program in hospitality management was so successful that in 1981 it was redesigned into a four-year, Bachelor of Science curriculum.

Establishing a baccalaureate school on a junior college campus was an example of Brandywine's creativity. But as the School of Hotel and Restaurant Management (SHRM) began to develop a reputation within the hospitality industry, concerns about the comprehensiveness of the student life experience were raised on both campuses. There was a need for expanded student services; for additional laboratory and library support; for enriched offerings in business, liberal arts, and general education; as well as for co-curricular and extra-curricular opportunities that are rightfully expected by four-year undergraduates. The list of needs in Delaware was significant enough to lead to a discussion about moving SHRM to the Main Campus in Chester. The move would provide hospitality students with a more appropriate and comprehensive academic and social experience. In turn, the students would increase the undergraduate enrollment on the Chester campus, an undoubted advantage given the projections for a regional and national decline in four-year students. The integrated nature of decision making at Widener was clearly on display in this period; discussions ranged across two campuses, several schools, and numerous programs.

The University had purchased a Sheraton hotel adjacent to the Delaware Campus in the belief that it would enhance the curriculum and provide invaluable internship experience for the students. Unfortunately, the Sheraton's bottom-line reality for profit greatly restricted the range and intensity of student integration into the hotel. It quickly became apparent that the true benefit of owning the Sheraton was primarily as a marketing tool. As a result, it was determined that there would be little impact on either the hospitality courses or the Sheraton-Brandywine Inn if the school were relocated and the hotel sold.

The move of the hospitality program would also help relieve the tension over space allocation that existed among the staff and faculties of law, hospitality, Brandywine, graduate business, and the University College programs that were also offered on the campus. It was clear that the Law School needed additional library space and classrooms. Moreover, it and other academic units serving adults in Delaware could only be encouraged to expand if SHRM moved to Chester.

The consolidation of all baccalaureate programs on one campus answered most of the academic, social and physical-plant issues. Given the decision to move the School of Hotel and Restaurant Management, the construction of an appropriate facility on the Chester campus became inevitable. The bottom line was, if Brandywine could survive, it would be an economic plus. If not, the Delaware Campus would continue to be financially viable through expansion of other campus-based programs.

Closing Brandywine College: Behind the Scenes

Brandywine College continued to weaken, raising the specter of closing. The elimination of an academic unit stirs the whole gamut of sensitivities including loss of morale and the creation of an atmosphere of hostility and recrimination. Most serious is the potential for litigation from faculty over tenure and seniority if the dissolution is not carefully managed.

Before closing Brandywine, we undertook serious study of all the attendant issues and included in the deliberations the faculty and staff who would be affected by the decision. To begin the process, in January of 1988, I requested the deans of Widener's schools and colleges to revisit and update the strategic plans that had been prepared five years earlier. They were to realistically reflect the shifting external demographics as well as potential growth opportunities. By including Brandywine in this planning effort, I avoided singling it out for speculation.

Assisted by a faculty member from the School of Management, Dean Bushko led a committee of Brandywine faculty and staff through an analysis that included two crucial issues. First was the identification of the enrollment level at which the academic programs would no longer be viable. Second was identification of the point at which the blend of academic and co-curricular activities would no longer be conducive to a good learning experience.

The Brandywine plan was submitted in April of 1989 and was complete with a projection that called for an enrollment increase over three years. In reality, the decline in the fall of 1990 was 23 percent. In a financial impact study conducted by Vice President Eckard, the projected deficit for Brandywine that academic year would reach $1.1 million. The outcome was painfully clear to everyone.

At an October 10, 1990 meeting of the Brandywine College Academic Council it was advised that after evaluation of all available data I had reached the decision that Brandywine College was no longer financially viable and could no longer provide an acceptable level of academic offerings. I shared that I planned to recommend the discontinuance of Brandywine to the University's Board of Trustees. In the same meeting, the council was asked to assist in preparing recommendations for phasing out the academic programs while meeting the college's obligations to its students.

As a consequence of its work on the planning document, the faculty leadership was uniquely familiar with all the issues, problems and financial numbers. They understood the conundrum facing the University. While obviously unhappy with the discontinuance, they reacted professionally in light of the analyses and data by accepting, if not fully endorsing, the decision.

Among the recommendations ultimately submitted by the council, the most significant was that Brandywine College faculty and students move to the Main Campus for the final year of operation. Separating faculty and students from the Delaware Campus was an excellent suggestion for many reasons, not the least of which was that it would provide a good collegial experience for the students.

One hundred and fifty of the 204 first-year Brandywine students elected to move to the Main Campus to complete their studies in academic year 1991-92. In fact, many elected to transfer to the campus as four-year baccalaureate students, an option made available to those who qualified academically.

The more complex personnel issues of faculty and staff were handled on an individual basis. Since the locus of academic appointment at Widener is by school or college, the issue of seniority or tenure was not a factor. The faculty handbook, section 2.2.4, states: "All faculty appointments, whether probationary or continued, have the locus of their appointment within the discipline of their school/college/library as stated in the annual letter of appointment.

"A faculty member's locus of appointment may not be changed from that specified in the initial letter of appointment in any manner disadvantageous to that faculty member with respect to employment protection in cases of program contraction or discontinuance without the agreement of the faculty member." (Widener 1987)

It was understood that the University had an obligation, when financial exigency forced program discontinuance, to assist faculty to find a position at Widener or to seek employment elsewhere. Some, nearing the end of their careers, elected to retire. A number of Brandywine faculty qualified for teaching positions on the Main Campus. One became the director of the Honors Program and another, the undergraduate assistant provost. Several faculty were given classroom assignments or administrative posts.

Four individuals filed claims against the University and those, curiously enough, occurred several years after the discontinuation when the claimants found themselves unhappy with their second-career choices. In all cases, the University was absolved of fault.

The closing of Brandywine, while regrettable, was accomplished smoothly largely because of the leadership of Dr. Bushko who was able to conduct his role as dean of Brandywine and assistant provost for the Delaware Campus without prejudice. His rapport with the faculty was instrumental in enabling them to examine the facts in a rational and collegial manner. No less important were the University administration's effort to share all information critical to the decision-making process, and the willingness of the Main Campus deans and faculty to welcome Brandywine faculty as true colleagues.

It was an extraordinary effort. Indeed, a member of the Board of Trustees wrote to me after the closing to say that he believed "your ability and those of your staff to accomplish the closing of an academic school without litigation and with the consent of the faculty and staff being affected, is beyond remarkable!"

Barriers to Merger

Over the years, there were conversations with several institutions, usually initiated by the other entity, often in the hope that a stronger, more stable partner would promote survival. Opportunities came to Widener because of its reputation as a creative, entrepreneurial organization.

Many times, as in the case of the Coombs School of Music, a private degree-granting music school located in Philadelphia, the addition of the program proved after analysis to be too risky. Despite adding a missing component to our fine arts curriculum, the prospect of Coombs contributing positively to the bottom line was too marginal to pursue.

On two separate occasions, a number of years apart, talks were held with Peirce College located in center city Philadelphia. The contact each time was the president of Peirce, a long-time colleague. The first conversation occurred at a time when Peirce was struggling financially and when Widener was expanding the Delaware Campus and contemplating opening a third campus. Taking on a struggling two-year college as a turn-around project was not the best use of Widener's limited financial and human resources despite the attraction of Peirce's center city location and valuable real estate holdings.

The second conversation was held under very different circumstances and the potential merger was quite attractive to the University. Peirce, by then offering both associate and baccalaureate degrees, was solvent and doing well as a four-year college.

The impetus for the discussion was Peirce's aspiration to aggressively pursue distance- and off-campus learning, a niche market it had begun serving within a largely minority and part-time student population both on campus and in corporate settings. Although the college had become a provider for center city businesses among the ranks of lower and middle management, expansion would come with substantial cost. Seeking to partner with an institution maintaining a sophisticated technology infrastructure with excess capacity that also shared an appreciation for creative and flexible academic programming made sense. The Peirce group, including the board chairman who was involved in the discussions, understood the necessity of a merger since Widener would be assuming the greater risk. The only non-negotiable item was that the Peirce name had to survive in some manner, a sensitive and reasonable demand.

The business programs and part-time nature of the Peirce student would have been an excellent fit with Widener's non-traditional University College. Because University College had no permanent faculty, the absence of tenure among the Peirce faculty would not become an internal Widener issue. Changing the name of University College to Peirce College of Widener University was a logical answer to the preservation of the Peirce name.

The use of University College as the structure to bring Peirce under the Widener umbrella, while presenting the possibility of some difficulty with AACSB in the area of Peirce's business education program, could likely have been managed.

Two issues ended the talks. In a meeting with the Peirce group, a discussion of AACSB restrictions resulted in their misperception that Widener's provost did not understand that they exclusively used contract and adjunct faculty. It was most regrettable, especially so since Provost Buck was always both creative and flexible in his approach to academic opportunities.

The second concern was more substantive. When asked how long I intended to remain at Widener, I replied that I planned to retire in two years. I later learned Peirce's comfort level with Widener was based largely upon my reputation, experience and relationship with their president. It was unfortunate the timing was as it was, for the merger of Widener and Peirce had the prospect of being an excellent one.

The University also looked at Spring Garden College, a private institution in Philadelphia faced with imminent bankruptcy. In this instance our interest was not to acquire the college – financially the numbers would not work – but to take on a small but excellent architectural program and several business programs that would have added strength to the student numbers of University College and the School of Business Administration.[4] However, after due diligence we concluded that the debt structure of Spring Garden, including several lease arrangements, was too risky to offset potential gains.

One of the more interesting conversations that occurred was with Westminster Choir College located in Princeton, New Jersey. The president and several of his senior staff requested a meeting to "pick our brains" about how to seek a partner because existence as a stand-alone institution was becoming financially more and more difficult.

Provost Buck, Vice President Eckard and I met with the Westminster group on a snowy evening. After a lengthy conversation, I expressed an interest in pursuing the notion of Widener's fit for the role of parent corporation. Westminster was a gem with a wonderful location next to Princeton University and an international reputation as a

---

[4] The School of Management became the School of Business Administration in 1986.

music college. Unfortunately, because of geographic distance the necessary synergism was not there. I do believe, however, that we assisted them in eventually merging with Rider University located only fifteen miles from Princeton.

Even a school with the improbable name of the Straight School of Chiropractic Medicine was considered. I personally thought it would be a good fit, given Widener's strength in allied and professional health offerings. It would have been an excellent revenue producer.

I was persuaded, however, by the deans of the Schools of Nursing and Human Service Professions that chiropractic medicine was not seen as a mainstream health provider and would not gain much favor with the accrediting bodies of our other programs. I still am not convinced it was the correct decision.

The strategies of merger, acquisition, expansion and reduction can each enhance an institution's growth and stability. It is the task of the university's president to weigh the impact and potential of each option.

Chapter 7

The School of Law

I was persuaded early in my presidency that the School of Law, if properly marketed, could be a major asset in creating an identity for Widener. The ability to promote it as one of only 175 law schools in the United States to have earned accreditation by the American Bar Association helped differentiate it among the competition. In addition, law schools – like medical schools – were perceived to have academic quality and greater societal importance than other graduate programs, making it easier to market than to attempt to establish a niche for business or education programs that existed elsewhere in abundance.

Society's growing complexity in the last decades of the twentieth century created new specializations in law: health, environment, credit, civil rights, age and gender among them. Concomitantly, the courts began to show a willingness to be involved in areas of society that had been considered outside the legal system in the past, including family and parental matters, medical decisions, and rights of children and minorities. This broadened role of the legal system attracted more and more people to the study of law. The national attendance at law schools increased dramatically in the early 1980s.

However, the "selling" of a law school owned by a Pennsylvania institution to a parochial "First State" mindset was an obvious challenge. While the legal community was pleased that Widener had acquired the law school, there were many in Delaware who felt it should have become a part of the University of Delaware. Actually, it was our understanding at the time of the acquisition that the University of Delaware had determined, given the size of the state, that a law school for Delaware was not practical. (Over the years, the president of the University of Delaware would occasionally ask me with a wry smile, "How's my law school doing?")

The key to success was to position the institution as a regional law school drawing students from the tri-state area of Pennsylvania, New

Jersey and Delaware. Indeed the geographic location, north of the city of Wilmington and easily accessible to Interstate-95 and the Philadelphia suburbs, was a positive influence in attracting both students and faculty. As the Law School developed and matured, the geographic span of the school provided unusual access to the judiciary and law firms in both states.

Firing a Dean

Every enterprise is dependent upon the skill of its leadership. Since it is they who provide the energy and vision, having the right individual in place at the right time is critical to the life of an organization. After my first year, Widener was fortunate to have a series of law deans whose skills uniquely fitted the occasion of their deanships. However, when I became president, one of my less pleasant chores was to fire the sitting law dean.

The dean had made it obvious in less than two years in the position that he had been a problematic appointment. Controversial since being hired during President Moll's last year in office, he had shortly thereafter made some very unflattering public comments about the University. Dr. Moll, in deference to me as the incoming president who would inherit the dean asked what action I thought he should take. My instinct and recommendation was that the dean be fired and we all accept that hiring him had been a mistake. Dr. Moll decided not to do so.

All law deans question the allocation of revenues for services from the parent corporation for areas such as finance, development, marketing support, space, overhead, etc. The issue arises because if the enrollment numbers are on target, most law schools regularly produce excess revenue over expenses. In this case, the dean developed a constant theme of complaint about what he saw as financial handicapping of the Law School by the University. When members of the Law School's advisory panel, known at Widener as the Board of Overseers, began to sound the same refrain, it was apparent that the dean had been proselytizing. His agenda was clearly to disassociate the Law School from the University.

His attempts to persuade the board to his position ultimately led several overseers to conclude independent of each other that the dean was not a good fit at Widener. Months after the fact, I learned that at an overseers' meeting he had complained that the budget for the law library was inadequate and asked what they, the overseers, planned to do about it. The response, correctly, was "How do you as dean plan to find, or raise, additional funds?" His answer, "That is really not my problem," was both inaccurate and inappropriate; certainly not the right retort to a group of senior VPs of major corporations and partners of law firms.

The event that helped finalize my decision to dismiss him occurred on the Delaware Campus at a meeting intended to clarify the relationship between the University and the Law School. It was late afternoon when Vice President Eckard and I walked into a moot courtroom packed with students and faculty. We presented our remarks on the structural and corporate relationship and how the allocation of revenue was reached. When I opened the meeting to questions, the atmosphere in the room became hostile.

Questioners asked what value obtained to the Law School from being part of Widener. Why did the University take revenue from the Law School? Why wasn't the dean more independent of University management, etc.?

There was the misperception on the part of some in attendance that the Law School was funding the University's debt; that without its contribution, Widener would be in financial difficulty. The perception was wildly incorrect and could only have come from the dean and those among the faculty who had been with the school from its inception as a freestanding entity and disliked being part of Widener.

At one point, as the dialogue became more heated, there was a loud explosive sound. I said, "Damn, somebody tried to shoot me!" The crowd roared with laughter, which let the air out of the adversarial tone. It was a good line and came at a very good time courtesy of a bursting balloon that had remained clinging to the ceiling from a celebration the evening before.

The discussion that followed the balloon incident was cordial and more civil as the students attempted to understand the issues. Law students are intellectually bright, inquisitive, and argumentative. They respond to logic and candid information. Since my relationship with students was always to be straightforward, never to obfuscate, the conversation concluded well.

I was convinced that the dean had motivated several of the heated questions. In fact, I saw him pass a note to a student, who in the next moment stood to ask me a question. On the way back to the Main Campus, I asked Dave Eckard if he had seen what I had. He corroborated my observation.

When, in confidence, I shared with several senior law faculty that I planned to replace the dean, I was advised that he was not universally liked. I was not surprised, but the reported numbers of those who disavowed him substantiated my initial advice to my predecessor. I also met with a group of overseers who resided in Delaware, several of whom were supportive of the dean. It was not the most pleasant breakfast I have ever had, but I felt it necessary to share my concerns and the reasons for my decision. It also illustrated my commitment to the simple fact that in every organization only one person is the final decision maker. Input from others is essential, but the responsibility for decisions lies with the CEO.

I called the dean to my office and informed him he was being relieved of his duties as dean but I would allow him to resign if he wished. He elected to resign.

Former dean Arthur Weeks, who had remained at the Law School as a member of the faculty, served as interim dean. A search committee headed by Esther Clark, a popular senior faculty member, was constituted immediately.

Reflective of its uncertain beginnings, the school had had three deans in nine years. Thus, I was convening a search committee for the fourth.

Professor Clark strongly recommended Anthony J. Santoro, then dean of the University of Bridgeport Law School. A graduate of Boston College who held a J.D. and LL.M. from Georgetown University School of Law, Santoro had teaching experience at the McGeorge School of Law, University of the Pacific; Western New England; and Marshall-Wythe School of Law, College of William and Mary. His wide network of associates also included good contacts in the American Bar Association.

Despite all of this, he used to say that working for his father in the clothing industry prepared him best for academe. "Working in the 'rag industry' is good training for being a lawyer and better for being a dean; it brings practical business experience to the task of advising clients and teaching students."

I always appreciated the added value of individuals with varied degrees of experience, social, cultural or professional, and looked for these traits when hiring senior staff. Anthony Santoro was a perfect match for the School of Law, for Widener University, and for me. We were both politically attuned and entrepreneurial by nature. We both believed that individual contacts translate into support and acceptance of the institution you lead.

On the day of our first meeting, scheduled for my office in late afternoon immediately before I was to fly west on a fund-raising trip, the campus had a massive blackout caused by the failure of a high voltage electrical system. My secretary had found several candles so my office basked in an atmosphere more appropriate to an intimate dinner than a job interview. After several interruptions for repair updates, Tony recalls I informed him, "It was a pleasure meeting you and I apologize for leaving, but I must catch a flight to Chicago" and left him sitting in the dark. Or as he says, "as usual, left me in the dark!"

Hard-driving, personable and experienced, Santoro had the instincts and knowledge to be successful at Widener. He understood the need to be involved in the internal and external communities. Under Santoro, the School of Law reached out to the legal community and afforded the bench and bar the opportunity to become prominent and consequential partners with the school. He also cultivated and strengthened ties in Philadelphia and opened new contacts in other parts of Pennsylvania, Delaware and New Jersey.

Legitimacy

The one individual who, in my mind, provided the impetus for the Law School's acceptance by the legal community was the chief justice of the Delaware Supreme Court. Chief Justice Daniel Herrmann, a gracious and kind man, embraced the Law School when it was unpopular in Delaware to do so. In many ways his approval was tacit, but in others openly acknowledged. His stature in the legal community made it acceptable to be involved with the school. In part his imprimatur can be attributed to the personal and professional relationship that had developed between Hermann and Santoro. The chief justice shared with me that he felt that the Law School could lend valuable support to the justice system. He was correct, for over the years the relationship between Widener Law and the bench and bar became a strong and effective partnership.

The chief justices who succeeded Herrmann, Andrew Christie and Norman Vescey were frequent visitors to the Law School. It was Chief Justice Vescey who scheduled the Supreme Court of Delaware – acknowledged by many as one of the most intellectual and capable courts in the nation – to sit in session in the Law School's new moot courtroom in the year 2000, a first in the history of American law schools.

Many members of the bench became members of the law faculty.

William Quillen, who served as chancellor of the Court of Chancery and as a member of the Delaware Superior and Supreme Courts for many years, had a long relationship with the school as did Justices Joseph Walsh, William Duffy, Randy Holland and G. Andrew Moore, to mention a few.

The senior U.S. senator from Delaware, Joseph Biden, taught one of the most popular and long running courses. His Saturday morning classes, "Selected Topics in Constitutional Law," were always wait-listed. Biden also spent time with the students beyond the designated class time, sharing his experiences as a national and international figure.

Board of Overseers

Bill Quillen not only taught at the Law School, he also sat on its Board of Overseers and then served for many years as a member of the University's Board of Trustees. The Board of Overseers provided the opportunity for leaders of the legal community from the tri-state area to become involved as advisors to the Law School. The creation of boards of visitors for each of Widener's Schools and Colleges grew out of the discussions of the Task Force for University Structure. Utilizing the professional skills available in the communities in which we operated provided an opportunity to expand community outreach. The Law School overseers also assisted the dean as a sounding board for academic direction while serving as advocates for the school to the public.

While participating on an ABA panel in Detroit, I spoke about the responsibilities of law school boards of visitors, saying, "One of the problems in academia is a tendency to listen only to ourselves. It is very helpful to have a board that consists of representatives from both the corporate and legal community to provide a link between a law school and the outside world." (Bruce 1985)

To better tie the Board of Overseers to the University and in recognition of the Law School's economic and academic importance, Widener's by-laws were changed to provide the chairman of the overseers a seat on the University's Board of Trustees. Given the fifteen-mile distance between the two campuses, the decision to integrate the School of Law leadership into the Board of Trustees enabled Widener to avoid the adversarial relationship between parent and subsidiary that often occurs with professional schools.

At one point the chief counsels of the major corporations in Delaware, i.e., DuPont, Hercules, Columbia Gas and ICI Americas, were members of the Board of Overseers. They and many others like them brought special skills and leadership to the Law School.

Faculty Development

One of Dean Santoro's principal objectives was faculty development. The process of upgrading virtually a whole faculty can be painful and is seldom undertaken unless necessary for the reputation of the school. The law faculty hired by Dean Avins, while acceptable, was not academically distinguished; it is a rare academician who is willing to place his or her career in the hands of an unaccredited school. Many appeared to have been hired more for their conservative political philosophy – reflecting the views of Dean Avins – than for their scholarly skills.

At the outset of the upgrade, personnel policies were changed. One change restricted the amount of external legal work faculty could undertake. Another restructured class schedules to ensure sections met Monday through Saturday. Both of these were aimed at some full-time faculty who were functioning on a part-time basis by scheduling their teaching on two or three days.

Another policy change instituted a residency requirement, demanding that faculty live within a 75-mile radius of the campus. Office hours were extended and enforced. Criteria for awards in academic scholarship were made more demanding. Expectations for scholarly work were established and made a part of the hiring process; no longer was good classroom teaching enough for tenure. As a result, the transition to a faculty committed to full-time teaching, mentoring and academic scholarship occurred in a remarkably brief period of time. Over the years, the faculty improved further, from marginal to outstanding, bringing a diversity of academic and practical skills and knowledge to the classrooms.

Target Admission Program

Widener's educational philosophy – to provide opportunity for students with potential to become successful – soon extended to the School of Law. The law admissions staff, while concerned with quality and student preparedness, was also committed to providing an opportunity to students who exhibited potential for success. Given the demand for law school seats in the 1980s, the recruitment of good, solid students who may have been overlooked elsewhere served Widener Law well while its reputation was being built.

Playing off its willingness to provide opportunity, the Law School introduced what was known at Widener as the Target Admission Program (TAP). A select number of students with high grade point averages from excellent colleges or universities but lower LSATs than required or, conversely, students with high LSATs but lower grades, were admitted to a summer program in which they took the equivalent of three law courses. The program was academically rigorous and held out the prospect of a seat in the entering fall class for students who successfully completed the program. Over the years, many Widener Law graduates who entered as TAP students went on to have outstanding law careers. I recall one young man who entered through TAP and was selected in his third year for the President's Award as the most outstanding individual in his class. The program was and still is highly successful.

A beneficial byproduct of the TAP program was its ability to satisfy requests from donors, alumni or political figures to give a less-than-qualified student a break. By offering a spot in the TAP program, we provided the opportunity for a student to prove his or her ability to succeed at law school academic work. Since exams at law schools are taken anonymously with assigned student numbers, any possibility of favoritism was eliminated. If a student performed, he was given a seat; if not, he had failed the generous opportunity to qualify for the study of law.

The Evening Division

One of the distinguishing features of the Widener School of Law is a large evening program, known as the Extended Division. Most traditional law schools do not offer an opportunity for the part-time study of the law – though, actually, the term "part-time" is a misnomer since evening students carry a full load of courses spread over four rather than three years.

A sizable evening enrollment brings a different vitality to the campus. The students are usually more mature and many are married. Most are actively engaged in a profession and see the study of law as career enhancing or offering new professional opportunities. Their experiences and mindsets are uniquely different from those of the traditional day students, a majority of whom enroll directly from undergraduate studies.

The logistics of running classes in the evening and on weekends necessitated the expansion of the core faculty with the inclusion of qualified practitioners and members of the judiciary. The resulting faculty mix of traditional academics and skilled practitioners provided students with a unique magnifier on the law. The opportunity to study with a leading criminal lawyer or a justice from the Delaware or Pennsylvania Supreme Court offered a perspective that cannot be found in the casebooks. Indeed, at Widener, many of the adjunct faculty were experts whose writings were highlighted in the casebooks.

New Scholarly Memberships Sought

The School of Law made the decision to seek accreditation by the American Association of Law Schools (AALS). The AALS, although not in control of bar exams or admission criteria, was considered by the faculty to be the primary association promoting scholarship within legal education; membership was seen as a seal of approval within the legal community. Its acquisition would be a significant achievement as a statement of the University's commitment to expending the necessary funds on physical facilities and human resources to achieve success.

To meet AALS requirements, Widener constructed a new wing of the library – thus accommodating the collection's 300 percent growth since the school's acquisition – and built new seminar rooms, a trial advocacy area and a smaller mock courtroom. After several years of self-study, site visitations by accrediting committees and the expenditure of several millions of dollars to expand facilities, membership was unanimously awarded by the American Association of Law Schools in January of 1987.

Widener Law continued to seek membership in organizations enjoyed by more established schools including the Order of Barristers, a national honorary organization dedicated to promoting oral advocacy and brief-writing skills. Our acceptance to membership in the Order of Barristers allowed Widener students to compete in regional and national oral advocacy competitions.

Clinics Become a Popular Venue for Skill Development

Under Santoro's guidance, the Law School also expanded academic and clinical opportunities for students. Clinical internships in a variety of agencies afforded students the opportunity to practice lawyering skills by representing clients at hearings or in court, always under the direction of faculty. The range of clinics included tax, civil, environmental, post-conviction relief (assisting individuals who felt legal errors had been made in their cases at the time of trial), and consumer credit (representing indigent persons in bankruptcy cases).

The Environmental Law Clinic under the direction of Professor James R. May became one of the more visible and successful clinics. It won sizable monetary awards from the courts in several cases brought against corporate environmental violators, and garnered considerable press coverage, usually with a "David v. corporate Goliath" slant to the story.

It also raised eyebrows among some business people who questioned the appropriateness of law students bringing suit against a corporation. This same tug and pull existed with most clinics. People questioned the correctness of students assisting convicted criminals with appeals, or assisting welfare recipients who questioned the system and the application of rules and regulations.

What most critics didn't stop to think through were the changes within society that had so dramatically broadened the scope of issues addressed by the legal system. Neither did they consider that all students in clinics were supervised by faculty who had standing before the courts. The clinical students represented individuals and cases that were researched and reviewed before being undertaken. They provided passionate advocacy for the underclass and gained legal experience.

Graduate Law Degrees

Graduate and international programs were introduced as part of a strategy to become a broad-based Center for the Study of Law. The American Bar Association approved a master's (LL.M.) in corporate law and another in finance and taxation. These academic programs joined the existing J.D./M.B.A. already in place.

The acquisition of the doctoral program in clinical psychology led to a J.D./Psy.D. program that required an extraordinary commitment on the part of the few students who were selected for it. The time to complete the course of study was seven years!

By my final year as president there were three masters and two doctoral programs offered by the Law School. The master's in health law under the leadership of a recognized academic scholar in the field, Professor Barry Furrow, earned a national reputation as being among the top ten programs in the United States.[1]

---

[1] Doctoral programs in 2001 were: S.J.D. (Doctor of Judicial Science) and D.L. (Doctor of Laws). Masters were: LL.M. (Master of Laws in Corporate Law and Finance, also Master of Laws in Health Law) and M.J. (Master of Jurisprudence in Health Law).

The number of students in graduate programs was relatively small in relation to the J.D. program. However, the impact on the reputation of the Law School was incalculable.

International Studies

The introduction of international studies was another thrust of Santoro's. The first program, in Nairobi, Kenya, was offered in cooperation with the faculty of law of the University of Nairobi and was designed with a focus on international environmental law. Subsequent International Law Institutes were opened in Geneva, Switzerland; Sydney, Australia; Padua and Venice, Italy. The Geneva and Nairobi programs were the most popular. One of the primary attractions to the Geneva Institute was the opportunity for some students to undertake internships with the many international organizations that called the city home, including the World Health Organization and the World Trade Organization.

My wife and I traveled to Geneva one summer when the program was being reviewed for re-accreditation by the ABA. I sat in on several classes during my visit and found the format fascinating. The classes were team taught in English by a Widener law professor and a member of the University of Geneva's law faculty. If the topic were corporate law, for example, the first part of the lecture would be a presentation applying American legal standards, immediately followed by a presentation on the same subject from the perspective of European legal standards. The final discussion among students and faculty would be related to forming an understanding of the differences between the two systems.

Dean James White and the Trip to Yeshiva

Thanks to the time I spent working with the dean on Law School issues, I became conversant with the workings of legal education and friendly with many of the leading legal figures in Delaware and Pennsylvania. Santoro introduced me to the group he worked with at the American Bar Association including Jim White who was then heading the ABA's Section on Legal Education.

On the occasion of an ABA meeting in Philadelphia, I invited Jim White to lunch. After the usual ice breaking conversation, I shared with him my vision for the Law School and its future. We then had a lengthy discussion about legal education and what he saw as the challenges for the legal community in the future.

In exchanging thoughts on the ABA accreditation process, I commented – a bit tongue-in-cheek – that the process seemed stacked against the parent universities since the team visitors were all from the legal community. Invariably, they concluded, or at least inferred, that if only more financial resources were made available to the law program it could take a quantum step forward. Some months later, an invitation arrived from Dean White inviting me to participate in an accreditation visit to Yeshiva University School of Law in New York City.

Of course I accepted, and became the first university president invited to join an accreditation team in the history of the ABA. It was a fascinating experience made more so since Yeshiva, an orthodox Jewish institution had several restrictive faith-based policies that were a cause for concern to the ABA. In the exit interview, with the president of Yeshiva present, I almost burst out laughing when the team leader began to speak about the need for additional financial support for the school of law. I had told my team colleagues that if this were to be raised, I would dissent then comment on the financial relationship of law schools to universities. I did so, and when I did, a warm smile blossomed on the face of my fellow president.

Chapter 8

Law School Expands to Harrisburg

The creation of a campus in Harrisburg, Pennsylvania to house a branch of the School of Law was one of the more ambitious undertakings during my tenure. Illustrative of the operating culture we had established at Widener – seek opportunity and implement creatively – it became the third campus of the University on August 21, 1989, although not before an odyssey through the state government and our own Board of Trustees.

In June 1986, House Resolution 313 was introduced and passed in the Pennsylvania General Assembly. The resolution stated that the "speaker of the house would appoint nine members to a select committee to study the feasibility of establishing a new law school in the Harrisburg area." The chairman of the committee was Rep. Mark B. Cohen (D-Philadelphia).

The possibility of establishing a law school in the state capitol had surfaced periodically. Harrisburg, like many capitols of east coast states, was not a particularly exciting city. The post-secondary education options were limited to a community college and a two-year branch of Penn State. There were no professional schools; the closest legal study was a traditional daytime-only program at Dickinson Law School, then a free-standing, private school of some 450 students located in Carlisle, 20 miles west of the city.

The intent of Resolution 313 was to assess the potential regional support for a law school in Harrisburg that would offer part-time studies with an emphasis on public law. Despite being denied during the study process, a factor in the passage of the resolution was interest by a number of legislators in attending law school without having to travel to Pittsburgh or Philadelphia.

After reviewing HR 313, Dean Santoro suggested that we investigate the potential of such an undertaking for Widener. I enthusiastically supported the idea. The interest level was high among key members of the Law School's Board of Overseers and within the Board of Trustees' Executive Committee. Leslie C. Quick, Jr., then chairman of the board, was skeptical about the undertaking, commenting that there were "already too many lawyers in the country!" From a corporate CEO's perspective, Les accepted lawyers as a necessity, but not an embraceable commodity.

When Chairman Quick requested the opinion of the Executive Committee, it was unanimous in its support of undertaking a feasibility study. The chairman agreed to support the study with the proviso that any recommendation for action would not add debt to the University. Thus, at the December 1986 meeting of the Executive Committee, approval was granted to explore the issue further. A subcommittee was established consisting of board members knowledgeable in the law. It was a powerful group including the general counsels of several major corporations, a managing director of a large law firm, and corporate leaders. Dean Santoro led the project, calling on associates from the Law School and University as needed.

During its hearings on the feasibility of a law school, the Pennsylvania house committee met with Bryce Jordan, president of Pennsylvania State University and Peter Liacouras, president of Temple University, to ascertain the interest of the two public universities in the project. Penn State was very interested because a school of law was the missing piece in its academic conglomerate. Temple, with a law school offering evening studies, saw the potential for additional part-time courses in central Pennsylvania. However, when it became evident that the legislature was not interested in appropriating large sums of public dollars to make a law school a reality, the interest of both institutions quickly waned.

At Widener, we were convinced from the beginning stages of the process that a private institution not dependent on public funding would be in the best position to pull off such a venture by establishing either a free-standing law school or branch campus of one already in existence. While it was beneficial to explore a partnership with the state government, we were convinced that the legislative committee studying the issue was somewhat naïve in its assessment of financial outlay and human effort required to achieve ABA accreditation.

After a year of demographic analysis and countless meetings, we concluded that an additional law school in central Pennsylvania could be academically and financially successful. Our studies showed that based upon the number of Pennsylvanians who applied to study law, the number of available seats in existing schools, and the projected population of the Commonwealth, there clearly was the need for an additional 250 to 400 full-time seats. There was also a need for an extended division, particularly among women and the full-time employed, but the number of part-time places was more difficult to predict.

The periodic progress reports to our Executive Committee and overseers always led to the decision to proceed. Ongoing conversations with legislators produced expressions of support, but little funding. Indeed, there was some hostility on the part of some legislators who as graduates of Dickinson Law School were concerned about the impact on their alma mater if a second law program competed in the region. They were right to be worried. Early in the study phase when we had decided that the key to success was part-time study, we had discussed our thinking with Dickinson Law's dean. Asked if his school were considering offering part-time study, the response was "no interest." If he had said otherwise, in all probability we would not have proceeded with the project. [1]

The decision to move forward was made with the full knowledge that our positive analysis of the Harrisburg potential was contradictory to the reality of declining national law school applications. Although Widener's enrollment numbers had steadily increased from 1983 to 1986, national law applications had declined 28 percent in the same three years. Many reasons for the decline were advanced: the numerical drop in undergraduate students that inevitably led to fewer available to enroll in law school; the public's perception that there were too many lawyers (reflecting Chairman Quick's opinion); more undergraduate students shifting from study in the liberal arts (the traditional feeders into law school) into professional or pre-professional majors, such as business, health disciplines and the sciences.

---

[1] Parenthetically, the decision by Dickinson was, to my mind, short sighted and analogous to the University of Delaware's failure to merge with the law school in Delaware when given the opportunity to do so. It was obvious to Dean Santoro and me that our presence in central Harrisburg would hurt Dickinson. This was proven correct. Eventually, Penn State merged with Dickinson School of Law, providing it with financial support and Penn State with its missing specialty.

Widener submitted a formal proposal to Rep. Cohen's committee, stating "Widener University is prepared to establish a dual division law school in Harrisburg by the fall of 1988." It was clear in the proposal that a capital appropriation of $8 to $11 million from the Common-wealth, plus the cost of land, would be required (despite the dim prospects for that degree of support). Given the regional interests that existed in a state the size of Pennsylvania, there was no political appetite to support a law school that would be perceived as only benefiting a small segment of the population. We hoped that the major selling point to the legislature would be the public-private nature of the partnership: once the initial start-up costs were borne by the state, there would be no ongoing annual public subsidizations; the law school would not become a burden to the Commonwealth budget in perpetuity. The rationale wasn't as convincing as we had hoped!

Discussions during the ensuing months illustrated that the options for space being suggested by the legislative committee were woefully inadequate. The proposal that the state law library be used as the foun-dation for the law school library was ill informed, not only because the library was physically inadequate but the collection would fail to meet ABA standards.

The report of the Widener trustee subcommittee on the opening of a third campus, presented at a special meeting of the board's Execu-tive Committee in July 1987, recommended that Widener proceed by using private funding rather than public funding. This proposal changed the ground rules from the earlier recommendation; going to private-sector funding would incur debt for the University. The ration-ale for this decision included avoidance of government oversight, and the fortuitous identification of a donor who had offered land and a cash gift to cover start-up costs. Finally, and most significant, it was an ex-cellent business opportunity that fit our academic mission.

The Chairman Objects

Following in-depth discussion at the July meeting, Chairman Quick asked each member of the Executive Committee to express an opinion, informing them that he could not support the project. With the exception of the chairman, the outcome of the vote among the oth-ers was unanimous; the project should move ahead. However, at the chairman's request, final approval was delayed until the full board could discuss the issue in September. He felt, and correctly so, that the

Executive Committee should not act on behalf of the board on an issue so significant.

Enroute to the airport immediately after the meeting, Les wondered aloud if he wished to continue as chairman. I understood his thinking. As a director of Quick & Reilly, Inc., I knew how his board operated. The chairman was *never* over-ruled by the board in a formal vote!

However, as president of Widener and as a friend, I was deeply concerned by his reaction to the vote and several days later asked him to meet me for breakfast in New York. As I left the house I told Judy, "I may not have a job when I return." Les and I met at the University Club on 5th Avenue and 54th Street and had a candid discussion for several hours. I told him I would have backed away from the project at any time if he had objected to it, but since he had agreed at each stage to continue the study, it was reasonable to assume that the committee was going to get continually more excited about the project. I shared with him that I was committed to the Harrisburg Campus because I believed, as did his Executive Committee, that it was a good academic and business decision. At this point in the conversation I offered to resign as president if he felt I had not been supportive of him, or had misrepresented his position, or simply believed it would be in the best interest of the University to change leadership.

Les assured me that I was providing the leadership Widener needed. He mused that perhaps he should be the one to resign since this was a philosophic disagreement over the need to train more lawyers. I remember him laughing when I said that I might agree, but "if someone is going to train them it might as well be us!"

Following the September meeting at which the board endorsed the project despite Les's negative vote, Les and I continued to speak on a regular basis. I argued that he should not step down as chairman, even though I understood that he was having difficulty accepting the vote. It was not a vote on his judgment, but support by the board for a good project. The situation was a classic study of the differences of the role of a chairman in a corporate setting vs. the role of a chairman in a nonprofit institution. To allow the project to be fully discussed in a collegial manner by the board members, he had permitted it to proceed at each stage, something he would never have done in his own company without making his objections public.

Several weeks later, Les told me that he planned to step down as chairman. He handled the meeting in which he informed the board very professionally, saying he would remain active as a board member, and would continue to support Widener, but not as board chairman. Following that meeting, the Executive Committee invited Fitz Dixon to resume the chairmanship. He accepted with the caveat that it would be for a limited number of years because he planned to spend more time at his home in Florida in the years ahead.

Les Quick and I continued regular contact. Over time he began to attend meetings on a regular basis and after two trustees traveled to New York to seek his opinion on some issues, one of his sons shared with me that he was pleased that the board had reached out to him.

Ironically, when Chairman Dixon stepped down, Les Quick was invited to reassume the chairmanship. He accepted and later said to me, "while I philosophically disagreed with you on a law campus in Harrisburg, you made a good business decision. It has been successful and has made money."

Without our mutual trust and commitment to Widener – the critical bonds between us – Les Quick might have disappeared. While at times we disagreed with one another, the disagreements never affected our ability to work together, or our friendship.

The enthusiasm and confidence that Widener's Board of Trustees expressed toward the development of the Harrisburg Campus confirmed beyond doubt one fundamental difference between public and private institutions. At a private university, the implementation of an idea can be swift; at the public institution financial constraints can impede the process, and approvals often take months, if not years.

Once the notion of a Harrisburg Campus had been articulated and was known to fit the mission, its viability and economic soundness were researched and the decision to move ahead was immediate. What we then accomplished in Harrisburg in two years could not have been duplicated in the public sector.

Widener Makes ABA History

The American Bar Association had never granted approval for a degree-granting branch campus but we believed that such a goal was attainable and were willing to breach virgin territory to accomplish it. While there were several states that operated two separate law schools under one university system (Arkansas and Indiana, for example) none had ever opened a fully integrated branch of an existing accredited law school. Adding to the complexity of the issue was the fact that the branch campus would be located in a different state from the home campus.

The key to making it work was Dean Santoro's understanding of the mechanics of the ABA process that governed legal education: He pursued Rule 33 of the ABA Standards. The rule provided that an already approved law school seeking to establish a branch location must apply for and obtain "acquiescence" before establishing the branch. In all likelihood, the originators of the standard had not anticipated any institution attempting to establish a branch with a wholly integrated law curriculum leading to the J.D. However, it was evident that Widener qualified under the rule to build and seek approval for a branch campus if the University and the School of Law continued to meet all ABA academic requirements and could produce the financial and physical resources needed for accreditation. In other words, the Law School had to own and control the physical facility, approximately duplicate the quantity and quality of volumes in the parent law library, employ a full-time faculty earning salaries competitive with other comparable area law schools, and maintain a student-faculty ratio of approximately twenty-two to one. Finally, the parent school had to be fiscally sound.

Despite the earlier suggestion by the state legislature that we lease space and consider the state's law library as our teaching library, the ABA standards forbade this route. The only way the project could be approved was to take the path that Widener proposed, to build an independent campus with private funding.

Our earlier improvements to the Law School, including the 1985-86 additions to the Delaware Campus and the faculty development that led to the 1987 acceptance to AALS membership, had positioned Widener well. Since we had met all the benchmarks set by the AALS and ABA, the University's credibility and position was sound. In light of the wording of Rule 33, Widener's proposal posed a true conundrum for the American Bar Association.

During 1987 and early 1988, we spent a great deal of time responding to ABA requests for information and in meetings, both with members of the Legal Education Section and separately with its head, Dean White. Within Widener, the enthusiasm for "getting it done" became pervasive among the University leadership and throughout the Law School. The school's Board of Overseers became deeply involved with the process. It was a challenge of great importance and significance: a "no" answer was unacceptable as an outcome!

In April the ABA granted acquiescence for the establishment of a branch of the Law School in Harrisburg. On June 5, 1988, formal authorization to proceed was granted by the Council of the American Bar Association's Section on Legal Education and Admission to the Bar. This was the first time in the history of American legal education that a university would be allowed to establish a fully integrated branch of an existing, approved law school. A remarkable achievement!

An interesting postscript to the Widener use of Rule 33 is that the ABA changed the rule soon after so it could never again be used to establish a branch law school. Harrisburg would be forever one of a kind! Allegedly some in the ABA were concerned that an unnamed university would start a series of franchised law schools in a number of states. They did not want any university to become the McDonald's of legal education. Internally, we felt the revised standard was directed at Widener and should be known as the Widener Rule.

We Meet the Harrisburg "Aristocracy"

The two most critical factors beyond ABA approval were to identify financing for the project and to choose an appropriate site. Some pressure was applied to locate the campus in downtown Harrisburg but the tracts of land available were either in the wrong location, needed extensive clearing, or were too expensive. While keen to bring economic value to its community, the local government was, as usual, reluctant to invest heavily in the infrastructure of a dedicated project like a law school.

A private individual became the catalyst for launching the Harrisburg Campus. John O. Vartan, a real estate developer in central Pennsylvania whose entrepreneurial instincts meshed well with Widener's vision, became responsible for the breakthrough on both the physical and financial structuring of the project.

Vartan was an interesting combination of a hard-driving businessman who was also willing to think boldly about projects that would make the community a better place to live and work. When we first met him, John was in his early forties and had already left his mark on the city of Harrisburg and its neighboring communities. In the mid 1980s, against conventional wisdom, he had built office space in downtown Harrisburg, then a depressed city. He was widely credited with sparking its economic renaissance.

Vartan was bright, inquisitive and an extraordinary self-promoter.

With John, the deal was the thing. It was always in John's best interests, and it was never done. Doing a deal with John was – for him – a gift that kept on giving! He also wrote poetry, collected art, lived in a large and lavishly appointed home, and drove around town in a chauffer driven Rolls-Royce or Bentley. As an individual, John was the equivalent of local aristocracy.

A Widener Law graduate and political operative in Harrisburg introduced Dean Santoro and me to John Vartan early in the planning process. Vartan and Santoro hit it off immediately. During the various stages of the feasibility study, John became increasingly interested in the project and began to introduce Tony and me to key legislators from central Pennsylvania.

I recall meeting with one Republican house leader who happened to be a graduate of Dickinson Law School. Vartan had set the meeting to discuss Widener's willingness to consider a branch campus in Harrisburg. What we received was a fifteen-minute rant excoriating Widener for thinking the University would receive any public funding for the project. He made it clear he would not support any legislation to do so. When he finally stopped wagging his finger, giving me an opportunity to respond, I stated that as a private university Widener was not dependent on the legislature for its existence and we had not visited him to lobby for funds. Additionally, I as president of Widener did not need to be lectured to. We thanked him for his time and left.

John had sat silent through the entire diatribe. When we got outside, I said, "Sorry John, Widener doesn't need that kind of intimidation." He smiled and in his quiet voice said, "I have raised a lot of money for that guy. He was embarrassing and will never get my help or money again."

Vartan was proud of his background as an Armenian immigrant. Like so many who become naturalized citizens he believed that all things are possible if one is willing to take chances and work hard. He loved America and its opportunities. I am convinced that John saw in Widener's project the same attractions to which he was predisposed in his business life: to do something others said could not be done and, equally as significant, to do a profitable deal while raising his public profile.

The Deal

The original cost projection for the campus was approximately $11 million, $3 million of which was dedicated to developing the law library.

The deal with Vartan to provide land and construction for the new campus was negotiated by David Eckard and Widener's General Counsel Rocco Imperatrice. The process took several months of conversation with John and his attorney before the agreement was signed on October 23, 1987. The decision to partner with him was clearly a win-win for both parties.

The terms of the transaction are interesting, and instructive as to Vartan's financial thinking. Widener agreed to purchase 13 acres located in Susquehanna Township from Vartan for a purchase price of $750,000. The University assumed an existing $1.5 million mortgage and received a $750,000 cash contribution from Vartan. Vartan donated to the University his 14,000 sq. ft. former home, with one acre of land, collectively appraised at $1.35 million. Widener executed a $6.8 million mortgage in favor of a Vartan family trust. Vartan Construction would build the 50,000 sq.ft. teaching center, a 300-plus-car parking lot, sidewalks, roadways, and utility connections for a price of $6.8 million. Of the $6.8 million purchase price, Widener would receive a $2.5 million allowance for shelving, furniture, equipment and books, which, if not fully used, would reduce the principal balance. Widener granted certain easements relating to Vartan's adjoining property. The University would pay all transfer taxes.

Mortgage payments would commence August 1, 1991, with annual installment payments of $661,000 until paid in full on August 1, 2019 with a final balloon payment of $800,000. The mortgage payments were "understood to include both principal and interest" but if Vartan could not procure financing at a rate of 10 percent or less, Widener would pay the excess over 10 percent to be calculated and adjusted on a monthly basis.

On the day the contracts were signed we emulated John Vartan by traveling to Harrisburg in a limo owned by the University's Sheraton Inn. On the way home we sipped champagne to celebrate the acquisition of the University's third campus.

A 15-Month Deadline for Construction

Late in April of 1988, a groundbreaking ceremony was held on the Susquehanna Township site. The groundbreaking was attended by some

100 people including many members of the region's bench and bar and then Attorney General of the Commonwealth LeRoy Zimmerman. Indeed, the investment in central Pennsylvania gave Widener legitimate access to four U.S. senators (from Pennsylvania and Delaware) and a number of U.S. representatives from several regions of Pennsylvania.

In mid June of 1988, construction began on the Law School teaching facility. The property, located on an attractive hillside across from an office building and business complex developed by Vartan Enterprises, was approximately eight miles from downtown Harrisburg. Similar to the Delaware Campus of the Law School, the location provided a safe suburban setting with close proximity to a major city.

Publicity regarding the Law School was extensive and virtually overnight made Widener a recognized name and educational player in the region. Vartan received much acclaim for his role in the partnership, adding more luster to his public persona.

The announcement that the first class of students would begin their studies in August of 1989 meant the construction schedule was tight, and at times tension-driven. Only minor renovations were needed to convert the former residence into administrative space, but design changes were occurring daily at the teaching facility, even as the building was under construction. Reflecting on the timetable, it was faith and goodwill on the part of the University and Vartan's people that made it all come together.

It is noteworthy that the facility was completed on schedule and the Harrisburg branch of the Law School opened in August 1989 with a combined total of 276 students in the day and extended divisions. It was a gratifying accomplishment given the time constraints for completion.

New Name, New Structure

The ABA approval for the Harrisburg Campus provided the University with an appropriate time to change the name of the School of Law. The name Delaware Law School of Widener University under which the school had been operating frustrated me and many others. The strategy to use the Law School as one of the lead programs of the University was compromised by the name Delaware Law School, which understandably created the impression that the school was a part of the University of Delaware. But Widener had been restricted from changing the name for almost a decade because its founding dean, Avins, brought continued legal action against the University until a federal court finally ruled against him. On June 9, 1988, the Board of Trustees voted to change the name to Widener University School of Law. No one was more pleased than I!

The proposed operation of a two-state, two-campus law school necessitated a realignment of the administrative structure of the school. Two associate deans were named, John L. Gedid for Harrisburg and Thomas J. Reed for Delaware. The associate deans were given responsibility for the day-to-day operations of their campus and reported directly to Dean Santoro.

Physical Plant: A Conservative Approach

While designing the Harrisburg Campus, we agreed that the first phase of the physical plant development would be accomplished conservatively over a period of five years. We did not expect the full complement of 800 students to be enrolled until 1992, in the third year of the five-year plan. By that time the first class would be graduating and our planning for the next five years would be underway. This approach kept the initial costs down and provided the opportunity to review the first several years of campus operation before making a large investment in additional space.

As a result, the early facility was comprised of a 50,000 sq.ft. building housing classrooms, faculty offices, and the 20,000 sq.ft. law library. The former Vartan residence of 14,000 sq.ft. housed the administration, student support services, a student dining area, and the bookstore.

Counter to the downward national trends in law school applications and enrollments, and as a result of pent-up demand for law seats in central Pennsylvania, the Harrisburg Campus reached the projected enrollment targets for the first several years of operation, 1990 (513 students), 1991 (736), 1992 (792). Thus, by 1992 additional space was required to accommodate (1) the Law Review, Student Bar Association, Moot Court Honor Society and other student activities and organizations, (2) the new Continuing Legal Education program, (3) the law clinics, and (4) expansion of the library. The planning document presented to the Executive Committee of the board in 1993 was approved for continued development and cost analysis.

Arthur Frakt Named Dean

Early in the spring semester of 1992, Dean Santoro informed me that he would be resigning his deanship at the conclusion of the academic year to become founding dean of a law school at Roger Williams

University in Rhode Island. I was disappointed but knew that what motivated and intrigued him was the challenge of building institutions. Tony had achieved his goals and felt it was time to move on.

Once again, I turned to Professor Esther Clark to chair the search committee for a new dean. The committee was unusually large and, by design, inclusive of every facet of the Law School – trustees, overseers, alumni, students, associate deans and seven faculty in addition to Clark. Since I was proposing an aggressive schedule to identify a new dean, there was wide speculation among faculty that unless someone had been pre-selected for the position six months was too short a time for the search process. I responded to these concerns in announcing the search, saying "there is no pre-selected candidate unless I can talk Dean Santoro into staying." I also said that I did not want to lose the very positive momentum achieved over the past nine years by appointing an interim dean, and that with the concurrence of the Executive Committee of the Board of Trustees and the two associate law deans, the search would be limited to external candidates.

The process was swift, thorough and successful. On July 14, 1992, we announced that Arthur H. Frakt, professor and former dean of the Loyola School of Law in Los Angeles had been selected as the fifth dean of the Law School. He was given the title dean of the Law School and vice president of the Widener University Law Center in recognition of the scope of the School of Law offerings.

Frakt had earned both his undergraduate and law degrees at Rutgers University in New Jersey and had served there on the faculty. He had also been a deputy attorney general for New Jersey. In coming to Widener, he was returning to his East Coast roots.

Harrisburg Campus Expansion

Shortly before the arrival of Arthur Frakt as Santoro's successor, the Board of Trustees agreed in May 1992 that Widener would again enter into an agreement with John Vartan to purchase a residential property contiguous to the campus which, with minor modifications, could provide 17,000 sq.ft. of administrative and clinical space. The trustees also approved the construction of a 10,000 sq.ft. addition for completion by 1993. The purchase price was $3.5 million plus transfer taxes of $70,000. Vartan agreed to make a $1,940,000 contribution to the project at a net cost to the University of $1,560,000.

In a separate agreement with Vartan, also approved at the May meeting, the University agreed to an option to purchase nineteen-plus acres contiguous to the campus before December 1 of that year. To be paid for in installments at a purchase price of $2,320,000 of which John would donate $1,070,000, the land would be used for further campus expansion, possibly for residential student housing. Again, the relationship with Vartan proved advantageous to both parties. The University gained additional space and John had excellent tax deductions at little more than out-of-pocket cost.[2]

The last purchase for the Harrisburg Campus was in March of 1993. A 37,000 sq.ft. structure built in 1986 and located across one street from the campus, it was bought directly from Midlantic Bank for the price of $1,075,000, or roughly $30/sq.ft. The building provided flex space needed for library expansion over ten years. Given that the campus was scheduled for reaccredidation visits by both the ABA and AALS, it was important to show that planning for the future was underway.

The purchase from Midlantic Bank angered John Vartan. It and the fact that Vartan and Frakt did not relate well, shifted the dynamic of the relationship between Widener and Vartan. The close partnership had ended early in Frakt's deanship when Vartan told me he could not work with Arthur. Thus the handling of daily details fell to Widener's Director of Operations Al Rollins, Vice President Eckard, and the University's attorney, Rocco Imperatrice. I became both negotiator with Vartan and the manager of conflict resolution among all parties for many unpleasant months. The final straw was Widener's direct purchase of the Midlantic Bank building which eliminated another of John's complicated deals.

John Vartan had clearly been instrumental in making the Harrisburg Campus a reality. Although it had been a unique and profitable partnership, the relationship was over.

Angst in Harrisburg

There is a tendency for faculty, staff and students located on a satellite campus at a geographic distance from the main campus to feel isolated. Overseer Scott Evans wrote to me in July 1992 that: "There is a

---

[2] Given today's laws for real estate transactions and charitable gifts, agreements such as the ones made between John Vartan and Widener relative to the development of the Harrisburg Campus would not be possible today.

feeling on campus of being an abandoned child. I believe its students are frustrated by their own lack of identity and any requests of the administration must be 'approved by Wilmington.' Its faculty, though wanting to have a close interaction with the prestigious and knowledgeable faculty of Wilmington, feels as though they have been sent to some frontier post. And lastly, its administration appears as though it is only interested with administrative functions and nothing more."

The comments helped spotlight where the new dean and I needed to focus in order to nurture the campus to maturity.

Over the next several years, the associate deans in Harrisburg, John Gedid followed by Chip Prescott, were given greater autonomy in managing the campus. Administrative operations, while still centralized for planning, became more campus-based; for example, the registrar, student life, admissions, and bursar functions were localized. Interactive video technology created two-campus courses and faculty were encouraged to teach the classes from both campuses. I, and others of the University's senior staff made a point of working on that campus several times a month.

Dean Frakt spent at least a day or two each week on the Harrisburg Campus. The responsibility of overseeing a two-campus law school was arduous, both physically and intellectually. The ability to delegate and serve as a benevolent and diplomatic arbitrator was a requisite skill to do the job successfully.

At a meeting with the law faculty on February 6, 1996, I directed comments specifically to the Harrisburg professorate:

> I understand the frustration and, at times, your concerns about your relationship with the University since Harrisburg is the youngest academic component of the University and is geographically distant from the rest of Widener.
>
> I assure you that the Harrisburg Campus is an important and integral part of Widener. I am pleased with the progress that has been made in the brief time that the campus has been in existence. It has become an established and important part of the central Pennsylvania region.
>
> The School of Law is a single law school; an issue, as you know, that was debated with the AALS and ABA over a number of years. Each campus is important and viewed with equal significance by the Board of

Trustees and senior administrators of the University.

Academic reputations are built over time: time for graduates to advance to significant positions of leadership; time for professional colleagues to understand the quality of programs offered; time for faculty to achieve professional leadership positions and recognized scholarly status. Do not become discouraged. The commitment to Harrisburg is long-term and complete.

What is now necessary is to find the appropriate size for the Harrisburg Campus. The challenges facing Harrisburg are no different from those facing the Delaware Campus and those faced by Main Campus faculty over the past several years.

With time, the campus identity evolved. As it did so, the perception in the central Pennsylvania legal community shifted from mildly interested to supportive. Students and faculty became more closely tied to the state legislative process; students in internships, and both faculty and students as resources for legislative committees.

The Law and Government Institute founded by Professor John Gedid helped to coalesce the campus identity. Focusing on statutes and statecraft as well as the rights of citizens in dealing with the government, this specialized program provided students with the skills needed to represent clients before state and federal agencies. It was unique and appropriate for a law school located in a state capital.

Projected Enrollment Downturn Becomes Reality

Law School enrollments reached their zenith of 1,396 in Delaware and 797 in Harrisburg in 1992-93, making the school the largest J.D. granting institution in the country and second only to the Georgetown University Law Center in total number of law students. Despite the large enrollment (remaining above 2,000 until 1995), by autumn 1994 it was manifestly clear that the national and regional trends in law school enrollments and applications were finally affecting Widener.

Between 1992 and 1997 applications nationally to ABA approved law schools dropped by nearly 20,000. Yet the number of students admitted in the same period stayed fairly constant at about 43,000. It was obvious that law schools were dipping down to fill seats at the risk of academic quality. It was also a classic example of organizational inability to rapidly counter a lesser demand by reducing costs. Despite a declining applicant pool of students, income from predicted enrollments had to be met in order to meet the costs of faculty (many tenured), utilities, library resources, etc.

For several years, Widener had been able to avoid the demographic decline with an aggressive marketing and recruitment effort, the ability to offer on-campus housing in Delaware, and its broad array of programs. The Harrisburg Campus for its first eight years had tapped into the pent up demand for legal education in central Pennsylvania. The fact that students applying to Wilmington were also offered acceptance in Harrisburg assisted in keeping student numbers constant. Indeed, the academic profile of the student body was upgraded by the expansion of the Widener Scholars program which offered merit-based scholarships to prospects with a 3.4 undergraduate GPA, or better, who attained the higher percentiles of the LSAT.

Additionally, because of its philosophy of accepting students with risk factors, Widener did not suffer the dramatic stress experienced by so many other law schools. Nevertheless, in December 1995, I outlined in a memorandum to Dean Frakt the steps I wanted him to consider in preparing a plan for reducing expenditures, increasing recruiting efforts, and sustaining tuition revenues. A three-year effort was set in motion to realistically rethink the size of the Law School. Since the rise and fall in enrollments would always be cyclical, our planning focused on targeting enrollment numbers that would be both attainable and sustainable.

Given the two-campus structure and financial significance of the Law School to the University (then 30 percent of revenue), it was important that the planning be done in an open and sensitive manner. The dean and senior staff understood that a strategic plan with a series of tactical steps toward the final goals should be developed, and written in a way that faculty and staff unequivocally understood the objectives. One of the challenges was to convince a faculty who had experienced nothing but growth in legal education that altered guidelines for admission and hiring would be necessary in the future. In my February 1996 address to the School of Law faculty, I addressed the issues confronting higher education and legal education, issues brought about by shifts in educational interests, reduced government support, and declining numbers of traditional college-bound students.

A paradox of the late nineties was the demographic projection that, despite the loss of the traditional student, the number eligible for college study would increase. The growth would be in African-American and Hispanic populations who had not traditionally pursued higher education in large numbers. The challenge for society was to increase efforts to make college, and beyond, a reality for these groups. The introduction of a minority scholarship program and a concurrent increase in women applying to law school assisted Widener Law in diversifying the student cohort.

In spring 1996, Dean Frakt shared with the law faculty a comprehensive academic plan that had been developed in alignment with a financial analysis by Vice President Eckard and his staff. The plan, which outlined the steps to be implemented as needed in response to the competitive environment, was presented so that faculty and staff would know the potential constraints and possible remedies facing legal education. This approach was a more effective way to frame the dialogue than simply announcing downsizing decisions. Among the options was the possibility of reducing the number of first-year sections in Wilmington from three to two and in Harrisburg from two to one. The faculty was alerted that notice would be given to all non-tenured members and that some positions would be eliminated in the next academic year.

On the positive side, discussions continued on a library addition and upgraded classroom space in Delaware. There was also a series of initiatives for faculty to consider: strengthening legal writing, refining the curriculum, rethinking grading and academic continuance, adding more peer reviews for faculty promotion and tenure. These complex and possibly controversial initiatives provided faculty with the opportunity to be deeply invested in the planning for the future of the Law School.

Did I ever believe the Law School was in serious difficulty? No. However, because it was a young school that had experienced extraordinary growth and success over a fifteen-year time span, careful management through a period of uncertainty was important for continued development. The five years beginning 1995 were exceptionally difficult.

Rumor and Reaction

Rumors and concerns continued to spread about the future of the Harrisburg Campus, prompting Dean Frakt to write a memorandum to faculty in May 1996:

"The Law School is a major component of the University. It will remain so. The Harrisburg program will be maintained as an integral part of Widener University. The University has a long-term commitment and substantial investment in Harrisburg. There is not now nor has there ever been any consideration for closing, selling or otherwise eliminating the legal education program in Harrisburg. Faculty should reassure their students and the legal community on this subject and should vigorously dispute anyone who spreads or creates false rumors to the contrary."

Unfortunately, much of the demoralizing speculation was attributed by Harrisburg Campus Associate Dean Prescott to several faculty members who tended to "think out loud" in front of students, staff and the community. To confront the uncertainties and attack the rumors, Pat Brant, Widener's head of University Relations, spent many days on the Harrisburg Campus developing and implementing an integrated media and public relations campaign. Directed at the bench, bar, legislature and general public, her effort promoted the importance of the Law School in the region. She arranged for the dean and me to speak at service clubs, created exposure for selected law faculty at public forums, and promoted the school on all local media. The PR campaign was successful and, more important, its mere existence gave confidence to the faculty and students that Harrisburg was not going to be abandoned. The quick intervention of the University administration in supporting the dean and calming faculty and students prevented a potential loss of momentum that would have had an adverse effect on the entire University, not just Harrisburg.

Following the commencement ceremonies in 1996, I met off-campus with several senior faculty members and enlisted their commitment to "stepping up" to their colleagues and in the community as ambassadors and cheerleaders for the Law School in Harrisburg. They were unanimously agreeable and in subsequent months reaped real benefits for the stability of the campus.

Partnership with Pennsylvania's State System

One of the announcements that received excellent press and that resonated well throughout the state was an agreement with the Pennsylvania State University System to reserve a defined number of scholarships for the Harrisburg Campus specifically for students graduating from the system's fourteen colleges and universities. These would be known as Dixon Scholars, named for Fitz Eugene Dixon, Jr. who not only served as Widener's board chairman for many years, but also as chairman of the state system.

In retrospect, all projections for Harrisburg were met! After the pent-up demand for law seats had been filled, the target range to sustain a viable campus had been set at between 450 to 500 students. From 1997 to 2000, the numbers were in the high end of the 400s. Since that time, they have continued to meet the mark, ranging into the low 500s.

Decanal Change: Arthur Frakt to Douglas Ray

While the major issue Dean Frakt faced during his tenure was enrollment, he implemented several positive changes that strengthened the Law School. One was a revamped curriculum introduced for the 1995 entering class. It placed greater emphasis on legal writing for first-year students and mandated their participation in two courses that emphasized the traditional aspects of legal education: the intensive one-week, first semester "Introduction to Law" and a second semester course in administrative law. Despite the two curricular additions, the number of courses for first-year students was reduced. Additionally, all classes were extended from 50 to 60 minutes.

Dean Frakt also introduced programs that, despite the negative market, upgraded the academic profile of the student body. Two of these were the expansion of the Widener Scholars program and the introduction of minority scholarships (that attracted students with academic credentials well above the national statistical average for minority law school applicants). He also mandated that the faculty adopt more rigorous academic standards and grading policies. These critical changes not only improved the school's bar pass rate but helped the faculty realize that keeping a student who is failing to make academic progress, and therefore has little chance of passing the bar, is unfair to the student both financially and morally.

In May of 1996, Dean Frakt was diagnosed with cancer. Major surgery was followed by radiation treatments that extended through the summer. It was an excruciating ordeal that Arthur confronted with courage and determination.

The faculty and administrators at the Law School rallied during that summer and during Dean Frakt's recuperation in the fall semester. Professors Louise Hill and Susan Goldberg provided administrative leadership in the dean's absence. Frakt returned to the deanship in late October and served as dean during academic year 1997-98. Midway through, however, he informed me that he and his wife Jana felt, given the seriousness of his illness and uncertainty for the future, that they would take early retirement after commencement. Judy and I were completely supportive of the decision, as was the entire University community.

A search committee was constituted under the capable direction of Professor Louise Hill that resulted in the appointment of Douglas E. Ray as dean effective January 1, 1999. Ray was then in Ohio serving as the Charles W. Fornoff Professor of Law and Values and the associate dean at the University of Toledo College of Law. Since there would be an interim period when Ray could be on campus on only a part-time basis, Professor Barry Furrow was named interim dean from July to December 1998.

Doug Ray brought a quiet, confident leadership to Widener (his first deanship) during his seven-plus years of service. Under his leadership, academic programs were expanded, applications steadily rose and, of greatest importance, the bar pass rate for graduating students improved each year. Toward this last goal, Doug had made a forceful case to reduce the numbers of students in order to improve the quality level. Despite the economic impact on the University, I supported his strategy, and was very glad I had.

Another major accomplishment during Ray's tenure was the expansion of facilities on both campuses. The addition of classrooms, library space and a new moot courtroom on the Delaware Campus provided increased visibility within the state's legal fraternity. Amenities for faculty and students on both campuses invigorated the sense of community. The physical facilities during his watch were very competitive with other law schools.

Doug's thoughtful advocacy enhanced the school's image and secured new ties within the legal community, particularly the bench. As a senior member of the University management team, he became fully engaged, contributing ideas beyond his primary responsibility. While a forceful advocate for the Law School, he understood its role as a component of the broader University.

Chapter 9

Holistic Baccalaureate Education

Widener's transformation from a small baccalaureate college to a sizable university of semi-autonomous schools was fundamental to the flourishing of the undergraduate segment. So, too, were the interdependency among the academic units that led to a holistic approach to baccalaureate education, and a myriad of academic support programs established to undergird Widener's mission to help students meet their potential.

In academic year 1983-84, the first full year under the new governance structure, over thirty new undergraduate courses were introduced throughout the University. Once the paradigm had been established, the accepted course of action for deans and faculty was to be proactive and innovative in posing ideas. The new environment generated much enthusiasm among faculty. Senior professors took pride in teaching undergraduates as well as graduates, while also producing publications of significance.

General Education Reform

The College of Arts and Sciences (CAS) proposed a redesign of the general education requirements for the entering class of 1987. A basic curriculum for all students would include a minimum of twelve semester hours in the sciences, social sciences and humanities, and additional courses in aesthetics, history, ethics, and laboratory science. Students would also study empirical approaches to human behavior in the junior- or senior-year Values Seminar taught by CAS faculty.[1]

The concept of requiring so many additional hours across all

---

[1] Interestingly, the Values Seminars became multi-disciplinary over the years with, for example, nursing and engineering professors teaming up with CAS faculty to explore topical issues such as bioethics and the impact of technological developments on society.

schools immediately met with resistance from Engineering and Nursing, disciplines that were heavily prescribed with course requirements by their national accreditation bodies. Both schools were concerned about finding time in the schedule to integrate the general requirements and the professional course material. Although both were among the schools that accommodated the general education requirements by adding to the number of credit hours needed for graduation, their concerns focused the level of debate on campus about the meaning of undergraduate education.

The ongoing national debate about appropriate educational standards had been fueled by the increasing interest in professional preparation and the dramatic technological advances, including the exponential expansion of desktop capabilities. The academic philosophy was more complex at comprehensive universities because by definition they include a mix of liberal arts, professional, and applied disciplines. This blend made it intrinsically more important to clearly articulate an institutional academic philosophy. Widener's was a commitment to embed writing skills, critical thinking, mathematics and science, i.e. general education, into all curricula. The reform was successfully phased into each school and college over a period of several years.

The introduction of the general education requirements coincided with the relocation of the School of Hotel and Restaurant Management to the Main Campus, requiring the development of other new courses by the Arts & Sciences faculty. It met the test admirably, creating new science offerings in chemistry and microbiology specifically for the hospitality management students, as well as courses in French, German, Italian and Spanish with an emphasis on conversation. Other undergraduate curricular revisions continued apace during the 1980s as the drive accelerated to attain appropriate accreditations by professional groups.

Education Reform Leads to Holistic Baccalaureate Experience

One of the most significant outcomes of the reform was the work of a task force charged with making recommendations for the integration of co- and extra-curricular activities with classroom themes. Some very creative recommendations were put forward and, although a few failed for lack of interest, many became a part of the life of the University. Beyond specific programmatic solutions, was the admirable recommendation that "service to students" be added as a factor for faculty merit compensation. Taking its place beside scholarship, teaching and academic citizenship, service to students required a unique commitment because, unlike the norm at single-purpose, residential colleges, most of Widener's faculty did not live within a block or two of campus but were spread across the Philadelphia-to-Wilmington area. The recommendation was nevertheless approved and resulted in a gratifying increase in interaction between faculty and students.

The embrace of this merit salary component, more than anything else, was the first small step that ultimately led the University to adopt a holistic approach to the baccalaureate experience. On campus, the effort to integrate museum exhibits, lectures, etc. with classroom content was bolstered by a new availability of financial resources to any unit planning a campus-wide cultural event. Expanded theater and music programs provided more opportunities for participation. Attendance at the vast array of offerings in and outside of Philadelphia and Wilmington was encouraged by faculty mini-grants, specifically appropriated to enable the arrangement of student transportation and admission.

Campus Outreach in the Early Years

In the early 1990s, class scheduling (with the exception of science laboratories) was revised to free the time between 4 and 6 PM daily for student activities and athletics. As intended, this designated Activities Period not only increased on-campus student participation but broadened student involvement in off-campus volunteer opportunities. Among the most popular Chester-based volunteer programs were child tutoring and aid to the disenfranchised through several religious and community groups including Big Brothers and Sisters, support of the local food pantries and environmental advocacy. Some programs began as ad hoc efforts among the students themselves but others reflected the interests of the numerous administrators and faculty who worked assiduously in the community, including Dean of Students Ray Becker, Assistant to the President Pat Brant, and faculty in several departments, notably Social Work led by John Poullin, Clinical Psychology led by Don Jackson, and Arts and Sciences led by Professors Alzono Cavin and Jean Godsall-Meyers. As happens regularly in higher education, these interest-driven efforts became institutionalized. Over the years, this "service learning" also became organizationally more sophisticated. While it was referred to nationally under the rubric of Campus Compact, the end product was the same: Students benefited from a holistic academic experience while the community benefited from their altruism.

Organization of the Honors Program

Accompanying the introduction of core baccalaureate requirements, the Arts and Sciences faculty also provided the leadership in designing an Honors Program that crossed disciplines and was offered to students in all schools and colleges. Program admittance was initially offered by invitation to incoming freshmen based on high school academic records and SAT scores.[2] In succeeding years, as a way to encourage achievement among the most able, invitations were also extended to students who had proven their academic ability at the end of the first or second semester of the freshman year.

All faculty members were encouraged to develop honors courses to prevent the program from becoming the domain of a small percentage of the professorate. Honors courses were offered in English, calculus, and other discipline-specific topics, and supplemented by a freshman Honors Seminar and junior-year Honors Colloquia. The course content was organized to provide greater discussion and experiential learning than regular courses. Additionally, honors students were required to attend a minimum of eight cultural activities outside of the classroom each academic year. These might include on- or off-campus lectures or performances. Designed to reinforce the holistic approach to undergraduate education, this component of the program was significant for all honor students, but especially instructive for those in the more applied majors such as engineering, accounting and nursing.

Initiated with seven students in 1987, the Honors Program averaged close to eighty students per year in subsequent years. To avoid the construct of a two-tier baccalaureate school, these men and women were fully integrated into general university life, living in campus housing and functioning no differently from other students. To remain active, each had to maintain a GPA of 3.0 in all courses, including the honors sections. Those who met the required honors hours, earned a Certificate of Honors in General Education presented at graduation. This certificate, recognizing proficiency across disciplines, was one of the first of its kind from a comprehensive university.

---

[2] These outstanding students were also given preferential status to receive the merit-based Widener Presidential Scholarships.

Honors Week

As the Honors Program evolved, we realized that public recognition of scholarly achievement was needed long before that received at commencement. The issue was first raised at a meeting of the Friday afternoon "pretzel club," a group of President's Staff members who met on a random basis to muse about the University while munching on pretzels and drinking sodas. Our ruminations, always informal and often insightful, encouraged the flow of stream-of-conscious thoughts. On one particular afternoon, while chatting about the publicity conferred on athletes – Widener had many sports standouts – I commented that "it's too bad there isn't some way to do the same for academic excellence." All present leapt into a conversation about how to implement campus-wide recognition of the "best and brightest."

Honors Week emerged from that afternoon's conversation. Five days were set aside each March to recognize academic achievement. The week was replete with lectures sponsored by various academic disciplines, meetings of academic honor societies, and a wide array of student presentations of research projects and creative work. As the years passed, the sophistication of the undergraduate presentations grew to the point that visitors often asked if the student presenter were in graduate school. It was not such a far-flung notion; in time, students from several of the graduate programs did begin to participate in Honors Week, making it a celebratory week of University-wide academic distinction.

Honors Week culminated with a convocation at which the top ten percent of both graduating seniors and graduate students were inducted into Phi Kappa Phi, the national honor society for universities. Every inductee was individually acknowledged by the provost, as were members of the twenty-two national academic honor societies that were chartered at the University.

The convocation became a special event in the life of the University. Faculty in academic regalia formally processed into Latham Hall filled with students and parents gathered to celebrate academic excellence. It was one of those moments on a university campus that brings home why you chose education as a profession!

As a link between the excellence of the past and of the present, each honors convocation featured an address by a distinguished alumnus or alumna who had once also been among the best students. The inaugural speaker, whose remarks set a standard of excellence for all who followed, was William Knaus, M.D., a 1968 graduate and former member of the Board of Trustees. He was then a professor, researcher and co-director of the Trauma Center at the George Washington University Medical Center.

An internationally recognized expert in trauma research and emergency medicine, Bill Knaus had been one of the first physicians to treat President Reagan following the assassination attempt on March 30, 1981. He also created APACHE, a computer-based emergency room protocol used across the world, and held a teaching appointment at the University of Paris. Interestingly, he was also *persona non grata* in the Soviet Union for many years thanks to his controversial book, written from first-hand knowledge, *Inside Russian Medicine*. (Knaus 1986)

Dr. Knaus's address was so well received by the students that the following year, at the request of the senior class, he again honored the campus as commencement speaker.

Faculty-Student Research

Research collaboration between faculty and undergraduate students began informally but spread rapidly, in part due to the invigorating commitment to holistic education and in part because faculty told one another of the satisfaction derived by sharing scholarly work with the undergraduate students. In a 1996 survey of Widener faculty over 55 percent reported involving students in their personal research. As the collaborations spread, professors began to encourage students to present research papers at national forums and conferences.

In academic year 1994-95 alone: a number of humanities students presented papers at the National Conference on Undergraduate Research, and all were accepted for publication; English students participated in the Undergraduate Literature Conference in Utah; biology, mathematics and engineering students won awards for research at their conferences. The success of these efforts was quite heady. Imagine what a leg-up an applicant to graduate school would have who had already done significant research or been published in a scholarly journal!

The relationship between student and faculty certainly corroborated the Widener motto "We take your education personally."

Brandywine's Legacy

But not everyone is an honor student or a good researcher. Nor was our motto just a slogan. It reflected our policy of admitting stu-

dents who could be nurtured to realize their potential. To help accomplish this mission, and in response to an internal attrition study,
Widener established a sophisticated network of academic support services. Several of the programs were originally offered at Brandywine College then, after its demise in 1991, became absorbed, with modifications,
into the academic services on the Main Campus. One such program
provided help for students with learning disabilities, specifically dyslexia
and math anxiety. Enormously successful at Brandywine, it became the
genesis for the equally successful Enable Program at the baccalaureate
level. Other programs and services that were successfully translated to
serve needs on the Main Campus included an orientation for freshmen
modeled after one at the University of South Carolina, and clinics for
both reading and writing.

The key to inclusion of these service programs into the academic
mix of the University was the willingness of faculty and staff to open
their minds to every possibility. Programs that initially appeared incompatible with our mission were tweaked time and again into a perfect fit. I was impressed with the Main Campus faculty's appreciation for
the skills their junior college colleagues had in dealing with students
who required extensive mentoring. Indeed, many broadened their pedagogic skills by utilizing techniques learned from their Brandywine College peers.

Academic Support Services

Data produced in 1989 by the National Institute of Independent
Colleges and Universities (NIICU) indicated that more than 20 percent
of first-year students enrolled in a four-year baccalaureate program did
not return to the same institution for the sophomore year (Porter:
1989).

The study prompted the University to initiate a four-year internal
attrition/persistence analysis. Although our attrition was below the national average, we learned that the majority of students who left the
University did so after two or three semesters and did so with a cumu-
lative GPA of 2.0 or lower. The obvious conclusion: early intervention
would make the chances for academic success greater.

In the academic year 1992-93, Dr. Andrew A. Bushko, the former
dean of Brandywine College, was designated head of the new Office of
Freshman Studies and Academic Support Services. The concept was
born of the notion that keeping students was a more cost-efficient ef-

fort than recruiting replacements. This was an era when national and regional applicant pools were shrinking annually, and when student transfers among institutions had become common.

Under Bushko's creative leadership, the Academic Skills Program (ASP) was strengthened by partnering a faculty member with a student in need of mentoring and support services. First introduced by the provost in 1989, the ASP was designed to identify and assist freshmen who were projected to fall below a 2.0 GPA during their first semester. Once enhanced with faculty ombudsmen, the program became remarkably successful. In the first year, 68 percent of the students in the ASP program improved their grades.

Dean Bushko also revitalized an Early Warning System that relied on faculty to notify the Office of Freshman Studies early in a semester if they observed a student floundering or failing. The adjustment to an environment of total self-responsibility and heightened academic demands overwhelmed a number of first-year students each year, but the Office of Freshman Programs mitigated the transition for many.

PAC Hall (personal academic coaching) was Dean Bushko's response to the request by the Athletic Department for a study program for athletes, notably members of the football team. With the enthusiastic backing of the football coaching staff, all players were required to attend an evening study hall in the first semester of their freshman year. Overseen by a member of the Student Services staff, PAC Hall also engaged a select number of upperclassmen to serve as tutors. Players could opt out of PAC Hall in the second semester if they achieved a targeted GPA, but many who appreciated the structured study time elected to remain despite obtaining the necessary grades.

PAC Hall's success was such that it was expanded, first to all athletic teams and then to all freshmen, including those already within the support system via the Academic Skills or Early Warning Programs. An unintended positive of the program was a greater meshing of students with different interests. Some of the stereotypical academic v. athlete perceptions that thrive on college campuses were dispelled by the interaction of the disparate students in PAC Hall.

In addition to being expanded, the PAC program was replicated under the name Academic Mentor Program (AMP) for those pledging fraternities and sororities. In this instance, the tutors and mentors were selected from upperclassmen who were also members of Greek organizations.

The PAC and AMP initiatives made a substantive difference in the lives of many freshmen. There were other rewards, as well: the University benefited from reduced attrition, academically troubled students improved study skills and their odds for success, and gifted upperclassmen were able to earn spending money serving as tutors and mentors. The success of the programs brought national recognition to Dean Bushko from the National Center for the Freshman Year Experience.

Counseling

The concentration on student support by so many Widener faculty and staff resulted in increasing traffic in the Student Counseling Center. It and the Psychological Services Center, operated for the public by the graduate Clinical Psychology program, ran independently for some time until the two were merged in an effort to maximize existing campus resources. The new unit provided Widener with expanded, high quality student psychological and behavioral counseling services while employing doctoral students in internships supervised by faculty and other professional psychologists. The counseling services continued to be available to the public on a referral basis by local social agencies.

While behavioral and psychological counseling were offered among Widener's student services, the term "counseling" more often referred to academic progress with a faculty member as the counselor. Although every professor was expected to participate, not all teachers excel at counseling or give it the commitment it deserves. Nevertheless, all Widener faculty were coached to become more aware of the necessity of checking student progress and keeping students knowledgeable about individual curriculum ladders. These efforts did not in any way negate the fact that the student always has the ultimate responsibility to be sure he has completed all academic benchmarks for graduation.

Emphasis on Skills Development

The Widener faculty constantly sought new ways to respond to issues that, while common across the academic spectrum, could become a barrier to the graduate's success. The introduction of the Writing Center was a response to an acknowledgement that students' writing skills had eroded, to a large extent as a result of the increasing use of computers and the informal writing style of students while using computers. At times it seemed most students were devotees of e.e. cummings. Additionally, students were arriving on campus with a lack of understanding of what constituted plagiarism and how to provide appropriate attribution of sources from the Internet and elsewhere. The Writing Center provided support to improve basic writing but also assisted more skilled students in perfecting their essay-writing and research skills. The same range of services from remedial to advanced was provided by the Math Center.

One of the most ambitious undertakings to improve student skills was the introduction in academic year 1998-99 of a campus-wide writing requirement for undergraduates. The program, developed by a team led by Arts and Sciences Dean Lawrence Panek, was designed to move students to a level of writing competency that could be quantified based upon mandatory regular writing exams. Starting with the premise that writing is a means of thinking and learning, not just of communication, students in the first year were required to take English 101 "Composition and Critical Thought." In the succeeding years prior to graduation, they completed a minimum of four additional writing enriched courses, each of which was designed specifically for a school or college and included at least three writing assignments, plus the requirement of a graded rewrite. The Writing Center measured each student's development by requiring periodic samples and offered assistance to those with less than satisfactory progress. All graduating seniors were expected to pass a writing sample at level five competency.

I was enormously impressed with the faculty's attention to this issue. Many colleges and universities assume that entering students have adequate skill sets to pursue higher education. In today's world, with staggering unevenness in the preparation provided by secondary schools, that is a false assumption.

Not all students will succeed, or are willing to try; this is an individual's choice to make. The obligation of the university is to provide the academic tools for potential success.

Chapter 10

Faculty Rights and Responsibilities

A metaphor for a university is a three-legged stool, the three legs representing faculty, students, and administration/trustees. There is a constant dynamic among the three for each plays a specific role within the whole but is dependent on the others to make the university a vibrant and intellectually sound place.

In my mind, the primary role and *raison d'être* for any administration is to assist the faculty and students in doing what they do best, teach and learn. If the complexities of a modern university could be managed without an administrative group, the teaching and learning functions could work as they did in the early days of education, as a contract between master and student. However, in the twenty-first century a university operates like a city or even a small country. Housing, food, medical care, parking, security, financial management, markets, marketing, technology, office and teaching facilities, and the supporting infrastructure are not only needed but expected by students and faculty. These among others are the administration's responsibility.

The life of a university is a unique blend of constants and change. Students arrive, bringing exuberance to campus, move through and leave. It is this constantly changing energy that makes a university setting so stimulating. Yet, paradoxically, universities adhere to many traditions and academic customs that have changed very little over the years. Unquestionably, the most discussed is tenure.

Tenure: A Call for Reform

As a result of tenure, faculty are the continuum of the academic structure. In place for years and years, they can be extraordinarily creative or doggedly intransigent. They can be instrumental in forging change or stolid obstructionists. The skills of the chief executive, particularly in personal style and diplomatic ability, are critical in shaping an environment of collaboration and shared vision. A chief executive without a harmonious relationship with faculty is in for a less than pleasant experience.

Many outside the academy, especially those in business, see the university employment structure as non-productive and incomprehensible. It is not fully based on quantifiable outcomes, provides lifetime employment to a substantial number of individuals, and appears to have numerous periods of time during the year in which the employees aren't expected to be present in the workplace. I cannot count the number of times during my career I heard the comment of how easy it must be to be a professor. Good pay and only nine months of work! As with many things in life, the perception is far from the reality.

The misunderstanding of tenure is a product of not understanding its historical antecedents and its uniqueness in today's market-driven economy. Many of the concerns that historically led to the institution of tenure have been subsumed by other legislative laws and regulations that afford protection to all citizens. The Age Discrimination Act of 1967, the Civil Rights Act of 1964, the Civil Rights Act of 1991, Title VII of Americans with Disabilities Act of 1973 are among the external protections now in law. These protections in some ways buttress the arguments of many who believe that tenure in today's society is unnecessary because of the wide range of protections in place for all citizens. Why then is it necessary for academics to receive additional protection?

Those in the academy argue that tenure is necessary in order to ensure academic freedom in teaching and research. To many outside the academy, tenure is seen as a sinecure, simply a means of guaranteeing job protection.

The principles of today's tenure policies were laid down in 1915 when the American Association of University Professors (AAUP) became concerned with the lack of protection for faculty as new and more controversial academic fields were being introduced on campuses. Many of the disciplines were challenged as inappropriate by observers and trustees of institutions. One can imagine the concern in various regions of the country with the introduction of Freudian psychology, Darwin's theory of evolution, cellular biology, and new approaches to economics and anthropology.

In 1940 the Association of American Colleges and AAUP published what is known as the *1940 Statement of Principles on Academic Freedom and Tenure*. This policy statement, still the benchmark for the principles of academic freedom and tenure, has been endorsed over the years by more than 135 academic societies. It established that tenure would, after six years of service, be granted in the seventh or equivalent year of probation; if denied, the seventh year becomes the terminal year. It also reaffirmed dismissal for cause as an integral part of the process (AAUP 2006).

It is important to understand the intention and content of "dismissal for cause." If a tenured faculty member fails to perform expected duties at an acceptable level, he or she may be subject to reassignment or dismissal. The clause is difficult to enforce but it sets standards for faculty and provides the administration with an option to terminate inadequate individuals. Faculty may also be dismissed for "financial exigency." In other words, when a university's economic conditions are such that the institution is experiencing severe financial difficulties, a reduction of the academic force is an acceptable, though unpleasant, path to maintain financial stability. Not surprisingly, the process to remove a faculty member under the above two options becomes quite adversarial in most cases.

The Age Discrimination Act of 1967 exempted colleges and universities from mandatory retirement at age seventy until 1993. The anticipated fear that older faculty would ride out the years, thus delaying the influx of talented younger faculty for six years, did not materialize in any substantial way. I believe that this was a result of institutional incentive plans to assist older faculty with the transition to retirement. While the occasional faculty member will remain in place beyond his or her productive academic life, most have other interests and are aware when their scholarly productivity and academic effectiveness begin to diminish.

A legitimate question then is "is tenure necessary?" Does the same need to protect free speech in the classroom and research exist as in years past? The issue of free speech has become increasingly moot, but protection for research has increased as the bounds of scientific investigation have expanded.

Unfortunately, much of the misunderstanding surrounding tenure results from the relegation of the core issue, academic freedom, to the periphery of the discussion. Blame for the distortion of the conversation should be shared equally by boards of trustees, administrators and faculty: The discussion of tenure as critical to academic freedom has been largely replaced by a discussion of job protection and economic entitlement.

For many trustees and administrators tenure is seen as anathema to providing greater flexibility for managing limited resources, particularly in difficult times. The inability to transfer assets, both human and financial, or to respond to new opportunities because of closed faculty positions is a legitimate concern. However, this begs the question is tenure itself the problem or is it the management of the process? I would argue it's a bit of both. Tenure is still needed, but in a more limited form, and universities can improve the administration of the process.

The presence of a heavily tenured faculty is a concern on many postsecondary campuses. Such a faculty is more manageable at a single-purpose, liberal arts college where changes to the core curriculum are usually incremental, allowing time to adjust faculty positions through attrition and retirement. The issue becomes more critical at a comprehensive institution that is adding new programs on a regular basis; there, maximum flexibility is needed if the institution is to expand.

Reform to Preserve

The traditional expectation for tenure consists of academic scholarship, teaching and service. However, the recent emphasis on scholarly recognition in that triad often leads to reduced contact with students and limited classroom teaching. Indeed, there is a growing debate in higher education, especially at the large research universities, as to whether the university is valuing research at the expense of undergraduate education and excellence in teaching. The fact is that, while scholarship is in itself a legitimate academic pursuit that produces many of the scientific, cultural and sociological advances in society, it alone would not be an appropriate criterion for tenure at liberal arts colleges or comprehensive universities. Any discussion of tenure must be done in the context of an institution's philosophy and academic objectives.

Widener, with its recent history of change, may be viewed as a classic comprehensive university. With its early roots as a traditional undergraduate college, Widener developed a mix of undergraduate and applied graduate/professional programs. Thus, the application of a traditional liberal arts or research tenure model would be inappropriate. Primary to the core academic values at Widener is the need for all faculty to be master teachers. Without this skill, the prospects for long-term retention are close to nil. Nevertheless, some angst occurred among the faculty when I, with the assistance of the provost, instituted a teacher/scholar model for faculty, rather than the more traditional scholar/teacher standard.

The teacher/scholar model as defined at Widener was appropriate for the mission of the University. One was expected to hold the terminal degree in one's discipline, i.e., Ph.D., Ed.D., J.D., D.N.Sc., Psy.D., be an excellent classroom teacher and communicator, provide evidence of scholarship in published books, refereed journals, or via original research. The faculty handbook, section 2.6.1, elucidates scholarship as "... intellectual contributions to the academic area of the faculty member. Examples include research that is empirical, primary or inductive; scholarship that emphasizes synthesis or integration or pedagogical work that focuses on the application or on the conveying of new information." (Widener 1987, 29)

Academic citizenship simply means institutional service. Service may be to the discipline, including professional organizations, to the school or college, to the university, or to "specified constituencies or affinity groups included within the faculty and student community of Widener University." The service component provides a wide series of options for faculty to be engaged both internally and externally with the life of the University and his or her profession. To just be an excellent teacher or just be an excellent scholar is not enough. These two attributes must be joined with an active engagement in the life of the academic community whether on campus or externally based.

One defense invariably raised when a faculty member is found deficient in the area of scholarship is "but he is so good in the classroom and with students." Individuals who fall into this category may find a place in the academic community teaching introductory level courses but know that the prospects for future advancement in academic rank will be unlikely. There are many superb teachers of basic English skills, mathematics, and introductory languages who find employment as contractual or adjunct faculty. However, they will not, except in rare circumstances, be considered for tenure. While this may seem harsh, consider the analogy of an auto mechanic who learned his trade on pre-computer vehicles and never took further instruction on how to use the appropriate diagnostic applications available for newer models, or the physician who does not stay current with new treatment modalities or pharmacological advances. Good classroom teachers become better teachers if they are active in their academic disciplines. This does not mean that their communication skills will necessarily improve, but the depth of knowledge and currency of their knowledge available to the student increases. A published author in English or history is certainly a better role model for students than one who has not published. A science or engineering faculty member engaged in research imparts a sense of intellectual enthusiasm to his students and a higher level of commitment than a professor whose knowledge is textbook only.

The teacher/scholar model provides the comprehensive university with a cadre of faculty who combine the best characteristics of the traditional liberal arts college and a research university faculty.

The diversity of academic offerings at a comprehensive university necessitates flexibility in the application of tenure standards. Each of the schools and colleges of Widener was allowed to develop the criteria specific to its needs. These criteria, published in the bylaws of the schools and colleges, were an integral part of the promotion and tenure process.

The scholarship component for faculty in the College of Arts and Sciences would be what most people would recognize as traditional scholarship. The number of books in discipline-specific fields and articles in refereed journals are usually greater in CAS than most other schools. Some disciplines are more practice-oriented; nursing, social work, education. As a result, the scholarship and pedagogy of the faculty in these disciplines is markedly different from faculty in CAS, Business or Law.

A challenge for a comprehensive university is to construct an environment that allows a diverse faculty to understand, appreciate and respect the professional demands and pedagogy of the different disciplines. This challenge is assisted by the third element of the teacher/scholar model, academic citizenship. Serving on college and university committees, ad hoc groups studying academic proposals, or being engaged with student-related activities contributes to the integration of knowledge and understanding.

Adjunct Faculty

Heightened financial pressure on both public and private institutions is forcing many colleges and universities to find ways to reduce the number of full-time faculty by expanding the number of adjunct faculty. The increasing number of adjunct faculty on campuses raises concerns among professors who have traditionally seen adjuncts in a different support role. Many senior faculty contend that while adjuncts play a valuable instructional role on a limited basis, charging them with the responsibility of academic advising and more teaching hours runs the risk of diminishing academic quality.

There is a growing movement to find a way to legitimize adjunct faculty through benefits, more professional security and a greater inclusion in the academic and social fabric of the campus. Adjunct faculty have functioned for decades as a nomadic tribe of scholars moving from position to position, from institution to institution, usually without benefits and at the low end of the pay scale. In many instances they are paid at a set rate per course taught and have little prospect for full-time placement in a tightening job market.

A catch-22 of the tenure process is that the recruitment of qualified younger faculty becomes increasingly difficult as individuals who may have joined the academic life apply their skills elsewhere. Practitioners in disciplines such as the cutting-edge fields of microbiology, as well as finance, languages and accounting, to name a few, have the potential for greater economic reward in areas external to the campus. It is recognized that a balance must be found between traditional tenure for all academic positions and the need to achieve maximum flexibility offered by part-time and adjunct faculty.

An approach to the current dilemma may be for each institution to identify the number of core faculty necessary to maintain the academic mission of the institution. Positions so designated would be recognized as tenured positions, with the commitment that as openings occur through attrition or retirement, tenure would be granted. Such positions would be subject to the understanding that a position could also be shifted to another discipline or department if dictated by the ebb and flow of student interest and societal demands.

In today's rapidly changing world, with the demands for new knowledge and training, the inflexibility of the traditional tenure structure supports the critics who oppose tenure. Faculty should embrace legitimate reform as a means of preserving the tenure system.

It is time to make contractual faculty a significant part of the academic workforce. An effort should be made to provide faculty, as a condition of employment, a degree of job security, benefits and greater integration into the life of the academic community. Contract faculty should understand that they hold the positions subject to the academic and financial needs of the college or university, and to peer review.

Many will dismiss this approach with the criticism that it divides a faculty into a two-class system. The reality is that the system already exists and unless modification to the traditional tenure system is made, further erosion to tenure will occur in an unsystematic way. It would be more valuable to recognize the need for change and to intelligently craft a structure that meets organizational need and reality than to have the system implode.

Without change, the pressures of financial shortfalls and the perception by the public that tenure is nothing more than an entitlement will continue to grow.

Collegiality: Managed Suspicion

It is always dangerous to generalize about groups but there are certain characteristics that apply to faculty. Individuals who spend their lives in the professorate are intelligent, analytical, idealistic, and skeptical of authority. Faculty members instinctively believe that they are the quintessential core of the university and *primus inter pares*. In matters academic, they are correct. In other matters, they are participants with an opinion. Nevertheless, because of their training and the nature of the academic commitment, they operate in a largely self-directed environment. A colleague once remarked to me that the faculty is "a Mandarin class." They resent and resist directives, expecting, instead, intellectual dialogue on why something should happen. Moreover, their years of study to obtain a doctorate are years spent questioning, inquiring, seeking flaws in research materials, and being critical. If they consistently challenge students to question and to interpret, why shouldn't they apply the same standard of skepticism to administrative policy and decision making?

As president, I spent countless hours communicating with faculty through deans and the provost, as well as in person. Except on rare occasion, I always listened rather than opining, engaged in dialogue rather than pronouncing. The nurturing of a collegial environment is not an easy task, but it is crucial if one wishes to lead a university. Faculty representation should be included whenever possible in the decision making process, and absolutely always in matters pertaining to academic decisions. Furthermore, decisions once made should include a process for reporting to the full faculty both the outcome of deliberations and the potential impact of the decisions upon the institution. Without faculty comprehension of the larger institutional vision, change may be warily viewed from the much narrower perspective of a department, school or college. It is human nature to wonder "how does this affect me?" with little concern for the greater good. Knowing the institutional priorities and objectives may not bring about universal consensus, but it does create an understanding of the *raisons d'être* for most policies.

Extending the Vision

The president's task is to create a vision that allows the institutional culture to develop and thrive. The larger the institution, the more difficult it is to convey that vision. The faculty is critical to making this happen. In fact, it may be the most powerful of the interested parties, as acknowledged in the classic book *Leadership and Ambiguity: The American College President* (Cohen and March 1986, 3): "The American college or university is a prototypic organized anarchy. It does not know what it is doing. Its goals are vague or in dispute. Its technology is familiar but not understood. Its major participants wander in and out of the organization. These factors do not make a university a bad organization or a disorganized one; but they do make it a problem to describe, understand and lead." In the 1978 edition of the work Cohen and March commented that: "the most potentially obstructionist of the possible anarchists are the faculty if not appropriately integrated into the decision making process." One vehicle for inclusion is to have a cohort of respected senior faculty, the so-called movers and shakers, serve in the role of quasi-consultants to the president. These individuals are asked for input and are kept in the loop as the planning moves forward. My group not only provided reactions that may have forestalled roadblocks from other faculty, it provided a sounding board of knowledgeable colleagues.

Obviously, there are times when the administration must make unpopular decisions. However, if an environment of collegial give-and-take has been the *modus operandi*, faculty oft times will accept a decision they are unhappy with because of the trust that has been built over time between them and the president and administration. Oversight of the academic structure, its quality and control, is the province of the academic vice president and provost. I was fortunate that Provost Larry Buck had the type of rapport with the faculty leadership that enabled this kind of pulse taking to be a regular working component of the decision-making process. It was a rare occasion when a new academic initiative or difficult administrative decision created surprise or unmanageable controversy when presented to the faculty. There are presidents who prefer to manage from an adversarial position. I firmly believe that the style only leads to conflict and narrowing of options. A heavy-handed management approach may work because the ultimate authority rests with the president through the board of trustees. However, such an approach can be demoralizing to faculty who may elect to opt out of any meaningful involvement in faculty governance.

The Challenges of Tenure: A Case in Point

The control of the content of academic material, the teaching style and the methodology to accomplish the task are the purview of the individual faculty member, a tradition that continues from the earliest days of organized teaching. Oversight of the academic process in each discipline is largely by peer review. Colleagues with similar expertise sanction the courses as well as the objectives and goals of the material. Colleges add or delete courses based on the curricular matrix determined by the departments, and on institutional degree requirements.

Especially in the years leading to tenure, faculty are subjected to peer review in the areas of scholarship, teaching effectiveness and style, and academic citizenship. Individuals are scrutinized on a regular basis. However, as in many human endeavors, colleagues often find it difficult to objectively criticize associates; thus, the process leading to denial of tenure is painful and often emotional.

There are many reasons for the angst attached to the tenure process. In some cases faculty are distressed when they realize that they have made a mistake in initially judging the capacity of a fellow scholar to reach the level necessary for a tenure appointment. If the decision is clouded by personal fondness for an individual, or other extenuating circumstances, rationalizations surface as to why a negative decision should be avoided. As one faculty member commented while reviewing a tenure candidate, "He would not be a *harmfully* inferior teacher!"

Because the body of knowledge is constantly evolving, faculty who were tenured at an earlier time may not meet the standards demanded of younger colleagues. This conundrum often makes older faculty uncomfortable with the tenure standards. It should not, basic skill sets are ever changing in nearly all fields of human activity.

In a large majority of cases, faculties approach the tenure process with consummate fairness. However the process, being both quantitative and subjective in nature, can provide opportunity for reasonable individuals to passionately disagree on the merits of a candidate. The quantitative benchmarks of teaching and scholarship are fairly easy to assess; more difficult is the aspect of individual "fit" as colleague and contributor to the university. A disruptive personality in a small department can render that department ineffective.

One tenure case at Widener led to two emotional lawsuits that created opposing camps within a department, a college, and beyond. One tenure candidate was popular with both students and colleagues and had been mentored for several years by highly respected academicians as to the need to produce more and better scholarship. His failure to measure up to the research standard resulted in a denial of tenure despite his acknowledged skill as a classroom teacher.

The denial of tenure was a correct one. However, the introduction of peripheral issues into the process made for a very unpleasant period of many months. Surprisingly, a second candidate for tenure in the same college (one who was well considered) became an outspoken critic of the process and his tenured colleagues. In defense of his friend and co-candidate, he created an extraordinarily disruptive environment through innuendo, half-truths and personal attacks on colleagues. Despite his good qualities and likely prospects for tenure, he self-destructed. This was a case in which the tenure standard of compatibility was appropriately applied.

Both candidates were denied tenure. Attorneys entered the process shortly thereafter, leading to the deposition of many faculty members in anticipation of lawsuits by one or both of the failed candidates. I was astonished at the issues raised during these depositions; politics, personal attacks for alleged interference in academic affairs, and accusations about private lives made the testimony sound at times like a grade B soap opera.

One of the key individuals in the process was terminally ill with cancer and, therefore, consented to be deposed on videotape. It was sobering to watch his hours-long testimony and to see his grace under ordeal. Had his tape (or the depositions of certain others) been aired at a trial, the private lives of several faculty would have been irrevocably damaged.

Many faculty fail to understand that when being deposed, the most acceptable answers are: yes, no, or I don't remember. Certainly, when asked a question by an attorney one considers carefully before expounding tangentially since that may create a record that can be used by your adversary in court. Happily for the University and for faulty both on and off the tenure committee, both cases were dismissed prior to a trial. Nevertheless, contentious tenure cases are expensive and disruptive and it takes time to heal the animosity created.

Ironically, I thought these two cases were easy ones to decide. It was patently clear that the likeable young teacher had failed, despite mentoring, to meet even the minimum standards for scholarship expected for tenure. The second candidate clearly displayed personality traits that defined him as unacceptable to colleagues and the University.

The inherent instinct of a vast majority of faculty is to do the right thing. A critical obligation of the academic system is the concept of peer review. Contentious promotion and tenure cases undermine the system and make it less likely that faculty, especially junior faculty, will want to participate. But, despite the untidy nature of the process, the system of peer review works well.

Denial of Retention: A Case in Point

In our litigious society, the potential for a lawsuit related to failure to retain, or to grant tenure, is ever present. In such cases, the desired outcome to the plaintiff is an economic settlement or a reconsideration of the negative decision. Reconsideration is rarely an option since the courts have traditionally given maximum leeway to educational institutions regarding tenure. If the tenure or retention process is followed as described in the faculty handbook the courts are reluctant to become involved, especially in the private sector.

Among the most vexatious cases to defend are those relating to a charge of discrimination on religious grounds. Given the political correctness pervasive on campuses and in society today, such charges are fraught with potentially negative implications for the university. One such case at Widener involved a faculty member who had been hired to fill a new position in the School of Human Service Professions, the Center for Education. When denied a continuing appointment, he sued based on a charge of discrimination because he was Jewish. He claimed that his failure to be retained emanated from an anti-Semitic culture at Widener and was the result of ethnic discrimination.

He had come to Widener with an excellent reputation that included classroom service as an associate professor, numerous publications and high public visibility on radio and television as an education expert. Regrettably, while his teaching and student rapport at Widener proved above average, his academic scholarship was neglected in favor of external consulting and promotional activities. It became unarguably clear to his colleagues that the University was simply a platform for personal gain and aggrandizement without sufficient effort to fulfill the required scholarship.

The lawsuit was tried in U.S. federal court in Philadelphia. The plaintiff's attorney had achieved a degree of fame for his success in discrimination cases (including that of an individual fired for having AIDS, later made into the 1993 movie *Philadelphia* starring Tom Hanks). The University's General Counsel Rocco Imperatrice, a skilled defense lawyer who is expert in higher education law, represented Widener.

One allegation presented in evidence of the University's supposed culture of anti-Semitism was the date of a social gathering for faculty and administrators at the president's home. Held annually on the opening weekend of the academic year, and announced months in advance without eliciting comment, the event had been inadvertently scheduled for the eve of Rosh Hashanah. As the fall semester approached and we realized the conflict, I had met with several Jewish senior faculty who recommended we send a memo acknowledging the error, avoid such a conflict in the future, and hold the event as scheduled since attendance was not mandatory. The meeting and recommendations defused the issue on campus.

The plaintiff's counsel's examination of the dean of the Center for Education, also Jewish, was fascinating. He claimed the she, too, was a victim of the culture of discrimination who had acquiesced to the negative retention review in an effort to protect her position. The fact that the senior faculty member who had written the negative recommendation was Christian was also carefully woven into the presentation. It was an exceptional piece of lawyering by innuendo.

In cross-examination, the plaintiff admitted to Mr. Imperatrice that he had no proof of any ethnic comments made about him; he "just knew they were anti-Semitic." In response to the plaintiff's claim that his principal interest and occupation was teaching, Rocco produced his tax returns for several years proving more income had been earned from external activities than from his faculty position. Our attorney further questioned one of the accused faculty, asking point-blank: "Are you anti-Semitic?" The professor said no and offered the facts that his wife was Jewish and his children were being raised in that faith. In dead silence, a recess was called. Widener presented no further defense; the jury was charged, filed out, and returned after a brief meeting to recommend that the case be dismissed.

Academic Freedom

At times campuses are not particularly well balanced in matters relating to societal or political issues. The combination of young, idealistic students and liberal-oriented, intellectual faculty leads to predictable responses to issues, as evidenced by the stance of colleges and universities during times of national debate on hot-button issues such as the environment, civil rights, and the use of armed forces.

The clash between the philosophic beliefs of academe and the reality that exists external to the campus can be paradoxical. After all, a universally subscribed tenet of higher education is to elicit and examine divergent viewpoints. The campus is ideally a place where all voices are heard and risk-free forums enlighten all who attend. The principle of academic freedom – accepted as an eleventh commandment, if you will – must be vigorously nurtured and consciously lived. Any insistence on "politically correct thought" or, more disturbing, the codification of "appropriate language and action" must be guarded against for it is contradictory to the ideal of free expression in an intellectual community. It is curious that many faculty who may inadvertently participate in establishing a restrictive campus environment are the same faculty who, in public, would man the barricades against codes of behavior that restrict the rights of any individual or groups.

Limits to Academic Freedom: A Case in Point

While faculties are the sole arbitrators of what is taught in their classrooms, they must consider course content within the context of institutional and intellectual inquiry. For example, espousing a particular religious view would be unacceptable unless one were teaching at an institution established to support a particular set of beliefs.

A classic case occurred at the Catholic University of America, a Vatican controlled institution, when a member of the faculty was dismissed for teaching against several basic tenets of the Roman Catholic Church. In the end, it was determined that the institution had not violated the professor's academic freedom since the faculty member was well aware of the philosophical and theological positions of the university when hired. Academic discussion of the validity of the church's position would have been acceptable; publicly denying its validity was not.

In the majority of colleges and universities an unwritten sense of the limits of what is or is not considered acceptable behavior for faculty develops through years of tradition. What may be considered appropriate at an Eastern, secular, urban institution may be inappropriate at a Midwestern, faith-based college. Faculty should be aware of institutional culture and characteristics before accepting a teaching appointment.

Many senior faculty are products of the 1960s and 1970s when society was in turmoil. Questioning traditional values and turning away from the American corporate culture was de rigueur, as was supporting civil rights, academic freedom, and political idealism. As students, many remained in college or graduate school during the Vietnam War thus guaranteeing an exemption from military service. The inherent unfairness of a draft that allowed a defined segment of the population to avoid military service still conflicts many faculty who benefited from the policy.

Despite the predilection for campuses to be liberal, and the concerns expressed by some segments of society about this bent, there is little evidence that an individual faculty member's political or philosophical views have any real impact on classroom instruction. In my experience, faculty are consummate professionals who would never use their positions to proselytize a social or political view.

But outside the classroom, it is equally as important that campuses maintain an environment in which a balanced exchange of ideas is encouraged and individuals are comfortable in espousing unorthodox views if they wish.

There are always those who will question or oppose the appearance of certain individuals on campus because of the views they represent. First amendment rights will always create thorny dialogue. Some rights are easier to grasp because of the apparent correctness of the issue. But what about pornography in the context of freedom of expression? The controversy over the artist Robert Mapplethorpe's work had continued for several years when the campus museum invited the director of the Cleveland Museum of Contemporary Art, who had been sacked for mounting a Mapplethorpe exhibit, to lecture on the subject of censorship. The lecture played to some 400 – in attendance for divergent reasons, I'm sure, including defense of freedom, art appreciation, titillation, and curiosity. During the lecture, the speaker used slides of the artist's less controversial, though still unsettling, work. The point is that he was there and so were the slides despite my receipt of calls prior to the lecture questioning the appropriateness of allowing such "a travesty" on campus.

At another time, I was questioned about allowing Senator Gary Hart to speak on campus when he was a Democratic candidate for President (and before the extra-marital controversy). I was similarly queried when George W. H. Bush, running against Ronald Reagan for the Republican presidential nomination, was provided a forum on campus. Again, in my opinion, no one has the right to dictate appropriate thought.

Who May Recruit?

The military's position on homosexuality is an issue that still divides law school faculties. Even President Clinton's infamous "don't ask, don't tell" policy failed to appease the AALS in its belief that the military is discriminatory and should not be granted the right to recruit on law campuses. It threatened to remove professional recognition from law schools that allowed the Judge Advocate General's Corps (JAG) to recruit on campus. Although the AALS is seen by law faculty as the intellectual arm of legal education, and its imprimatur is important to the status of a law school, the threat was without teeth. The AALS has no authority to prevent students sitting for the examination: that is the purview of the American Bar Association.

The debate raged for several years until it was made moot by the Soloman Act, an act of Congress that stated that law schools or universities must allow the military the same right to recruit on campus as any other recruiters. Failure to meet the law would mean the loss of all federal aid to the institution. The amendment forced many institutions to conclude that the loss of financial aid and/or research funds was more significant than concerns of any single discipline. Widener took the position, well before the Soloman Act was adopted, that since the military was an agent of the U. S. government performing a legal duty under the law of the land, it would be unlawful to deny it the right to visit the Law School.

In reality, the passage of the Soloman Act did not end the debate. Numerous law professors from leading schools filed briefs asserting that a university should be allowed to accept federal funds while opposing the policy of the military regarding homosexuality in the armed forces. They posited that restriction of access to law campuses was a matter of civil rights protection for gays and free speech. They were stunned on March 11, 2006 when the Supreme Court rejected their position in an eight to zero decision.

As human beings, albeit more learned than other segments of society, faculty should not be universally brushed with a patina of always being correct.

Professors obviously have the right to speak outside their areas of expertise but should be mindful when in public that others may accept their information as fact rather than opinion simply because they are faculty. Despite the fact that I have known several academically brilliant faculty who thrived in the protected environment of campus with absolutely no "street smarts," I've also worked with countless extraordinarily intelligent, caring, gifted and savvy professors. They've been flexible and supportive in the face of daring reform. Teaching is a noble calling and a unique profession; its practitioners stand the line between ignorance and knowledge. Those who are deaf to applause for their influence are treasures.

On Faculty Unions

Organizational communication is always a concern. Shortly after University Council began to function, I spoke at length with the academic deans about the importance of the communication flow from it to the collegiate units. Some schools had done a good job in creating an opportunity for the council representative to report to colleagues, others had not. The deans were instructed to provide regular and adequate time at each collegiate faculty meeting for a report on University Council deliberations. The shift from a single undergraduate faculty meeting to a representative form of governance gave rise to the potential for faculty to begin to concentrate more exclusively on department or school issues. But all faculty needed to be kept informed about the more global discussions and thinking in council so that misunderstandings would be avoided.

In extreme cases, administrative mismanagement of the shared governance process can lead to talk of unionization. Unions are more prevalent in the public sector of higher education where work rules are driven by state government regulations and political whim and agenda. In the private sector, if a union exists at all, it is most probably the AAUP which is managed by academics, not trade representatives.

My personal bias is against faculty unions. If one accepts the premise that a university is an institution in which all parties have a vested interest, then the mission should be to debate, enhance and implement progress in a collegial manner, not by a set of rules hammered out in collective bargaining. An institution does not need a union to define the well-understood roles of faculty and administrators. Certainly, no one denies that final decisions are the CEO's purview; it is how input is provided to the decisions that makes the university different from other organizations. When positions are dictated, trust lessens and creativity in problem solving can be lost. Personally, I believe that if the faculty in a private college is seriously considering a collective bargaining unit, the president and board of trustees have stumbled rather badly. [1]

Some of my presidential colleagues preferred dealing with a collective bargaining unit because it simplified the relationship with faculty and staff: whatever the issue, it is either in the contract or it isn't; if it isn't, don't ask until the next bargaining session! I found this approach counter productive and was on record as saying I would have been uncomfortable serving as CEO of a university with a faculty union.

From the start, my meetings with the AAUP campus chapter to discuss my view of the faculty's role at Widener were cordial. (While AAUP did not represent the Widener faculty, a long-established chapter existed on the Main Campus.) Usually called by senior English Professor Diana LeStourgeon, the meetings provided opportunity to exchange views as colleagues, not adversaries. Since my management style was to be candid, I shared my beliefs without reservation.

Questions at the first few meetings were broad ranging, including my position on tenure and sabbaticals – and the role of the Academic Committee of the board in these matters. Regarding the latter, I explained that the chairman of the board adhered to one rule for all board committees, "keep your noses in and hands off!" which always brought a laugh. We also discussed the external forces that would continue to impact the University, including: government intervention through

---

[1] A 1980 landmark labor decision by the U.S. Supreme Court in the case of the National Labor Relations Board (NLRB) v. Yeshiva University effectively denied faculty in private universities the right to engage in collective bargaining. In its five to four ruling, the Court held that faculty, because of the nature of shared governance and participatory decision-making in private schools, were managerial employees excluded from certain protections. While a footnote to the decision stated it was not intended as a blanket prohibition against private college faculties organizing, it was perceived as just that. The AAUP failed in its legislative efforts to have the decision overturned, and, though often challenged by faculties, the Yeshiva ruling prevailed except in very few cases. One of the most interesting of the successful challenges turned on a misstep by the management of Manhattan College. The NLRB ruled that the Manhattan faculty was not management with decision-making input when it was shown a 1994 memo from the administration in response to faculty concerns over a proposed reorganization of the college that said, in effect, that the college did not have to speak to or consult with faculty before making the reorganization decision. The faculty successfully argued that the directive negated the claim they were a part of management.

controls on budgets or on academic programming via regional duplication and research regulations, law suits for value not given, the right
to privacy, fraternities, civil rights, civic activism, and others.

I also called their attention to certain statements in the AAUP *Statement on Government of Colleges and Universities:* "... the distinction
should be observed between the institutional system of communication and the system of responsibility for the making of decisions." Also,
"the sign of a healthy, vibrant governance structure is simple to see, a respect for the various constituencies and the role each plays in the
process." (AAUP 2006)

Our meetings alleviated some of the concerns of faculty regarding
academic policy but reinforced the understanding that while certain
AAUP policies pertaining to tenure, faculty rights and dismissal would
be followed, a carte blanche adherence to the so-called "AAUP Red-
book" would not happen.

The significance of not fully adhering to AAUP policies was clearly
demonstrated in academic year 1994-95 when demographic shifts in
the undergraduate population resulted in steep enrollment declines in
several academic programs. In addition to an administrative reorganization, 14 faculty positions were eliminated. Under AAUP guidelines,
the University would have had to declare financial exigency, producing
low morale and an unwanted public perception. Instead, we had the
option clearly stated in the faculty handbook that allowed for the termination of faculty as a result of bona fide contraction of enrollments
in a program or department.

From Experience: Personal Recommendations

Shared governance is exactly what the words imply, an agreed upon
organizational structure that provides an environment and forum for
the exchange of ideas relating to academic and structural policies. The
decision-making process is well defined so that all parties are aware of
the respective roles of the various constituent groups and the parameters of each group's authority.

The structure of the faculty input varies, largely by the size and traditions of the institution. At liberal arts colleges, faculty traditionally
meets as a whole; all individuals holding academic rank are entitled to
attend and to vote. Additionally, some institutions assign faculty rank
without tenure to senior administrative staff, providing them the opportunity to be full participants and voting members. At other colleges,

all members of the campus community, whether administrative or academic, are invited to attend and participate. The results are faculty meetings in the form of the New England town meeting.

At many smaller institutions where faculties meet in plenary session, the president often chairs the meeting. I believe this format to be fraught with potential problems since the chair is traditionally expected to moderate but not to participate in the discussion. Such a role limits the ability of the president to respond to issues or, if need be, to mount the bully pulpit.

Presidents who find themselves in the position of having to chair faculty meetings should appoint a faculty parliamentarian to whom procedural questions can be deferred. Absent that, they should become experts on *Robert's Rules of Order*, still the authority on parliamentary procedure. One of General Robert's comments is a lesson not only for faculty meetings but for life: "The object of the Rules of Order is to assist an assembly to accomplish in the best possible manner the work for which it is designed. To do this, it is necessary to restrain the individual somewhat, as the right of an individual in any community to do what he please, is incompatible with the interests of the whole." (Robert 1990, 14)

Larger university faculties often meet as a senate to which representatives are elected by faculty, usually in a proportional representation based upon the size of the various colleges and schools within the university. This format has as its antecedent the original concept of the House of Representatives with elected members for a definite number of constituents. It is an efficient way to gather faculty input but changes the dynamic from a fully engaged faculty to a general opinion from an academic department, college or school to which the representative belongs. Beyond providing input, the representative shoulders the responsibility to disseminate information and frame discussions of policy among his or her colleagues. In short, it removes most faculty from the primary discussion of issues.

My preference, as president, was to attend faculty meetings that were chaired by the provost or faculty chair, listen, and be available to respond to questions when directly requested. On occasion, I requested the opportunity to speak on a specific issue. This provided a forum to address issues that were being discussed on campus, especially those that had the potential to become controversial. At times, being able to clarify a policy decision or changes being contemplated was hugely helpful.

Faculty meetings are often intense and erudite. On occasion, they are frivolous and comedic. I recall listening to a passionate debate in one meeting over an arcane rule that required all baccalaureate candidates to be able to swim the length of a pool. The debaters waxed eloquent and at length on what values constitute a liberally educated individual, one even using the swimming pool as a metaphor for the whole man. A pragmatist finally ended the debate by observing that the business of a university is not to teach swimming.

At Widener University, a governance structure founded on mutual respect between faculty and administration became the framework and catalyst for positive change. It reflected the realities of the institution and the idiosyncratic traits of the University.

Chapter 11

Heart of the Enterprise: Students

The choice of a college or university to attend is both critical and formidable for a high school student and his or her family. For the student, the selection is a first step into the future. It means focusing on the preparation for a career path or exposure to new concepts through the study of the liberal arts. For the family it means making, often at great sacrifice, a major financial commitment. For both student and parent it signifies the beginning of the transformation of a teenager into an independent and self-reliant adult. In the continuum of life's choices, it is often the first major one to be faced.

Of the many factors that contribute to the selection of a college or university, several are objective, among them: location, size, residential or commuter, and academic specialization. The more abstract factors include comfort level in the environment and social suitability. If possible, prospective freshmen and their parents should visit campuses while classes are in session to observe faculty in their classrooms, to meet other students, and to develop a sense of the institution's style. At the fall open house we called Widener Day, I always reminded prospective students that while parents, friends, and literature may be helpful resources, the choice of school had to be theirs. If the chemistry of the campus did not feel right after a visit, they should move on regardless of what anyone else said.

Freshmen, particularly residential freshmen, often find the transformation from high school to college difficult. In most cases, they leave a nurturing and structured environment populated by family and friends to enter the domain of strangers and the seduction of freedom with self-responsibility for one's actions and time management. The culture shock can be compounded by the move into a room with someone met largely through emails and phone calls.

The institution's role is to make the transition as seamless as possible. Each year, Widener introduced increasingly sophisticated opportunities for peer bonding. What worked, stayed, what didn't was discarded. Overnight visits in the summer for accepted students, early assignment of academic advisors, pairing with an upperclassman, and an intensified orientation period for networking and sharing activities were all mainstays in creating a platform for a successful first semester.

Of course, all new students experience the same transition (and insecurities) together. I remember our son Scott, who in high school had been student government president, an athlete, and a member of the National Honor Society, calling home after several days at Colgate University: "I think" he said, "They are all valedictorians and have higher SATs than mine." This exaggeration was a remarkably accurate expression of the impressions of most first-week college students.

There is, however, a college out there to suit any student's needs and preferences. The number and diversity of colleges and universities from which to choose is among the great strengths of American higher education. From multi-campus systems to small sectarian or single-sex institutions, the options are wide ranging. Thankfully, too, the days are long gone when college was the sanctum sanctorum of an elite class, when social standing and pedigree were on a par with intellectual ability as an admission criterion. Today, over 60 percent of those graduating from secondary school go on to some type of higher education. This is an extraordinary change from the early 1950s when only approximately 35 percent continued on. Attending college then was a process of pre-selection, since many students were placed in the non-collegiate tracks in secondary school.

The Disease of Prejudicial Opinion

If one of the greatest achievements of the post-WWII era is a tremendous gain in educational equality, a discouraging counterpoint is the increasingly prevalent tendency both on and off campus toward egocentric agendas. The historic tenet "the greatest good for the greatest number" no longer informs the majority of today's opinions. Too much is weighed in terms of individual needs, inspiring the dramatic growth of single-issue advocacy for ethnicity, politics, religion, or, simply, personal opinion. It is not surprising that this emphasis has precipitated a decline in civil discourse on campuses and across society. The inability of individuals to listen, *really listen*, to someone else without pre-conceived prejudice is becoming a lost art; comprise and mutual beneficence are more and more difficult to achieve. Given this, it is imperative that a critical goal of today's university is to make dialogue frequent and inclusive. The commitment of a university to maintain an environment that respects the idiosyncratic characteristics of its students and faculty is not an easy task, but is fundamental to its existence. Classes and numerous extra-curricular and co-curricular activities offer opportunities to promote cross fertilization of ideas, and thus to nurture civility as well as personal development.

Each year at the New Student Convocation, I addressed the need for individual responsibility. My position was that each listener had choices that would affect his or her success and happiness at Widener. Theirs was the choice of how to exercise the freedom and independence afforded each student on a campus, of academic success or failure, of how to spend their time, of what activities to pursue, of which relationships to embrace. But I also emphasized that student choices are significant to the life of the institution. Because a university is a place where all sides of an issue should be heard in a reasonable and non-threatening environment, where each individual's contributions enforce or undermine civility and others' ability to learn and mature, it is important that every student accept responsibility for his or her actions.

Parents Beware: Opportunity Comes With Responsibility for the Self

Responsibility for the self can be a heady, sometimes intoxicating, concept for a freshman. It can also be difficult to embrace for several reasons, one being the involvement of parents in the lives of their sons and daughters at college. I have been amazed at the increased unwillingness of parents to accept any failure as the fault of their child: A poor grade is interpreted as the ineptitude of faculty; lack of playing time for an athlete reflects the failure of the coaching staff to appreciate talent; disciplinary issues are a result of someone else leading the student astray, and often, poor institutional supervision. Too many parents believe that college tuition guarantees success and happiness for the student. It doesn't.

On more than one occasion I shared this fact with a parent who raised the issue of Widener's cost of close to nearly $40,000 per year. I explained that the University did not owe an education to any student who elected not to be an active participant in the process, nor was it a baby-sitting service. On several occasions, I and other members of the senior staff suggested that perhaps the student would be better served at another college. Curiously, that option was rarely chosen.

The involvement of this generation of parent in the lives of their students is breathtaking. This intense indulgence began in the 1970s; today, because they are always hovering, these parents are commonly known as "helicopter parents." The overarching prevalence of the cell phone and text messaging can create a seamless stream of contact between parent and student. I have known students who contacted home several times a day, supposedly just to kill time. This nearly continuous communication makes it too easy for the student to pass on to the parent – and for the parent to accept – the burden of problems that would be far better resolved by the student.

Learning to cope is supposed to be an integral part of the collegiate experience.

Selecting Students

While every college and university seeks to enroll the most capable students possible, that number is finite and statistically small. Fewer than ten percent of all high school graduates rank at the top of their class and fare equally well on standard achievement tests. It is disingenuous for over 3,000 colleges and universities in the United States to claim that these are their target students.

Each institution must realistically define its target population, and should do so with consideration of the student mix. In short, the selection of students should be based on institutional philosophy. I was struck quite often by how many colleagues offered mean SATs, aggregate GPAs and class rank as the benchmarks in discussing prospective or current students. I believe that a more important benchmark is the composition of the class. Even the most competitive colleges do not strive for each and every student to be the brightest from their high school. It is not a question of the best and the brightest, but of enrolling students who are capable of achieving academic success at a particular school. This is admittedly a more subjective basis for student selection, but it encourages a class of diverse talents and gifts in many areas: academic, athletic, cultural, special interest, etc.

As a comprehensive university, Widener had considerable leeway in recruiting students across a broad spectrum of academic and interest levels, students with vastly different skills and preparation. We were philosophically committed to providing students with an opportunity to succeed and aided them with a network of support programs. It was gratifying to see weaker students reach new heights of understanding, but just as delightful when a standout was academically fulfilled. There were very fine students in all of the University's schools but the Honors Program and a widespread construct of student/faculty research increased the number of exceptional students in the College of Arts and Sciences. Because of the nature of the disciplines and the emphasis on math and science, the School of Engineering also consistently attracted excellent students.

Diversifying the Experience

Bob Strider, president emeritus of Colby College and a mentor of mine, used to liken the four-year cycle of undergraduates to the seasons. Each year a crop would be harvested and be replaced by a new, young, untested group that would grow to maturity, be harvested, and the cycle would begin again. It was true and, unfailingly, watching students enter the University each year instilled a renewed sense of excitement. Each class brought its own distinct set of talents and personalities, and in subtle ways (and sometimes not so subtle) each impacted the life of the campus.

One of the goals Widener established early 1980s was to raise the percentage of international students to five percent of the undergraduate population. We recognized the increasingly global environment in which our graduates would compete and believed that mixing the domestic student with those from various parts of the world would benefit both and enrich the campus. Of course, the international market was a means to expanding recruitment opportunities.

The five percent goal was phased in over a period of time, making assimilation and the development of a critical mass of foreign students gradual rather than sudden. The strategy worked well. We never experienced any cultural hostility within the student body, nor the unwanted creation of a foreign enclave on the campus. Other institutions were not so well prepared. When the downturn in domestic students became a reality, many colleges reached out to the international market, all at once bringing in large numbers from abroad. Oft times this proved to be disruptive because the campuses were not prepared to assimilate so many undergraduates from different cultural backgrounds.

To facilitate the integration of international students into the life of our Main Campus, Widener created an Office of International Student Services. The office served as liaison with the immigration agencies to assist in smoothing entry into the U.S. for international students. The office also became the focal point for the counseling and academic support for those students. Recognizing their difficulty in adjusting culturally and socially, including adaptation to the colloquial language of the campus as well as the formal English used in the classroom, Widener contracted with an independent language institute that became resident on campus, offering intensive study of English as a second language.

While it was largely the support network that helped create an attractive environment for international students, it was the geographic location that made Widener unique among independent private universities in its ability to attract minority students, especially African-Americans. Because we were located on the edge of a predominantly black city, Chester, and within fifteen miles of Philadelphia, the environment for recruiting and integrating urban minority students into the campus was as close to ideal as it could be.

It was an excellent environment for all students. The minority numbers were sufficient to avoid the trap of promoting diversity on a campus that has too few students of color to fully integrate them into campus life. The stigma for a student of being part of a "special group" is a difficult one to work around. As a result of the numbers of minority students it enrolled, Widener was more successful than most institutions in graduating minorities.

Yet, the societal problem of attracting and graduating minority males was then and remains a challenge. Despite the massive efforts with financial aid and incentive programs by the federal and state governments, the number of black males enrolled in college remains relatively static. On the other hand, African-American women continue to increase as a percentage of undergraduates and to achieve academic success. Unfortunately, this disparity has generated additional challenges for talented black women. I well recall a conversation Judy and I had with a group of black women students who expressed recognition of the fact that as their numbers grew, the options for social relationships and marriage within their race diminished because the scarcity of college educated African-American males.

A typical diversity of the Widener undergraduate student body is evidenced by the student profile of academic year 1995-96: 115 in the Honors Program, 240 international students (5 percent of the population), 14 percent minorities (10 percent African-American, 2 percent each Hispanic and Asian). There were very few institutions, public or private that could boast of that type of profile. Indeed, at that time Penn State University, the flagship public university in Pennsylvania, was under a mandate to raise its total minority enrollment above 5 percent.

Evolution of the Widener Student

When I first visited the Widener campus in the 1970s I recall being struck by the number of students who were the first in their family to attend college. They were representative of the widely expanded range of students taking advantage of the "opening of higher education." Having been a first-generation college student from a lower-middle income family, I easily related to those early Widener students.

As the University itself transitioned, the student body evolved so that, if asked now to apply an adjective to the Widener students throughout my years there, I would say "eclectic." Some were wealthy, some not. Some were sophisticated, many were not. There were brilliant students and those who entered with academic deficit. A unique aspect of Widener was that if those who had been admitted applied themselves and took advantage of what Widener offered, they could excel.

In the early years of my administration, the undergraduate enrollments included a preponderance of students from Pennsylvania and New Jersey, many from parochial schools. We used to joke that the football team in the 1980s could have been named "St. Widener's," given the number of student athletes from Catholic schools. In many ways, the students mirrored those who had attended the institution throughout its history: unwilling or unable to travel far from family and neighborhood, and seeking a relatively conservative college. For student athletes, the ability to play at a demanding level of competition without leaving their community was especially appealing. Additionally, the curricula of applied disciplines attracted students who wanted to leave college with the knowledge and skills to immediately begin a career.

The Personal Approach to Student Progress

The home environment significantly impacts the preparation of a student for college. Families in which reading and an interest in the arts are common better equip their children for college work. The differences between graduates from highly ranked high schools and those from poorly rated school systems are initially quite striking.

However, one of Widener's strengths was the ability to look beyond the raw data and intuit the ability of the students who applied for admission. I was often quoted as saying, "I am more concerned with the output than the input." If after four or five years, an individual had expanded his intellectual horizons and become academically directed, the University had been successful.

A *sine qua non* for a faculty member to be successful at Widener was to embrace the mission of stretching and cultivating the talents of each and every student. Obviously not all students succeeded; some with talent never made the transition or commitment to college work. The counterbalance to those who left, however, was the number who exceeded expectations and became stars.

Widener's approach to students was very simple: students come first. As much as humanly possible, a personalized concern for and handling of each student was the operative style on all of Widener's campuses. The slogan "We take your education personally," coined by Pat Brant, became not only the guiding principle in dealing with students, but was referred to on campus as the "Widener mantra." Its pervasive influence guided most of what happened on a day-to-day basis from the Maintenance Department to the clerical staff to the faculty and administration. Vice President Michael Mahoney was fond of publicly saying: "I have heard the president say hundreds of times over the years to faculty and staff, 'You cannot shortchange the students.' No matter what we were talking about, or what plans were being developed, that was the underlying theme of his philosophy."

At times, attempting to resolve student issues on a personal basis put the staff under real stress, but the student-based approach paid maximum dividends over the years by creating a campus environment in which student/faculty or student/administration issues could be dealt with in a civil and reasonable way. The designation of an assistant provost as ombudsman for undergraduate students on academic matters allowed a student to feel comfortable in discussing a policy issue or faculty member with a neutral academic observer. The assistant provost, as a faculty colleague, could then intervene and seek resolution from a non-threatening position.

Good PR

There will always be occasional negative headlines but by publicizing the positive aspects of campus life, faculty, and its student body, a university can usually escape an unwanted reputation. For example, it is unfortunate that intercollegiate athletics in general attract a disproportionate share of bad publicity. At many schools, including Widener, there are excellent athletes who are also outstanding students. For example, Widener's 2001 valedictorian and salutatorian were both members of the track and field team.[1]

Academically successful student athletes deserve better press coverage than they usually receive; it takes a good sports information director (SID) to generate interest. During the decade that Susan Fumagalli served as Widener's SID (1994-2004), she introduced an almost missionary zeal to promoting athletic achievement. Her efforts resulted in 31 student athletes being named Academic All Americans, an extraordinary number for a small, regional university considering that Widener's candidates for the distinction were competing on a national basis.

Fraternal Societies: To Be, or ...

For several decades, the hottest issue in academe was the purpose and role of Greek societies on college campuses. The fate of many local and national fraternities and sororities was sealed in the 1980s when prestigious liberal arts colleges, among others, disbanded their Greek organizations in an effort to change the campus social patterns. To some, it was an emotional issue that reflected societal engineering and political correctness – a plot to make college campuses as homogeneous as possible. To others, it represented an effort to eliminate organizations with restrictive membership.

In reality, much of the national debate grew from the increased awareness of underage drinking and alcohol abuse, not only on campuses but in society. The Greek organizations were in a catch-22 situation. As one of the primary social forces on campus, they were vulnerable to criticism and became the focus for negative publicity vis-à-vis the "ideals of campus life." For years, and largely by default, fraternities had been the hub of collegiate weekend social life. Indeed, prior to the change in attitude regarding alcohol on campus, fraternities were semi-autonomous and were able to avoid the issue of underage drinking and alcohol restrictions – often with the tacit assent of the college administration. The prevailing attitude was that students were going to drink, so wasn't it preferable to have them do so on campus

---

[1] Indeed, the salutatorian Kate L'Armand was both an academic and an athletic all American. She had also been selected in 2000 as the NCAA's Academic All-American of the Year in the Women's At Large Program.

rather than driving to off-campus watering holes? The evolving societal approach and intolerance to alcohol during the 1980s changed campus policies.

I personally believed that, if properly channeled, the good that could come from the Greek organizations far outweighed the negatives, a belief that was echoed by Widener's senior administrators, most of whom had participated as undergraduates in fraternities and sororities. A dispassionate look at all student activities made it relatively easy to judge the worth of each organization and, more important, easy to see if the potential for improvement existed. The Greeks were no different from any other group, just more visible. Thus, the issue at Widener was not whether to join the anti-Greek movement, but rather how to encourage fraternities and sororities to recognize their potential for positive leadership on campus.

In 1987, at the request of the University, Tau Kappa Epsilon (TKE) was suspended by its national organization for two years. In 1988, Zeta Beta Tau (ZBT) was closed by the University due to inappropriate behavior. Having gotten the attention of the Greek organizations, the administration presented its demands for the role the Greeks would play on campus. It was then that the IFC and Pan-Hel began to work with the Office of the Dean of Students to restructure Greek life.

The transformation took several years but was done cooperatively. Academic standards went up, rules and regulations for parties were enforced, and involvement of the Greeks in University-sanctioned activities became accepted behavior rather than the exception. As a result, the Greeks assumed ever greater leadership in campus organizations.

In 1993, I shared with the Board of Trustees my concerns about the condition of several of the privately owned men's fraternity houses. The properties, individually owned by the Greek national or alumni organizations, were technically outside of University control. Our method of influencing the upkeep of the properties was to threaten the loss of University approval as designated housing for enrolled students. However, this potentially adversarial stand strained the budding partnership between the two entities.[2]

The board approved the administration's proposal to purchase all fraternity houses. It was made clear to the chapter house owners that a

---

[2] At this time sororities were housed in the residence halls.

failure to sell at a mutually agreed-upon price would result in Widener exercising its right to not recognize the organization, which would effectively end the fraternity as a part of the University.

At the same time the board approved the purchase of these properties, it also approved the construction of new fraternity and sorority housing, to be owned by the University and assigned to Greek organizations in good standing. A classic carrot-and-stick approach to resolving a problem, the strategy worked well with the exception of one angry group. While unanimously accused of playing hardball, the transfer of property to the University was accomplished with relatively little ill will.

The fraternity and sorority leadership were treated as important contributors. At a cost of over $6 million the brick houses were designed to replicate a Victorian street and, as such, both established a distinctive identity and blended with other campus architecture. Completed in time for occupancy in 1994, Greek Row also housed all but two sororities that were relocated into nearby, renovated mansions owned by the University (Manor House and The Castle). It was a win-win for all concerned.

The integration of the Greeks into the campus leadership was successful because the senior administration and student-life staff avoided the adversarial approach. Rather, they undertook the difficult task of working to overcome the traditional but often undeserved image of Greek life. Although a small percentage of the undergraduate population, the fraternities and sororities eventually provided a disproportionately high percentage of student leadership.

From the Students' Mouths

I found all students engrossing. I loved their enthusiasm, their "can do" attitudes, their passion, and their curiosity. Even on those occasions when the issues were serious and negative in nature I found the interaction with students instructive.

I made a point of attending as many undergraduate student activities as possible and visited the dining hall several times a week, occasionally sitting down at a table with students. At first, this intrusion caused consternation but invariably led to good conversation about their status, activities, and the campus issues that concerned them. I visited the Harrisburg and Delaware Campuses, too, meeting with the student bar leadership each year, but mostly just strolling the campus.

My philosophy was "management by walking around," speaking casually with students, faculty and staff. I was amazed and pleased how many times parents would tell me that their son or daughter said that they "knew the president" or "had spoken to the president last week." Even more amazing is what one can learn by walking through a campus and really listening!

I must confess that as a former student athlete I had an affinity for the men and women who played sports and became well acquainted with many of them. Quite a few were also among the campus academic and political leaders so they were a source of pride to the University for the diversity of their achievements.

Judy and I entertained the Honors Program students on a regular basis and enjoyed meeting all the others who, as a result of their academic accomplishments in specific disciplines, were inducted into their national honor societies. These evenings at our home were wonderful. It was a real joy to see students who had been shy and socially awkward as freshmen gracefully engage others in a social setting four years later as seniors.

I invited AnnElise Collier, the valedictorian of the class of 2000, a superb student and member of several athletic teams, to speak at a trustee luncheon before the annual meeting of the board. When I introduced AnnElise, I concluded by remarking that she would be attending medical school in the fall and perhaps I might someday become her patient. Her rejoinder when she stood up was, "President Bruce, I don't plan to practice geriatric medicine." The comment brought unanimous laughter.

The relationship any president hopes to have with students was exemplified by AnnElise in a quote she gave to University Relations on my announcement that I planned to retire. "The characteristic I admire most about President Bruce is his ability to interact with people on a personal level while maintaining an excellent level of professionalism. In my future practice of medicine, I hope to emulate that quality..."

Who Could Ask for More?

A final word: One of the objectives of a university is to help young adults, a majority of whom are 18 to 22 years of age, respect the collective good. It is not an easy task! It depends on the role models provided by faculty, student staff, coaches, and upperclassmen. While the goal may be idealistic, and hovering parents a hindrance, one of the most valuable outcomes of the college experience is the change that occurs in so many students. The four- or five-year experience provides a platform to experiment, test oneself, stretch the mind, and learn through trial and error. The college experience is one of the most significant periods in the life of an individual. Much of what a student encounters and learns provides the basis for what will follow in life.

Chapter 12

Intercollegiate Athletics

One of the interesting aspects of collegiate life is the passion engendered by athletics. From the largest mega-university to the smallest college, the role of athletics often appears out of proportion to all reason and to the expenditure of time, energy and resources. Athletics, although peripheral to the *raison d'être* of a university, certainly generates more ardor than any academic discipline. No one regularly reports the results of the chemistry labs or the achievements of students in a German class, but sports has its own section in both the public media and collegiate news outlets. Perhaps athletics assumes its stature because it is part of the American tradition to compete, to win. It also teaches life lessons in team building and participation. It validates the inclusion of all of the extended supporters of an institution including parents, alumni, and local residents. Successful athletic programs may also assist an institution in attracting financial support. Conversely, many universities find themselves struggling with the dilemma of what to do with a program that year after year produces losing records.

Athletics can also generate institutional pride, provide name recognition and underpin marketing efforts. Villanova stepped up from a regional to a national admissions recruiter following its 1985 NCAA basketball championship. At Widener in the 1970s, with its structural and cultural transformation from military college to civilian university, athletics played an important role in promoting the new profile. The success of two of its graduates, Billy "White Shoes" Johnson'75BA and Joe Fields'75BS, both all-pro in the National Football League (NFL), reinforced the name of Widener in the public mind.[1] To hear on national television that "Billy 'White Shoes' of Widener" had returned another punt for a Houston Oilers's touchdown was pure platinum for the college. The

---

[1] Johnson played for the Houston Oilers and Atlanta Falcons. Fields played for the New York Jets and New York Giants.

decision to contract with the Philadelphia Eagles to hold training camp at Widener also resulted in wonderful regional PR. Each summer evening on the news, the sports lead, "today at the Eagles training camp at Widener …" brought more recognition than could have been purchased to promote the transformation from PMC Colleges to Widener.

Whatever the reason for the often rabid interest in collegiate sports, the administrative objective for intercollegiate athletics should be twofold: first, to keep them in appropriate balance to the academic mission of the college and, second, to be sure that the young men and women who represent the university are talented, competently trained, and equipped to be competitive. All else is peripheral.

There is nothing more discouraging for an athlete than to know he or she does not have the athletic skills or team depth to compete successfully. That does not mean that the team should win every time, although that is every athlete's hope, but rather that it should be competitive. I always found it peculiar that some institutions with exceptional pride in their academic programs were willing to tolerate mediocrity or worse in their athletic programs. I believe that espousing and supporting a philosophy of excellence should include all of the campus endeavors.

Football, the Benchmark of a Program's Success

To understand the place of athletics on a campus one has to understand the culture and history of the institution and the role that athletics plays at that school. At most universities where football is played the sport becomes the driver of the institution's athletic reputation. We have to wonder if this arises merely from the fact that it is played in the autumn. At the beginning of a new academic year, the excitement of the weekly game becomes a focal point for student weekend activity. It is also the anchor for most of the alumni entertainment, always including Homecoming and Parents Weekend, thus perpetuating the memories of one-time students who remain associated with any post-secondary institution, particularly their alma mater. As the weeks of football success build, the excitement draws more and more fans.

In my first year as a new president, the Widener football program reached a pinnacle that would not be repeated in my administration: Widener won the NCAA (National Collegiate Athletic Association) Division III national championship by defeating the University of Dayton 17 to 10 in Phenix City, Alabama. The victory, Widener's second national championship in five years, concluded an undefeated season of 13-0 and established Widener Coach Bill Manlove as one of the premier head coaches in the nation. Later, I'd remark that "I thought everyone was supposed to win a national championship their first year in office." The closest we came after that was in the fall of 2000, my final year as president, when Head Coach Bill Zwann guided the team to the national semifinal round in which we lost to Mt. Union College of Ohio.

I was delighted by Widener's 1981 season. Judy and I, usually accompanied by Board Chairman Fitz Dixon and his wife, Edie, attended all of the games. In December, we flew to the championship game in Alabama aboard the Dixons' private jet. Once there, we were welcomed at the airport then led to the television booth by a member of the NCAA committee. In contrast, at the end of the game as Fitz and I arrived on the field for the presentation of the championship trophy an Alabama state trooper stopped us. Although I tried to explain that I was the president of Widener and Fitz was the chairman of the board, the trooper was singularly unimpressed. I still see in my mind the moment when Fitz opened his rolled-up program and pointed to a picture of me under the Widener write-up. "There he is," he said, "*this* is the president." We were allowed on the field only because Dixon had forgotten to leave his program behind at his seat!

The 1981 team was enormously talented with two players, Hal Johnson and Doug Schultz, signed as NFL free agents and Tom Deery, a junior on that squad, drafted by the Baltimore Colts. Deery later joined Billy Johnson in the National Football College Hall of Fame. Two of the 1981 co-captains, Tony Britton'82BSB and Jim Hirschmann'82BS, were young men with whom I became close and stayed in touch. I was proud that during my tenure as president Jim was appointed to the Board of Trustees in recognition of his highly successful career in the financial world. Over the years I knew, mentored and counseled many players, but the group from 1981 will always remain special to me. It was a year that provided lifelong memories for the players and for hundreds of dedicated fans.

The Most Winning Coach: Bill Manlove

The architect of the Widener football phenomenon was Bill Manlove, one of the most successful coaches in NCAA history at any level. Manlove joined Widener in 1969 from an assistant's position at Lafayette College. He inherited a struggling football program and closed his first year with a 2-7-0 (two wins, seven losses, no ties) season. From that slow beginning, he built an extraordinarily successful program. In fact from 1973 to 1982, Widener had the most wins of any NCAA team in any division, compiling a record of 96-10-0 for a percentage of .9057; Alabama and Oklahoma followed. During that decade Widener was in the NCAA Division III playoffs seven times, winning national championships in 1977 and 1981. This invaluable name recognition came during the institutional change from PMC to Widener.

Manlove was quoted in the *Chronicle of Higher Education* as saying: "When I first came here, with my emphasis on winning, people were suspicious of me." (Monaghan 1984, 24)

If at first he had to convince people that he was interested in playing good football, not in building a powerhouse, later when Widener had reached the top of Division III, Bill Manlove had more convincing to do. He believed the Division III national title was as far as it should go, was as good as it should get. There was never a discussion or suggestion about moving to Division I-A.

Manlove earned an exceptional record over his years at Widener, 182-53-1. More significantly he impacted the lives of countless young men who had the pleasure of playing for him. His wife Edna and their three daughters were integral members of the University community and all three girls graduated from Widener.

Manlove's success continued unabated through the 1980s although not at the remarkable level of the previous decade. Still, everyone expected that every week Manlove's team would win. This was doubly remarkable because sustaining a winning tradition with the academic and financial restraints inherent in Division III is not easy.

In the eighties, recruitment for football was seriously affected by several factors: increased competition for student-athletes, the loss of players who once would have been admitted but no longer qualified, and the increasing cost of attending Widener combined with the fact that our comparatively lower endowment meant more financial aid packages in the form of loans than grants. There were external agents of change as well. With a decline in the number of traditional age students attending college, many members of the Middle Atlantic Conference placed greater emphasis on recruiting student-athletes as an enrollment management tool, a change that dramatically increased the level of competition in the conference. Greater parity among institutions meant that all games were difficult and of equal importance. It was no longer possible for one institution to be easily dominant.

All of the above affected football recruitment in general and

Manlove in particular. He began to question how much longer he could maintain the level of success everyone, him included, expected every year.

Manlove's Decision to Leave

The pressure to achieve, to excel, is found in every endeavor but perhaps nowhere more so than in coaching. The coaches' egos are involved and winning is the benchmark of their success. They take their jobs very seriously despite knowing that in Division III no one is going to call for their heads. I firmly believe that the pressure III coaches have, they put on themselves. If the student-athletes were being treated appropriately and enjoying the athletic experience in a competitive environment, the win-loss statistic was secondary to me. How a coach comported himself, how he represented the University and how he dealt with the students were the critical factors in whether he or she continued at Widener. On several occasions during my tenure individual coaches were dismissed, not for the win/loss record, but as a result of actions that reflected badly on the institution.

In the late fall of 1991, following the first losing Manlove football season since 1969, Bill and I had several discussions about the program and his role. He informed me that he might move on. I urged him to think about it carefully and to consider staying in his position of director of athletics if he truly did not wish to coach any longer. He told me, "I want to coach, that's what I do. I really don't want to be an athletic director!" Having won two national championships and countless conference championships he felt that he was unable to rebuild his program, and resigned.

I believe that Bill Manlove became a victim of his own success. His decision to leave came after several seasons in which success was achieved but not at the level that Manlove had set for himself or the program. Unfortunately, his decision was not accepted at face value. Many speculated that the University's lack of support had led to the decline of the football program and resulted in his departure. Unfortunately, the speculation was reinforced by comments made by Bill and some attributed to me that were taken out of context. However, much of the acrimony was generated by outsiders who felt that they had to weigh-in because they were sure they, and only they, knew the facts. These included former players, sportswriters, and former coaches with an ax to grind. The University's position was always one of praise for Manlove and for his accomplishments as a coach and as a human being. It was a position that never wavered. He had earned his excellent reputation and Widener's appreciation.

The New Head Coach

Bill Manlove's decision to leave was made in the spring before recruiting had been finalized; it left the University with the need to move quickly to fill the position. There wasn't time for a drawn-out search so I turned to Ken O'Brien, a Widener graduate of the class of 1975 who had been an outstanding quarterback and baseball player. An assistant to Manlove for many years, Ken was intelligent, loved the University, knew the local scene and had an excellent football mind. We met for lunch to discuss the football situation and the possibility of his leaving the business world to return as head coach at Widener. He subsequently refused the career change, feeling the travel and time-consuming nature of the commitment was not in his family's best interests.

Instead, Ken recommended a friend of his, Bill Cubit, then an assistant coach at the University of Akron in Ohio who had also coached at the University of Florida. Ken shared with me that he had spoken with Cubit who was interested in submitting his résumé. After reading it and speaking with him on the telephone, I invited Cubit to campus for an interview. On paper, he seemed superior to other candidates interested in the position and, in person, I was impressed with his knowledge, enthusiasm and personality. He made an excellent impression on the Athletic staff and the campus administrators he met.

The deal was done when I tracked him down on an Akron recruiting trip to Florida and offered the position. In his first visit to campus after accepting the job, he met with the players and told them Widener football was one of the best programs in the country and they were going to win. End of story. Bill Cubit was the right person at the right time for Widener.

Besides possessing an alert and creative football mind, Cubit was a charming and unabashed con artist! This is not a pejorative statement, it's written with amusement and delight. He worked the faculty, instituting a "coach of the week" designee by which a faculty member was invited to daily practice and into the locker room at game half-time. If they wished, they could call one play on Saturday afternoon.

It went over well and faculty, particularly some of the women, began to view football in a different light. (Although one blushing professor shared with me that she wasn't sure "a football locker room was a good place to be when the coach was angry.")

Cubit also made friends with the administrators who controlled the budgets and admissions, the maintenance people responsible for the fields, and everyone else who could help the program. His style was a fresh breeze but he was deadly serious about restoring Widener football to a position of preeminence.

Cubit had a mischievous sense of humor, which occasionally led to laughs at his expense. On his 40th birthday, as the Friday afternoon practice concluded, a group of administrators who were also among his many golfing partners presented him with 40 black balloons while singing "Happy Birthday" in front of the squad.

One of Cubit's first moves was to hire another Delaware County product as an assistant, Bill Zwann. The two Bills had played together at the University of Delaware and coached together in Florida. It was a fortuitous hire for several years later when Cubit moved on, Zwann took over the program.

Bill Cubit organized an extensive recruiting network, reaching out to areas beyond the greater Philadelphia region. His good contacts in Florida, a major student exporter state, helped attract players where little interest had ever before been expressed in Widener. With the creative input of assistant Dave Wood '91BSB, '93MS, Cubit also introduced a computer program to more efficiently track recruits. This software was sufficiently successful that in subsequent years it became the recruitment tool for all Widener athletics.

It is not an overstatement to credit Cubit with saving the Widener football program from years of rebuilding. After a first-season record of 3-6-1, a good showing considering he had little time to recruit, his teams garnered a 34-18-1 record over five years, including two conference championships and two appearances in the NCAA playoffs – an exceptional showing for a transition period.

In his second year, Cubit was given the position of athletic director. It is a common practice in Division III to combine the position of head football coach and athletic director. Often, the football coach is one of the more senior and externally visible Athletic Department staff members and one of the most difficult to hire if you are seeking a seasoned professional. The practice of combining the two positions allows for the development of an appropriate financial package without upsetting the university's compensation policies.

Cubit Moves On

Cubit was first and foremost an ambitious football coach. I was under no illusion he would make a career at Widener. Having had a taste of Division I at Florida, he was bound to use Widener as a stepping stone after returning the program to a high level of success.

My philosophy for all staff is to be supportive of their efforts to move up in their careers. Once an individual has decided to leave, it does little good to attempt to talk him or her out of it. If you succeed you too often have an employee who keeps wondering if he made the right decision.

Thus, I always made it clear to my staff that if they walked into my office and declared their imminent departure in the hope I would convince them not to go, they would be sorely disappointed with my best wishes. However, they also knew that they could be comfortable discussing a job possibility with me and that I would give them my best counsel on the pros and cons of the opportunity. To me, commitment is a two-way partnership.

After five successful years at Widener, Cubit took a position as the offensive coordinator at the University of Missouri. This was the big time, the level he wanted to coach. Unfortunately, Missouri hired a new head coach after Cubit's first year, and when head coaches leave, so do their staffs. He moved to Rutgers for several years then to Stanford as offensive coordinator and finally in 2004 became head coach at Western Michigan.

When Bill Cubit departed from Widener in 1996, he left the Athletic Department as well as the football program in a healthy state. The majority of Widener's teams had improved as the result of both better recruiting techniques and the stability and accountability resulting from the decision to hire only full-time head coaches.

New and Improved Athletic Facilities

The University's commitment to expand and improve all athletic facilities began with the planning for a new stadium in 1989. The project was complex with ramifications beyond athletics for it necessitated the removal of the venerable Memorial Stadium. Built in 1923 in the center of the campus as the focus of cadet activities, Memorial Stadium remained the site of commencement and, under the tiers of seats, the home of the student radio station. Both of these uses, and technical issues, presented problems that took several years to resolve, but the removal of Memorial Stadium was a critical component of the long-range campus plan articulated early in my tenure that called for a series of grassy quadrangles surrounded by dedicated academic and student functions. The elimination of the old stadium obviously required construction of a new one, on a new site.

In October 1994, the Leslie C. Quick, Jr. Stadium was dedicated prior to the homecoming game with Albright College. Built for $3.5 million, the stadium was named for Trustee Les Quick '50BS, who had made a generous challenge donation for its construction. Located in a natural bowl – a former quarry – near the Schwartz Athletic Center, Quick Stadium seated over 4,000 spectators and press. Its natural grass field was inside an eight-lane artificially surfaced track of the caliber needed to hold championship track and field meets. At Les's request, the track was named for former track-and-football coach and athletic director, George Hansell, Jr.[2] The Quick Stadium was the missing piece that provided Widener with one of the finest NCAA Division III athletic complexes in the country.

A feature that tied the school's history to the present was the embedding of the PMC motto, "*Mens Sana in Corpora Sano*" on a wall of Quick Stadium. Below that inscription, a wall of honor recognized project donors of $3,000 or more, among whom were many PMC graduates.

When the Quick Stadium was being designed, Cubit asked if he could have input on the colors in the stadium locker rooms. The response was "of course"; his input in the entire project was invaluable. As the facility was nearing completion, Dick Eusden, the director of maintenance, casually said to me one day, "have you seen the color of the visiting men's locker room?" I responded, "no, why?" Dick smilingly said, "its pink." Cubit's sense of humor at play, or a tactical decision? Probably both.

During the summer of 1996 the Schwartz Athletic Center was renovated at a cost of over $1.5 million. In recognition of the increased number of women athletes, the updated facility featured expanded women's locker and dressing room space, new exercise rooms, coaches' offices, weight rooms, and training rooms. In addition, a much needed practice field with lights was added near the athletic complex.

Zwann in Charge

With Cubit's departure, his successor was an easy choice. On January 14, 1997 Bill Zwann was appointed the twentieth head football coach in

---

[2] Mr. Quick had served as a student manager when Hansell was the PMC football coach

the history of the University. From his arrival in 1992 as the defensive co-ordinator, Zwann had played an integral part in the program's success. Moreover, he had impressed the campus with his concern for students and his commitment to their academic, as well as athletic, success.

Before he became head coach, Zwann heard me express my concern that there were too few juniors and seniors on the team. Either players were losing interest or we were not recruiting athletes willing to make the academic as well as the athletic commitment to be successful at Widener. Zwann's philosophy was to recruit academically sound students who, while not all exceptional athletes, would be with the program for four years. I was further impressed with his understanding that large numbers of transfer athletes were not the key to long-term success. While helpful in filling gaps, transfers could be disruptive as well as discouraging to players who had served their time as freshmen and sophomores and expected to move into starting roles.

During his tenure as head coach, Bill Zwann met all the expectations set out for him. His six-year record of three conference championships, two NCAA III playoffs (five wins, two losses) and a 33-12-0 record produced a winning percentage that was among the best of any coach in the more than 121 years of football at the institution.[3] More important, Bill Zwann was not just an excellent football coach, but superb campus citizen and dedicated athletic director. He represented Widener well to the University's many publics.

It was unfortunate for Widener that in the year following my retirement Bill elected to accept a position as the head football coach at West Chester University, a Division II institution able to provide athletic scholarships. It was a natural step for him as a coach. The good ones keep moving on!

Having been an athlete, my interest in the programs at the University was an extension of one of my own personal interests. Following my appointment as president, a local columnist quoted Bill Manlove as saying: "At least we'll have a president who knows a football is blown up, not stuffed." Not a bad line. (Finucane 1984) As a result of my years as a football player in both high school and college and a stint as a coach while in graduate school, I did understand the game and its nuances. But my only nod to my experience was each fall Monday morning when I phoned the coach to talk about Saturday's game. I always enjoyed hearing his post-game perspective.

---

[3] Football has been played at the school since 1879.

Impact of Athletics on Enrollment

Widener athletics have long been important to the admissions effort for both freshman and transfer students. Recent coaches have unanimously supported the notion that they were recruiting for Widener, not just for their particular sport, and many have begun JV programs to increase the opportunities for as many as possible to play.

As coaches and athletic directors, Bill Cubit and Bill Zwann worked hard at recruitment. I recall one entering class during their tenure in which combined freshmen and transfers numbered 700 students; of these, 140 had been recruited by the football staff! Coupled with the recruitment efforts for other sports, the impact on enrollment was significant. For example, track and field under Coach Vince Touey had an exceptional recruiting program. A strong coach with good student rapport, Touey's male and female athletes tended to compete for the full four years.

The commitment of Widener's coaches and athletic staff to the University's student-athletes was exceptional. Many were long-term employees who served with extraordinary commitment and dedication to the institution. Individuals like Fred Dohrmann in men's soccer and women's softball, Vince Touey in men's and women's track and Bob Piotti, men's and women's swimming, were not only superb coaches but individuals who provided a caring and ethical environment that embraced the athletes who played for them.

In an age when individualism is a dominant characteristic of young people (an attitude instilled by many parents), the role of the coach is increasingly important. Coaches are among the few authority figures in today's society to whom students listen. They serve as mentors, ombudsmen, consultants, disciplinarians, and sometimes friends, shaping and inspiring the individual as well as his or her physical talents. It is what makes the profession transcend being "just a job!"

Termination of a Coach

There was one unfortunate episode at Widener. Several years after Bill Manlove voluntarily left Widener, a second case involving the departure of a long-time coach produced ill feeling and ripples for a number of years. Widener's Basketball Head Coach C. Alan Rowe had coached the men's program for thirty-three years when he was terminated at the conclusion of the 1997-98 season.

Rowe, like Manlove, was one of the most successful coaches in

Division III winning over 500 games, many conference championships, and making two NCAA Division III national Final Four appearances. Unfortunately, his inability to accept the attitudinal changes between PMC players of the 1960s and student-athletes of the 1990s led to a widening gulf separating him from both the athletes and the administration.

Rowe's philosophy, "my way is the only way" is a common doctrine in the coaching fraternity, especially for a successful veteran. However, such a philosophy creates a reluctance to change leading to inflexibility. As a result friction develops and grows between the coach and his players.

A number of students and parents were expressing concerns and sharing their frustrations with various administrators about the experience the young men were having playing basketball at Widener University. The number of student-athletes who played in the program for all four years of their enrollment began to diminish, and player evaluations of the program began to slide toward negative.

When confronted with these concerns, Rowe dismissed them. He seemed not to understand that not only had Widener changed as an institution but the students attending the University had changed as well. Students were more questioning, less willing to simply accept what a coach decreed.

Coaching today's players is challenging because they are less disciplined, more independent minded and in many cases buttressed by parents who are heavily involved in their lives. Students' egocentricity leads them to a tendency to personalize everything, viewing coaching directions and decisions from the perspective of how it impacts them as individuals. One coach at another institution shared with me that he could only keep his team happy if "they were allowed to use five basketballs at the same time!" Compounding the difficulties, more fathers today seem to live their athletic ambitions or fantasies vicariously through their sons.

But Rowe summarily dismissed these concerns, saying the coach was in charge, and was right. A prime example of this coaching philosophy was Bobby Knight, the former coach at the University of Indiana (now at Texas Tech) whose temper tantrums were a cause célèbre of big time college basketball. I recall sitting in an airport one evening following an NCAA meeting with the then athletic director of Indiana and asking how Coach Knight got away with his behavior. The AD laughed and replied that one of the key aspects of his position was to try to keep Bob Knight out of trouble with the press, referees and university administration. He then made a statement that encapsulates the dilemma of big time athletics: "I can take Bob Knight to a luncheon in downtown Indianapolis and have standing room only; the president of the university can't fill the seats."

Dismissal

While lack of sensitivity and arrogance may be tolerated in Division I, it is unacceptable in Division III. The tipping point for Coach Rowe came in academic year 1997-98 when the evaluations of the players, including the tri-captains, unanimously rated their experience for the year as a negative one. Coincident with the player evaluations was the independent decision by Athletic Director Bill Zwann and Vice President Mahoney that Coach Rowe should not be retained. At a meeting called in March 1997 by Mahoney, I listened to their analysis and recommendation that a change be made. Zwann was particularly concerned that the program was in the process of self-destructing, that without a coaching change, the expected quality could not be maintained.

We discussed at length whether to replace Coach Rowe immediately or allow him a farewell season in 1998-99. Given his years of service, this option was attractive. I thought long and carefully about the two options, finally concluding that, given the coach's resistance to change, it would be best to make the move immediately. More important, given the player evaluations there was a serious question of who would play if Rowe were retained.

Following a meeting between Athletic Director Zwaan and Coach Rowe, I met with the coach. I stated that, while I respected his years of accomplishment and loyalty to the University, I felt that the problems confronting the basketball program necessitated a change. Indicating that I wanted to move in a new direction, I encouraged him to announce his retirement so the University could appropriately honor his years of service. Additionally, any public announcements concerning his retirement would be done jointly so he would be comfortable with the language. Finally, the coaching change would not affect his position as an adjunct instructor of mathematics.

He asked what his options were and was told that if he did not announce his retirement or resign, his contract as basketball coach would not be renewed. Regrettably he informed me that he would neither announce his retirement nor resign. The meeting concluded with him being terminated as Widener head basketball coach.

The next morning my son called to say: "Hey, Dad, I never knew you were such an SOB! Have you read today's paper?" There was a scathing article in the *Philadelphia Inquirer* by sports columnist Bill Lyons on the travesty done to C. Alan Rowe with me as the prime culprit. The comments attributed to me indicated that I wanted the program to move in new directions but would not say why. The piece even included quotes from John Chaney, the Temple basketball coach, supporting Rowe and excoriating Widener. It was not a pleasant weekend.

The conclusion: There are no winners in cases such as this. Coach Rowe ended a long career in bitterness and anger. The University looked heartless in public and to many on campus but we could not counter the public utterances without further injuring Coach Rowe and generating more acrimony. When dismissing an employee, the employer who does not provide details to the public is in a vulnerable position since only one side of the story is told. Nevertheless, Widener stood by its policy.

Dave Duda, the head coach at Delaware Valley College, filled Rowe's position as Widener's head basketball coach. Duda came highly recommended by many sources including Phil Martelli '76BA, the head basketball coach at St. Joseph's University.

Alan Rowe remained at Widener as an adjunct faculty member teaching math during the academic year and in the summers. His wife, a long-time employee in the Registrar's Office, also continued at the University. However, the loss of the coaching position led Rowe to file a grievance to the Pennsylvania Human Rights Commission (PHRC) on the basis of age discrimination, which was dismissed. He next filed a suit for age discrimination in the Delaware County Court of Common Pleas. The court found in favor of the University on July 16, 2004. Further appeals were denied.

NCAA Division III Athletics: Students First, Athletes Second

It is hazardous to comment in general about intercollegiate athletics because of the breadth of the programs that compete under the NCAA banner. However, it will surprise most to learn that the largest percentage of student athletes who participate in NCAA sports is in Division III. The primary difference among the divisions is the absence of athletic scholarships in Division III: in effect, students pay to play, a simple rule that dramatically changes the calculus.

Widener has always played in Division III but over the years there were occasional efforts to have the basketball program join Division I. I always rejected the idea because philosophically I disagree with the notion of having a group of scholarship athletes on a mid-sized campus. Introducing a separate class of students would change the culture and balance of the campus in many ways. Of equal importance, I believed the argument to be specious that a higher division basketball program would bring financial benefits to the University. Few Division I programs make money unless they become one of the country's elite.

The challenge in intercollegiate athletics is to sustain equilibrium between the competitive urges of coaches and players, which are unlimited, and a departmental budget that is not. Since there are no separate foundations to support Division III sports, the athletic programs are just one of many departments competing for funds from their university's operating budget. I am a confirmed believer that this fact allows athletics, at least at the small college level, to be kept in proper perspective. Students are students first and athletes second. Financial decisions should be made on this same basis.

My philosophy was put to the test in 1982. During a strike by the NFL players, CBS decided to fill the insatiable appetite of the viewing public for football with four regional Division III games. Having won the national championship in 1981, Widener was asked to participate, requiring us to move our Saturday game with Moravian College to Sunday afternoon. Naturally, the students were intrigued by the prospect of going "big time" on national television. Unfortunately, it was Homecoming Weekend. With many alumni on campus and events scheduled around the Saturday afternoon football game, the decision to me was simple: We wouldn't move the game.

Other than the normal human disappointment, the decision was supported by the entire Widener community including Coach Manlove, players, students, faculty, et al. This one event is a snapshot of the difference between Division III and Division I athletics.

When asked by a reporter what I would have done if the $30,000 offered to us to move to Sunday had been a $1 million, my response was "I'd like to think the answer would have been the same." In later years when I was involved in NCAA policy making, I saw how difficult it was for my Division I colleagues to maintain a balance within their universities that included but did not overly weight the revenue generated by big time athletics.

Understanding the NCAA's Structure and Impact

The governing body for all collegiate athletes in the United States, the NCAA is a large, complex organization that attempts to regulate a very diverse and often philosophically disparate set of colleges and universities. The membership varies in size from multi-campus research universities to small, single-purpose colleges. The NCAA is such a "large tent," embodying such a diversity of interests, it can easily be made ineffective in the way the United Nations is; too many voices clamoring to be heard. Despite the association's best efforts to be inclusive, some voices do count more than others since they are the revenue providers.

The NCAA divisions can be confusing to the uninitiated. All schools that participate in NCAA intercollegiate athletics fall into one of eight districts based upon geographic location. A further distinction is made by the level in which an institution elects to participate, Division I, II or III. Division I has subdivisions, with different rules and restrictions relating to scholarships. The big-time athletic programs reside in Division IA, others in Division IAA or Division IAAA. In Division II, comprised principally of institutions from public state university systems, a defined number of athletic scholarships may be awarded.

Division III is the largest grouping and is dominated by private institutions. It includes colleges with enrollments under 1,000 students, and some with over 20,000. In Division III, athletic ability is not supposed to be used in the financial aid or admissions processes. All standards for admissions and aid are to be applied equally to all students who seek admission to a Division III institution. Does this mean that III athletes are never given preferential treatment? Regrettably not, but the ability to maintain a semblance of parity between athletics and academics is far greater in Division III.

While the desire to be competitive in Division I and Division III may be the same, the stakes in III are much lower. Revenue from television, sporting goods companies, other corporate sponsors, and marketing rights to products bearing athletic logos are virtually non-existent in III.

In the early days of my presidency, the extent of my involvement with the NCAA was to discuss issues to be voted at the annual convention with our representative Bill Manlove, who participated in his role as athletic director. When I became more involved, I was astounded by the number of presidents who were unaware of the issues being decided at the conventions, which meant that the athletic staffs were de facto determining facets of institutional policy. For example, the topic of freshman eligibility for varsity sports is among the myriad of issues the NCAA dictates. We should remember that eligibility is not just about athletics but is intertwined with civil rights, the rights of individuals, factors of diversity, the rights of minorities, gender issues, etc. It is an example of the complexity of the issues the NCAA attempts to regulate. College presidents with any sense pay attention! [4]

A View From Inside the NCAA

In the fall of 1987, in anticipation of the NCAA annual meeting in early 1988, Ithaca College President Jim Whalen, then chair of the Division III Presidents Committee, invited all Division III presidents and athletic directors to participate in a survey assessing the operating philosophy of the division.

Among the key findings of the survey was a reaffirmation of the philosophy statement that broadly says institutions want as many students as possible to participate rather than to spectate, that the division stands for an appropriate integration of academics and athletics, and that athletes should be treated the same as all other students. The survey also addressed financial aid and academic eligibility.

My response to President Whalen went beyond the survey questions. In a separate letter, I outlined a series of steps that I felt would reaffirm the Division III philosophy while strengthening oversight. The result was an invitation to speak at the NCAA national convention in

---

[4] The freshman eligibility conversation has gone on for decades. In 1906 the Big Ten Conference prohibited graduate students and freshman from participating in varsity sports as did Harvard, Yale and Princeton, then athletic powerhouses. The NCAA constitution later allowed "home rules" with eligibility left to individual institutions or conferences. Then in 1922 the NCAA urged participating institutions to deny varsity competition by freshmen, which all did. In 1944, during WWII, freshman eligibility was reinstated because of manpower shortages. In 1947 freshman participation in varsity sports was again banned. In 1968 freshmen were allowed to participate in all championship events except basketball and post-season football. In 1972 freshmen were allowed to participate in all NCAA championships including basketball and football. Today the issue is not whether freshmen may participate, they do, but whether an athlete who leaves college after the freshman year is eligible to play in the professional leagues.

Nashville, Tennessee in January of 1988. Little did I know that this appearance would be the start of a deep involvement with the NCAA, including a term on the Presidents Commission from 1992 to 1996.

My first NCAA service was as a member of the Postgraduate Scholarship Committee, a group of athletic directors and presidents who review the credentials of student athletes from all divisions who have been nominated for awards. The scholarships at that time were worth $10,000 but in later years were increased to $18,000. The committee work was time consuming. We closeted ourselves for several days reading files and rating both male and female student athletes from a cross section of sports. I recall being impressed by the credentials of the potential scholarship winners, especially from the Division III institutions. Many of the outstanding student athletes held 3.8 to 4.0 GPAs.[5]

Programs such as the post-graduate scholarships are important to the NCAA's public profile. Too often the only image that the public associates with high profile athletics are a low graduation rate, misbehavior, and recruiting scandals.

In the 1990s I made a recommendation that the NCAA give consideration to establishing a fourth division for the smaller private colleges and universities unable to compete with the lower-priced publics and the larger privates that play in Division III. The proposal never gained approval outside of committee because my more idealistic colleagues objected to separate public and private divisions. Ironically, many of them were the ones in Pennsylvania who expressed concern about competition due to pricing differentials from the State System of Higher Education and Penn State University.

An NCAA Split?

The NCAA has struggled for years with its mission to serve and regulate diversified members. When serious issues have arisen, the usual response has been to add another regulation or rule. The NCAA rule book now reads like the IRS Code. A former president of the

---

[5] During my presidency, eight of Widener's student athletes were awarded postgraduate scholarships from the NCAA, thanks to the good work of Sports Information Director Susan Fumagalli. Also, football players Steven Cianci '91BSB, '92MBA and T.J. Hess '03BSB were chosen for the National Football Foundation and College Hall of Fame Scholarship. Hess received his award in 2001, the only Division III athlete selected that year.

NCAA, Cedric Dempsey who headed the organization when I was a member of the Presidents Commission, once commented that the NCAA has "regulated itself into paralysis."

In part for this reason, there is ongoing concern that the organization might split in two with the big-time programs banding together in their own association. The financial impact of such a move would be seismic. Funding for the NCAA and its Divisions II and III is a by-product of the revenues generated by the major programs. Since 2002 when CBS signed a contract with the NCAA to pay $6.2 billion over 11 years for the right to broadcast the NCAA men's basketball tournament, that championship alone has generated over 90 percent of the NCAA revenues. Without a similar revenue stream, II and III would become pay-as-you-go organizations. It is not too far a reach to state it would be the end of national championships for all but the major programs.

Philosophical Debate at 1988 NCAA Conference

The invitation to speak at the 1988 National NCAA Convention was on the topic "Is the Philosophy of Division III Working as it Should?" The address was framed by Proposition 48, a controversial ballot question that not only set minimum entrance requirements for athletes in all divisions but approved the inclusion of athletic skills in determining scholarship assistance, which is forbidden in Division III.

Ken Weller, president of Central College of Iowa, spoke in support of the existing Division III philosophy that guaranteed institutional autonomy in the matter of entrance requirements. His quite valid theme was that "the essence of imposing academic standards seeks to legislate . . . integrity on the members in an atmosphere of assuming the worst. Who we admit and who we permit to play ought to be determined by our institutions and our conference, not by the (NCAA) association." (NCAA 1988, 175)

Ken's position was simple: Those who want to cheat will find a way to do so. To change the rules of an association of institutions that operate on mutual trust simply to address violations of the minority would be wrong, and probably ineffective. "If," he continued, "we are going to introduce those kind of restrictions, it seems to me that it behooves us as a division to do it on the basis of allowing for *modifications* in the requirements based upon the profile of the students who attend the institutions."

In closing, Weller quoted from the Division III Philosophy Statement: "The Division III approach is to have consistent, equitable competition and to do so in ways that minimize infringement on the freedom of individual institutions to determine their own special objects and programs." (NCAA 1988, 175)

While agreeing in principle with President Weller, I argued that issues of concern should be recognized and addressed without violating the fundamentals of the Division III philosophy.

On the issue of misuse of autonomy, I expressed concern that "there are a number of schools that seem to be seeking and finding loopholes in the existing Division III philosophy standards relating to financial aid packaging. When that occurs, the opportunity for diminished academic standards often becomes a reality." I quoted a statement on athletics from the AAUP bulletin, *Academe*: "A pledge to remain competitive commits a school to a course in which the determinants of success are frequently being influenced by the preferences of the lowest common denominator." (NCAA 1988, 178-179)

On the issue of attempting to legislate standards for Division III, I offered the following: The very pluralism and diversity existing in Division III makes it difficult to try to legislate a codified statement of academic standards. The academic pluralism that exists within our division is reflected in our current statement of philosophy and approach, for it offers each institution, and I think correctly, the task of defining within its own stated mission exactly what it considers appropriate academic progress and acceptable admissions standards.

In the best of all worlds, self policing is the first choice of solutions. However, the pressures and cynicism of forces beyond our campuses suggest that a more defined approach to quality control is needed. To accomplish this, there must be recognition of two facts. One, a recognition of the direct linkage between financial aid packaging policies, academic standards and alumni and public pressures for athletic competition; and secondly, the acceptance by the presidents of our colleges and universities in Division III for the responsibility to control the academic standards for our athletic programs.

Now, given the acceptance of these two assumptions, I would like to offer three recommendations for consideration, and I believe that they meet some of the philosophic statements President Weller presented this morning.

We should endorse the financial-aid package amendment presented by the Division III Steering Committee, essentially that member institutions should not consider athletic ability as a criterion in the formulation of financial aid packaging.

That each college or university in Division III prepares an institutional policy statement of academic standards and the minimum for satisfactory academic progress for all students within that institution. These policy statements should be filed annually with our respective conferences and with the NCAA and should be open to public review.

That the president of each member institution in Division III annually signs these statements before submitting them to our conferences and to the NCAA.

I would suggest these recommendations are in keeping with our Division III tradition of having each individual institution set its own standards consistent with its mission. I also believe that these recommendations support the true philosophy of Division III for all students to be treated equally. Further, and in conclusion, I would again state that the way to achieve our objectives is to endorse need-based financial aid packaging and to publish individual institutional academic progress statements and have them attested to by the chief executive officers of all of our colleges and universities. (NCAA 1978)

The presentation was well received and contributed to a 172-61 vote against Proposition 48 in favor of Proposition 93. Proposition 93 read: "The composition of the financial aid package offered to a student athlete shall be consistent with the established policy of the institution's financial aid office for all students; however, a member institution *shall not consider athletic ability as a criterion in the formulation of the financial aid package*." (Italics added) It was in keeping with the Division III philosophy of institutional autonomy but made it difficult for institutions to defend leadership grants to athletes of lesser academic quality than other students. It became effective September 1988.[6]

My recommendations to publish statements on policy and to have institutional CEOs attest to their validity never made it out of com-

---

[6] Memorable tongue-in-cheek observations pertinent to this issue were made by two of my colleagues. From Jim Whalen, at the '88 convention, "I want you to know that if we vote No. 93 in there are going to be a hell of a lot of football players at Ithaca in the choir." And, from another whose programs had fallen on difficult times, "Concerns by opponents as to whether you are playing by the rules go away once you stop winning even though your policies are exactly the same!"

mittee. I think too many presidents were uncomfortable with having the onus for financial aid reporting vis-à-vis athletics fall directly on them. However, in the Middle Atlantic Conference, in which Widener competes, there is an agreement that if coaches bring a complaint to their president, he or she will contact their counterpart and raise the issue. I did that on several occasions and was satisfied after being given the facts that the scholarship awards were appropriate for the college or university in question. The difficult thing for coaches to accept is that under the Division III philosophy, each college or university sets its own academic standards. What qualifies a student for aid at one institution will and should be different from another. If, for example, the accepted norm was a 1250 SAT for a President's Award at Widener and 1100 at another institution, that was legitimate as long as it applied to all students.

The Presidents Assume NCAA Leadership

Continued concerns about the pervasive impact of big time athletics on college campuses led the John S. and James L. Knight Foundation to establish the Knight Commission in 1989. Driven by concerns that athletics at colleges and universities in the United States were out of control, the commission set as its objective a reform agenda for intercollegiate sports. In 1993 it recommended a series of improvements, including holding the presidents responsible for intercollegiate athletics in the areas of academic integrity, financial integrity and certification.

It took three years but in 1996 the NCAA finally voted to change its governance structure from an organization controlled by athletic administrators to one dominated by presidents. Thus, the formal responsibility for athletic planning, policies and budgets were at last in the hands of the men and women with the most global view of their institutions. When the restructuring was completed in 1997, the NCAA was controlled by a Presidents Commission comprised of an executive committee with three divisional organizations. A group that came into being, as one colleague said, "to allow the presidents to take back intercollegiate athletics," the Presidents Commission consisted of chief executive officers from forty-four member institutions – twenty-two from Division I, eleven from Divisions II and III – each of whom were elected by their divisional counterparts to serve four-year terms.

My term on the commission, 1992 to 1996, coincided with the implementation of the Knight Commission findings. The dynamics were fascinating, and at times most artful since compromise and trade-off among the three presidential groups was an integral part of policy making. One example of how the process worked remains in my mind. A decade ago, just as today, the question of a Division I football championship playoff similar to that for NCAA basketball was a perennial issue for discussion. The several factors against such a playoff were: the extension of an already long football season by several additional weeks, which would be detrimental to the athletes; the potential loss of revenue from the long-established bowl games; and existing relationships between individual conferences and bowls.

The first argument was somewhat specious since athletes continue to practice for many weeks after the season in anticipation of bowl games, and all other NCAA divisions have a national playoff without untoward damage to the players. Considering that Division I football is broadcast nearly every evening all fall, there is no question that maximizing revenues through bowl games was a major influence in the decision not to have a playoff.

I well remember that at one meeting the Division I presidents voted to endorse the establishment of a football playoff system for their division, a policy change that had to be approved by the Presidents Commission. Several Division I colleagues from the Big Ten quietly asked selected Division II and III presidents to vote against the proposal, saying that most Division I presidents were against it.

When I was approached, I asked why it had passed in division caucus and was told, "given the pressure from alumni, fans and the media, how can we be seen as being opposed to a national playoff?" The proposal was defeated on the strength of the votes from Divisions II and III; all presidents understand the ramifications of institutional pressure.

In Division I, priorities begin with maximizing revenues. Salaries for coaches far exceed those of the president and too many players believe the rules for them are different.

Academics at some institutions are adjunct to athletics. One NCAA graduation report showed only 40 percent of Division I-A football players and 34 percent of basketball players earn degrees in six years! The NCAA attempts to do the right thing but has the impossible task of trying to legislate its stakeholders, notably the stakeholders who supply the funding. The huge amount of money involved with Division I athletics will always hover over and impact discussions upon what I see as the Sisyphean themes of intercollegiate athletics: academic standards and eligibility for student athletes, financial aid to athletes and recruiting standards.

Given the extraordinary amounts of money involved with big time sports, the change to a Presidents Commission and with it the introduction of new policies was an ambitious undertaking. Moreover, the athletic personnel of the various conferences who had run the NCAA for years did not give up power easily.

The formation of the Presidents Commission introduced a political force with the power to implement dramatic change if it chose to do so. However, so many presidents are uninformed about, or not interested in, athletics that the task of engaging CEOs in the NCAA was and still is difficult, especially in Division III. Because of the financial stakes, Division I presidents are by necessity more attuned to athletic issues.

NCAA Reforms Lead to Significant Advancements

Despite its very difficult mission, I am impressed with the NCAA. I am impressed that it attracts so many intelligent and gifted individuals who truly believe intercollegiate athletics are a positive force in society. The numerous accomplishments the organization has achieved are often overshadowed by the media fascination with the ills rather than the good. For every illiterate athlete who gets into trouble there are thousands who perform with integrity both academically and athletically. They do not make the headlines but they too are part of the NCAA.

Despite the enormity of the issues, the initial NCAA reform agenda was largely successful. Eligibility standards were established and clarified. Important reform discussions were begun regarding the role of minority and women athletes.

One of the most significant advances in athletics has been the result of the NCAA Gender Equity Task Force dealing with what has become known as Title IX. Title IX refers to Title IX of the Education Amendments of 1972, a federal statute that prohibits sex discrimination in campus programs that receive federal funding. The application of Title IX to athletics fostered a clash within the traditionally male dominated NCAA when some very gifted women athletic administrators aggressively used the Office of Civil Rights and the courts to provide increased opportunities for women.

Under the law, the resources provided to men's and women's sports must be equal. Budgets for travel, coaches, etc. all come under scrutiny.

There must also be parity in the number and amount of scholarships awarded and in the number of athletes of each sex. In order to achieve compliance, the scholarships to males have decreased.

Football scholarships in Division I have gone from 105 to 85 per team. I find it hard to sympathize with coaches who claim that number of scholarships is insufficient.

The issue of proportionality as a test for Title IX is very controversial. The requirement states that the number of male and female athletes at a college must be equal and they must be treated the same. Not surprisingly, the area of greatest tension is football with its large numbers of participants. Because of the imbalance created by the size of a typical football team, men's teams have been reduced in number and women's sports have broadened to include a host of new opportunities, i.e. crew, lacrosse, softball, ice hockey.

Title IX has done wonders for the participation of women in intercollegiate athletics. One simply has to look at women's soccer and basketball that now rival the popularity of many men's programs on some campuses. During a time of civil rights progress in other spheres of society, Title IX became the catalyst for the inclusion of more women in leadership positions in the NCAA and in athletic departments across the nation.

Among the sports that have been decimated are men's wrestling and gymnastics. Tension continues to exist between what is seen as an intransient stance on the part of many women's athletic groups toward proportionality and the need in the minds of others to seek an accommodation that exempts the number of football players because they place an undue burden regarding proportionality on institutions with a football program. Many argue that the demand by women for proportionality is impossible without penalizing male athletes, that reducing or dropping athletic programs to meet equal participant numbers is artificial and prejudicial.

At issue is not Title IX, but how to seek an accommodation that protects both men and women. In 2000, the Knight Commission reconstituted itself to review the progress of the reform effort. It again reported grave concerns surrounding intercollegiate athletics and issued a series of new recommendations, many quite controversial. The major ones call for the elimination of post-season play for institutions that don't attain a 50 percent graduation rate among its athletes, a reduction in the number of athletic scholarships, and a redistribution of broadcast revenues. It will be interesting to see whether the recommendations will be implemented.

The NCAA's decision to become a presidents' organization was among the association's finest. It was rewarding to be a part of the transitional period.

Chapter 13

Political and Civic Engagement

One of the more compelling aspects of a university presidency is the opportunity for involvement with groups external to the campus community. The demand upon your time for these efforts grows exponentially the longer you stay in office and as your knowledge base and familiarity with issues becomes more sophisticated. Serving national, state and local organizations can be beneficial to the institution and personally rewarding.

The title of president provides access to a diverse cross section of individuals and organizations that under other circumstances would be difficult to gain, and these contacts result in personal and business connections that benefit many. Examples of this synergism are my service as a director of two corporate boards, Quick and Reilly, Inc. and General Accident Co. The friendship with Les Quick that grew from my board membership at Quick and Reilly enhanced his understanding of Widener and our working relationship when he became board chairman.

At General Accident, I convinced a board colleague, Jack Bogle, founder of the Vanguard Group who did not usually accept such invitations, to receive an honorary degree and deliver a commencement address at Widener. Further, I was able to recruit the chairman of the insurance company's board after its merger with Commercial Union to join the board of directors of Crozer Keystone Health System, where after one term, he succeeded me as board chair.

Grappling With a Dysfunctional Host Community

My external activities ranged from local to national and from professional to social. That said, I must admit that Chester, Pennsylvania, the hometown of Widener's Main Campus, was a difficult place to form lasting and productive partnerships and relationships. For many years the city operated on the verge of bankruptcy. While much of its difficulties could be traced to a declining economic base and shifting demographics, a large part of the decline and inertia was the result of dysfunctional political leadership.

A prosperous and productive industrial city in the early part of the twentieth century with a slogan "What Chester Makes, Makes Chester," the city found itself in a downward spiral in the years following WWII. There was an out migration of its industrial base and an influx of a less skilled, poorer, minority population. The real backbreaker, however, was a political stronghold by a single party that practiced patronage with great skill; while not inherently bad, too much power in the hands of a single group for too long becomes counterproductive. The result, after several decades, was a weakened tax base, chronic unemployment, and the creation of a permanent welfare class with all the attendant problems.

Very early in my administration, I was fortunate to have the wise counsel of Bill Coopersmith, a longtime resident of Delaware County and a Widener supporter who was politically well connected. As a friend and confidant, he counseled me against being perceived as too close to the mayor, a man who ruled both the city and his party with an iron fist. To avoid the potential ramifications of dealing directly with city hall, I asked Bill to serve as liaison for the University, which he did for several years. This arrangement undoubtedly saved Widener considerable embarrassment when the mayor was indicted, convicted and sent to federal prison.

On several occasions, the business community proposed reform efforts to help rejuvenate the city and its reputation; all were rejected by city council. One suggestion in particular struck at the heart of the problem. A proposal that the city adopt a city manager form of government died aborning because the existing mayor-and-council structure ensured maximum citywide control over jobs and the departments that provided city services.

For many years, Chester treated Widener with meager cooperation or, more often, benign neglect. Widener couldn't be completely ignored: we were one of the largest employers in Chester and a stabilizing force in the neighborhoods contiguous to the campus; at times our security forces had more officers and patrol cars on the streets than did the city. There we sat, too large to ignore but unembraced by the political leadership. It was a frustrating reality in which to work. In fact, the relationship with Chester reached a point where we contemplated legally annexing the University to the Borough of Ridley, a possibility because a portion of the property on which the athletic complex sat was situated in Ridley. Additionally, when we were acquiring property in Delaware for the second campus, I let it be known that Widener was considering relocation in its entirety. I'll never know if either of these proposed actions had much effect but I did receive calls from some in the city expressing concern over the University's possible departure.

Tensions common to all urban campuses were constantly in play. Ongoing issues included access to campus facilities by community groups who felt the campus was a public entity not a private institution, the erroneous perception that all students were wealthy and privileged, and expansion of the University through the purchase of real estate that took tax ratables off the rolls.

A University Zone

A university surrounded by residential properties is nearly always held in distrust by its neighbors for obviously the only way to expand is by encroachment. Ironically, it is often the presence of the university that stabilizes property values during a time of serious decline in the real estate market. Such was the case with Widener.

Over a twenty-year period, Widener purchased more than sixty contiguous properties. For many years, we discussed the concept of a university zone with the city. Such a zone would facilitate the acquisition of property by minimizing the zoning application process for each purchase. The city never finalized such an agreement, instead using it as a bargaining chip for many years. We simply moved forward using existing thoroughfares including Interstate-95 to the south and Providence Avenue to the north as boundaries for a University footprint, and purchased within those boundaries. When the city finally proposed the creation of the university zone, we declined since we had already created it de facto and to have it legitimized would add no value.

The Chester Academy

The Chester-Upland School District was among the poorest in the commonwealth, and had been for many years. Prior to the passage of legislation that introduced charter schools, Widener entered into a planning process with CUSD to develop what was to be tentatively known as The Chester Academy. The concept was to develop a track within the existing school system for the most gifted and motivated students. Selected teachers would be mentored by Widener education professors; a new curriculum emphasizing math and science would be at least partly taught in Widener's laboratories with Widener science faculty serving as advisors; and, most creative, an agreement would be signed by both parents and students committing students to full participation or expulsion from the program. For its time, it was an innovative approach to educational reform within an existing academic structure.

Unfortunately, the endeavor was doomed by the political maneuvering of the then superintendent of schools who was under fire for his performance. In the spring, with planning still in its infancy, the superintendent chose to announce via a local newspaper that the academy would open in September. In this apparent attempt to save his job, he was pushing Widener into an educational endeavor that was so unformed, so insubstantial, that it could have seriously damaged the University's academic reputation as well as the academy's chances for success. In a meeting with the press, Widener's spokesman made it clear that the University had not been consulted prior to the announcement and, further, that it was withdrawing from the planning meetings. Once again, a personal agenda of one individual led to a missed opportunity for Chester and its residents.

Voluntary Contributions to a Host City

During the lowest ebb in Widener's relationship with Chester, a statewide controversy arose over whether or not nonprofit, independent institutions should be required to reimburse their host city for services. Widener elected to make an annual contribution to Chester in the amount of $100,000, a realistic figure for the fire protection and police support received. We then launched a concentrated public relations effort to provide tangible evidence to the community of Widener's stake in the city, pointing out that our voluntary $100,000 donation was further bolstered by our social and cultural contributions to the city and region, by wages and wage taxes paid, by a long list of student and faculty volunteerism, patronage of local businesses, safety assistance, and other details of our economic impact.

The Bottom of the Spiral

The city hit bottom in 1995 when the recently elected mayor, the first Democrat to hold the post in decades, realized that she and her colleagues were incapable of handling or resolving the city's financial difficulties and thus, under Act 47 of state law, petitioned the commonwealth to intervene. I imagine that the expectation was a state bail out followed by a return to business as usual. Instead, the Commonwealth of Pennsylvania effectively placed Chester into receivership and implemented strict controls that successfully created an environment in which major changes could occur.[1]

Widener saw this as an opportunity to be actively involved in what it hoped would be a renaissance in Chester. The senior staff and other interested employees formed a Political Action Committee (PAC) to raise funds in support of city council candidates with a new vision for the city. It is important to note that since it was individuals forming the PAC, the University did not run afoul of the law preventing nonprofits from doing the same. On the other side of the city, the Crozer-Chester Medical Center (CCMC) employees joined the effort, thus creating a substantial and substantive group willing to support change.

The principal city council candidate supported by the PAC was Dominic Pileggi, a bright young lawyer who was also honest and politically savvy. He knew that the Republican Party in Chester had a leadership vacuum ripe for filling. He also understood the value of the two nonprofits (coincidentally, then the two major employers) as assets and resources for Chester, and reached out to the medical center and the University. Over time my relationship with Councilman Pileggi developed into one of trust, friendship and mutually defined objectives. In 1998, he was elected mayor (and in 2002, a state senator, subsequently becoming the senate majority leader). Under his leadership the city began an impressive turn around and today is on the verge of real economic development.

Reaching Out to CCMC

As I write, I am in my second decade as a board member of the Crozer Keystone Health System, one of my most personally satisfying examples of presidential engagement at the local level. My initial involvement with the health system began as a member of the board of the Crozer Medical Center. A mutually beneficial relationship had long existed between the hospital and the University. Widener students served there in numerous clinical placements, including those in nursing, social work, and clinical and neuro psychology, then often became

---

[1] Chester remains in receivership as I write in 2007 but the daily management is in the hands of local officials.

employees, occasionally returning to the University for an advanced degree under the CCMC benefit plan. During my terms on the medical center's board, I served as its chairman and also among those who initiated a merger with Delaware County Hospital, the first step in developing what is now the Crozer Keystone Health System.[2]

Following my service on the medical center's board, I was invited to membership on the board of the parent health system. I was fortunate to serve as chairman of that board for five years spanning the presidencies of both Jack McMeekin and Jerry Miller. Under their leadership, the health system's financial and clinical strength grew exponentially. It was, and is, rewarding to be a part of it.

The Partnership for Technology Park

Because Jack McMeekin and I respected each other and worked well together, when a new city management team took over we agreed to undertake a project to stabilize and develop the corridor between Crozer and Widener. The undertaking was not pure altruism since it provided the opportunity to own and control the acres of undeveloped property between the University and the medical center.

Our concept was to develop a technology park that would attract start-up companies to Chester. It was an ambitious undertaking since the reputation of the city was not conducive to a good business image but the incentives would include very good technological capability and support as well as proximity to a major teaching medical center and a university with an engineering department. Most important would be the low rental rates.

To begin the process Jack and I met with the CEO of the University City Center Science Center (UCSC) located in Philadelphia contiguous to the University of Pennsylvania. Founded in the late 1960s by a number of area universities and colleges for the purpose of promoting scientific research, UCSC became interested in our concept of establishing a replica in a distressed suburban city. The result was a partnership among UCSC, Crozer and Widener. Although, in the

---

[2] The largest health care provider in Delaware County, Pa., CKHS is now comprised of five hospitals, 7,100 employees with over 2,600 physicians and nurses, the only trauma center in two counties, and a regional burn center.

end the partnership was dissolved, the input and guidance by UCSC was invaluable.[3]

University Technology Park (UTP), as the project was known, was financed by a combination of federal, state and institutional funds. The first building, opened in 1998, was a 35,000 sq.ft. structure that was followed in 2000 by a second building of 40,000 sq.ft. The City of Chester contributed infrastructure changes and enabled the acquisition of the land. A third property acquired through a purchase from the city was also made available for future development. UTP, the first privately owned structure built in the City of Chester in twenty years, has demonstrated what can be accomplished when committed CEOs conclude something needs to be done in their host municipality.

On his retirement from Crozer Keystone, Jack McMeekin accepted the presidency of UTP while I assumed the chairmanship. He devoted several years to promoting, building and expanding the enterprise and it was his dogged commitment to the project that allowed it to survive.

Knowing the Neighbors

Although those who are fleet of foot or well insulated usually avoid meeting the neighbors under anything but their own terms, presidential civic and political engagement not only includes national committees and ranking politicians, but also falls under the rubric of town/gown relationships. Ours ran the gamut from neighborly indifference to formidable tension. Several instances became full-blown chapters in the history of my administration: the attempt to purchase an elementary school, the attempt to save art "for the people," and the debate over access to our athletic facilities.

The Stetser School Sit-In

Among the instances when residents thwarted initiatives between the city and Widener was the University's proposed purchase of the administration building of the Chester-Upland School District and the

---

[3] When it became apparent that the interests of the partnering organizations were moving in separate directions, Widener and Crozer Keystone bought out the interests of UCSC. The Science Center was committed to the development of projects in the City of Philadelphia with a long-term objective of generating income from the projects. Widener and CKHS were exclusively committed to Chester and had determined that any profit from the UTP venture would be put back into further development opportunities.

adjacent Stetser Elementary School. Occupying a full square block on the University's periphery, the property was of considerable value to Widener as a cost effective way to acquire academic and administrative space contiguous to the Main Campus. For the city it meant an infusion of cash for a financially strapped school district. Conversations between the city and the University went on for years but resident outcry prevented the sale. Indeed, one morning when word leaked out that the school board was contemplating closing and selling Stetser, a large band of elementary age children, their teachers and parents marched into the corridor outside of my office chanting "leave our school alone!"

Eschewing the first instinct to ask security to clear the hall, I invited the children and teachers to sit down, ordered cookies and juice to be served to them by our food service, and took a representative group of parents into my conference room to discuss the issue. I made it very clear that the University was not trying to close the school, but if the school board did just that, we were interested in buying it.[4]

I explained, too, that I agreed they had a valid case; the elementary school was one of the safest (largely thanks to Widener) and highest rated in the city. It was also the magnet that had drawn many residents into Chester's First Ward.

The conflict ended amicably, which was one positive derived from the years of negotiations over the acquisition of the administration building and/or the elementary school. I suspect that the city never had any intention of selling either building; it was a classic illustration of the carrot and stick.

Sun Hill

The University's athletic complex was most easily reached from the center of the Main Campus via the streets of intervening Sun Hill. Pedestrian and automobile traffic were irritants among Sun Hill residents that festered for many years until the city finally acted on a proposal by Widener to build a dedicated access road from the campus to the athletic facilities over a long-abandoned railway bed. Running along one side of the community's Washington Park, the bed was situated on land that sat below the garages that backed the row homes up on the adjoining hill. A direct access road there would benefit the entire com-

---

[4] The reasoned discussion resulted in a far more equitable relationship with our immediate neighbors than had existed for some time and ultimately led to a Community/University Task Force that met as needed.

munity. However, because it would also benefit Widener, there was neighborhood opposition.

At a public hearing held on campus packed with angry neighbors, I became the gratuitous target of hostility, despite support for the lease from the mayor and Council, who sat on their hands during the dialogue. The "discussion" was a circus, and most unpleasant. But having jumped through that hoop, the University was given a 25-year lease with the proviso that we supply security, maintain a public children's playground on the property, provide lighting and pay rent, all at no cost to the city.

The Deshong Museum

In any city with a myriad of economic and social ills, activist groups that cannot unseat the existing political structure often find it strategically useful to attack selected policies of whatever large, successful business is in town, quite frequently the local university. The city government may quietly encourage such activism in order to shift the heat from its own policy making or latent inadequacies.

A prime example was the fire storm surrounding Widener's takeover of the failed and decaying Deshong Museum located just off the Chester campus. The museum, built in the 1920s, not only resembled other Greek revival buildings in architecture but also in lack of air conditioning, art storage, humidity control, alarms, and any security beyond a lock on the door. For more than fifty years, it had housed the impressive art collection of Alfred O. Deshong, a Chester businessman who amassed a fortune in the late nineteenth century in banking, gas and stone quarries. In his lifetime, his was one of the most discriminating art collections in the country.

When Deshong died in 1913, he directed in his will that a trust be established to administer and display the collection in a museum for which he bequeathed funds for construction and maintenance. To be located in Chester, then the county seat and home to the wealthy, the museum was to exhibit the collection "for the pleasure of the citizens of Chester." The trust was founded in 1916.

By mid-century, Chester was well into its economic and social tailspin. The three trustees of the Alfred O. Deshong Museum grappled with such serious difficulties as lack of participation by the public and lack of funds. In apparent desperation, they seriously jeopardized the future of the collection and the building by allowing a public library to cohabit the premises, creating a security nightmare.

Over three decades, some one hundred artworks were stolen. In just the period from 1972 to 1979 an estimated fifty paintings and seventeen ivories were taken by a local high school dropout who hid himself in the building until after closing hours then took the works of art out an unalarmed window on the first floor. While it is hard to fathom how a high school dropout was able to place stolen works at one of the most prestigious art auction houses in the country, much of the stolen Deshong art ended up in auction at Sotheby's in New York City. [5]

Finally admitting their inability to properly administer the collection, the trustees entered into an agreement with Widener whereby the University leased the museum for three years at $1 per annum. In return the University became responsible for the salary of a curator, the cost of utilities and the maintenance of the building and collection. The trust would pay for security and the upkeep of the grounds.

At the conclusion of the three-year lease, with an annual financial loss of $45,000 to the University, it was clear that the attempt to revitalize the museum was a losing proposition. The trustees then concluded that it was financially impossible for the trust to continue to maintain the museum and its collection and, thus, petitioned the Court of Common Pleas of Delaware County to terminate the trust and distribute the assets in a manner that would as nearly as possible honor the wishes of Mr. Deshong. What ensued was a classic town/gown political conflagration!

Once it accepted the termination appeal, the court scheduled hearings for the distribution of the assets. In its petition for the art collection, Widener noted the desire of Mr. Deshong to keep the collection in Chester and open to public view at no charge. The University was the only entity in the city with the resources, expertise and presence to manage and exhibit the collection.

Over a period of several months a series of articles appeared in a local newspaper inferring that Widener had covertly conspired with the trustees to end the trust in order to gain control of the collection. It was

---

[5] The thief was finally caught living in an upscale apartment near Philadelphia's Academy of Music when police responded to a shooting there and noticed his extraordinary collection of art, presumably bound for auction. Subsequent investigations into his lifestyle led to a conviction. The FBI recovered thirty-two paintings and seventeen ivories out of the estimated one hundred missing works. A few others have been returned over the years.

essentially senseless for the University to respond to such innuendo. More vocal attacks on Widener's petition came from a local activist whose rallying cry, accepted as truth by many citizens, was that Widener was "stealing the people's art." This was an interesting and subtle twist on the truth of Deshong's will that called for the preservation of the collection *for the enjoyment of the citizens,* not for their ownership.

The request by other petitioners, including the Brandywine River Museum, to take only parts of the collection contravened the original trust language and would have had parts of the collection leave the city. Thus, on July 19, 1984 Widener was awarded the art collection and $500,000 to restore and preserve the works. The Delaware County Industrial Authority was awarded the land known as Deshong Park for the purpose of creating tax ratable properties for the city and the remainder of the estate, some $800,000, was awarded to the general fund of the county. The book value of the estate was $1,222,260 although the art collection's market value was twice its book value.

Appeals filed by citizen groups were dismissed by the superior court. The art collection was moved from storage to the University's on-campus art museum in December of 1986 when both the art and the funds legally became Widener's. Controversy and rumor were perpetuated by the welfare activists for several years but eventually died a justified death.

In 1998, with the election of Dominic Pileggi as mayor, the attitude of the city toward the University changed dramatically: an elected city official actually visited me asking how we could work together! While the difficult times prevailed, something positive was finally in place.

Political and Social Engagement: National

The good that can inure to a university and its reputation by appropriate presidential engagement can be far-reaching. It is, after all, human nature to assess an organization by the individuals who serve it; good personal relationships raise the approval ratings. I recall that as my involvement in state and national activities increased over the years, more and more people spoke positively about Widener. This was true within AICUP (Association of Independent Colleges and Universities of Pennsylvania), PACU (Pennsylvania Association of Colleges and Universities), NAICU (National Association of Independent Colleges and Universities), and MAC (Middle Atlantic States Collegiate Athletic Association), all of which I chaired at least once, and the Presidents

Commission of the NCAA (National Collegiate Athletic Association) on which I sat for six years. In reality, my colleagues in these organizations knew little more of Widener University than they had in the past. The only thing that had changed was the development of a working relationship with me. For Widener, an old institution with a new name and new persona, such contacts were invaluable in promoting its reputation and name recognition.

Parenthetically, I found my interaction with colleagues across the country intellectually stimulating and enjoyed my small part in making policy for private higher education. It was also useful to see the interplay among men and women with differing regional perspectives and management styles, although I admit having had a great deal of opportunity to observe the manifest dissimilarity of styles from one state to the next as I traveled between Widener campuses.

A Two-State Charter

As president of a university chartered in both Pennsylvania and Delaware, I was fascinated more by the differences than the similarities between the neighboring states. The college and university presidents in Delaware could sit together around a conference table; the same group in Pennsylvania needed a ballroom. The governor of Pennsylvania usually traveled with state police; the governor of Delaware often arrived alone. I remember one Lincoln Day black-tie dinner in Wilmington when the then governor Pete Dupont came in late and someone had to find him a seat. That would never have occurred in Pennsylvania, nor in most eastern states; dinner would have awaited the pleasure of the governor. Because it is small Delaware comes as close to a "participatory democracy" as exists today.

Widener's dual charter served it well on political initiatives for we were the constituent of four U.S. senators and several congressmen. Indeed, whenever I was traveling by train from Wilmington to Washington, I would usually share the depot platform with Senators Biden and Roth who commuted to the Capitol most days of the week. If invited to sit with one or both of them, I had a chance to weigh in on pending legislature, an opportunity that would have required a formal audience in Pennsylvania.

Testifying Before Congressional Committees

My trips to Washington, and thus my conversations with the senators, very often supported the business of the National Association of Independent Colleges and Universities, an organization principally intended to influence public policy for higher education. The group's agenda was advanced via the multitude of relationships among elected officials and the presidents of the NAICU institutions.

This involvement in the national scene was personally rewarding because of the excellent caliber of those representing the interests of independent education. Leo O'Donovan, S.J., president of Georgetown, and Mike Adams, president of Center College who would become president of the University of Georgia, were among NAICU colleagues who became friends. At the first meeting I attended as a board member, I sat next to Derek Bok, president of Harvard University. After we'd chatted for a time, he commented, "I hope you get more financial support from the Widener family than Harvard does!" I replied that we probably did, and smiled at how large a shadow the Widener name spreads, from Hialeah to Harvard.[6]

I must tip my hat, too, to the savvy staff of NAICU who, like so many of their peers across the city, knew all the inner workings of Washington and were an absolute necessity to any organization or person attempting to push legislation, understand the system, or develop policy. "Beltway mentality," an unconscious mindset that nothing matters outside of Washington, flourishes within these staffers many of whom become "lifers," moving from legislator to legislator and organization to organization.

During my time with NAICU, I appeared on several panels testifying before congressional subcommittees. The process was interesting. One is seated at a hearing table with a series of lights that signify the length of your testimony, green for start talking, yellow for time is short, and red for you're finished. Some chairmen cut you off when the red light winks on, others allow you to complete your thought. The lights always reinforced my notion that public testimony is really political theater giving the elected officials starring roles before the public and the media. They look engaged and ask questions prepared by the staff, all the while knowing that the entire testimony has been sub-

---

[6] Bok's comment was in reference to the Widener Library at Harvard that was constructed as a memorial to Harry Widener, Fitz Dixon's uncle who along with Fitz's grandfather died on the Titanic.

mitted in writing and so they are, in fact, just following the script.

On occasion, I was asked to testify or carry out an assignment that, on reflection, I should have declined. When the Financial Accounting Standards Board was proposing that accounting standards for colleges and universities be changed from fund to cost accounting so that the public and private sectors would be on the same accounting system, I was asked as a member of the NAICU board to represent it at a hearing in Connecticut on the impact on higher education of the proposed changes. While I knew enough to read a balance sheet or an audit report and was able to ask the right questions of my financial personnel, I was not equipped to speak in depth on the technical and finer points of the rules that apply. Widener's CFO had spent enough time with me so that I was reasonably literate on the subject, but I spent a painful thirty minutes testifying beyond my depth at what had been projected as a philosophical discussion, not a technical one. The lesson learned was to stay within one's knowledge set and not to speak on matters beyond your expertise just because you are a college president!

While congressional hearings took place in very impressive surroundings, my most memorable meeting venue was the Roosevelt Room of the White House. A group representing NAICU, of which I was then chairman, were screened through the elaborate security process and led to the room in which even the most jaded of us sat in awe of the many historic moments that had taken place there.

In Washington, the subject matter of a hearing usually dictated the extent of congressional attendance. I once testified on a long-forgotten topic in a very large hearing room with just one congressman (the chairman of the committee) and a handful of staffers in attendance. On other occasions the hearing rooms were packed with reporters and a complete panel of congressmen.

The hearing on unrelated business taxes was one such jam-packed meeting. I testified with other university presidents before a committee of the U.S House of Representatives on the issue of unrelated business income and the tax-exempt status of certain services provided by higher education. Bookstores, rental of facilities to outside groups, student housing and food services were all called into question. I recall a colleague from a Catholic university being questioned as to why a cemetery the university maintained should be tax exempt. While it existed to bury deceased clergy the issue of how germane this function was to the education of students was left unanswered!

University Accreditation by Peer Review: The Adelphi Lessons

Higher education operates a unique accreditation structure of peer review managed through regional accrediting associations that are responsible for evaluating, reviewing and accrediting all colleges and universities in their respective regions every ten years or more frequently if needed. As a member of the Middle States accrediting body, I served as a team leader on several occasions, usually to review colleges or universities that were on the edge of financial or academic crisis.

The accreditation process is rigorous in application with the real value in the institution's preparation for a peer review visit. When properly undertaken, the preparatory self-study engages an institution over a lengthy time span in reviewing and assessing its stated goals and outcomes. The reviewers who visit then offer recommendations or critical analyses of weaknesses and shortcomings as benchmarked against the institution's self-analysis. On occasion, if concerns are raised during the site review, a follow-up report or special campus visit may be required as part of the accreditation process. Problematic institutions may be put on probation or, more rarely, have their accreditation rescinded.

One of the most extraordinary cases in the history of higher education, now a case study of how conflict between an administration and faculty can threaten the existence of an institution, occurred at Adelphi University in the late 1990s. I had a front row seat to the drama, having led a special Middle States' team to Adelphi in 1990.

The saga began in 1985 when Peter Diamandopulos was appointed president of Adelphi University. He had left the presidency of California State University under a cloud with a reputation as "polarizing and arrogant," and had been the recipient of three votes of censure and one vote of no confidence by the faculty. Adelphi was then a small, comprehensive university with a good regional reputation for both undergraduate and applied graduate programs taught by a faculty specifically structured over many years to serve that mission.

The Diamandopulos appointment set into motion dramatic changes in the Adelphi academic profile. With three degrees in philosophy from Harvard, he was committed to what he called academic excellence in the most classic meaning— the study of the liberal arts. To that, he welded a belief in a corporate model of governance that considered faculty as employees rather than partners. He further believed in institutional governance by a self-perpetuating board of trustees. His vision for Adelphi was summed up in a marketing piece that raised eyebrows: "Harvard, the Adelphi of Massachusetts."

From the outset a faculty group had communicated to the Adelphi board of trustees its concern about the new academic direction, stating that Adelphi had never had any pretensions to be a small Harvard. It feared that the seismic shift from what existed to what was envisioned was doomed to failure. The stage was set for conflict.

During the first three years of the Diamandopulos administration Middle States received enough complaints regarding the deteriorating relationship between him and his AAUP-organized faculty that its 1988 reaccredidation report included a caution regarding sensitivity to the issue of shared governance. The complaints continued. Thus, in 1990 my small team of Middle States visitors headed to Adelphi.

The president was my first interview. I found him to be charming, autocratic and totally committed to his belief that his was the correct vision for Adelphi. It was also very apparent that the alienation between faculty and administration was fast approaching mutual repudiation. In my exit interview, I suggested that his unionized faculty so obviously lacked a collegial relationship with the administration that the environment would inevitably preclude consensus unless he immediately reached out to change the operating ethos of the campus. His response, said most pleasantly, was in effect: "I will break the union and faculty and I will win." My rejoinder was "if you don't find a middle ground you may win, but it will be a Pyrrhic victory!"

A Complete Breakdown of Principles

As the situation at Adelphi worsened, it sadly became a media topic, fostered by a group known as the Committee to Save Adelphi that went public in 1995 following a faculty vote of 131-14 calling for the resignation of the president. The impact naturally led to admissions and financial difficulties; enrollment dropped from over 4,000 in l987 to 1,900 in 1997. Finally, in February of 1997, following years of complaints and a four-month review by the governing body for higher education in New York known as the Board of Regents, an unprecedented decision was made to replace eighteen of the nineteen Adelphi trustees, including Diamandopolus. The first action of the replacement trustees was to fire Diamandopolus as president.

Although the intervention of the regents caused concern that it would set a precedent for public oversight in the affairs of private colleges, the autonomy of the private sector was safeguarded because of the egregious circumstances leading to the intervention. The regents took action because the institution's board did not. Indeed the board had already exhibited a monumental lack of prudence in setting the president's compensation, which included a salary of $837,113 in academic year 1995-96, a severance contract of $3 million, a $1.2 million Manhattan apartment with an option to purchase at a discount, and a lavish expense account. Worse, numerous trustees had exclusive and lucrative business arrangements with the university. The regents pointed to "a complete breakdown of the principles of governance" at the institution.

Following the replacement of the board of trustees and the president, I was asked to chair a team for Middle States to determine the accreditation status of the university. The contrast between this visit and the last was extraordinary. With impressive new leadership, the entire Adelphi community was enthused and committed to, as one professor said, "bring it back from the brink of extinction." The positive site report called for continued accreditation with periodic updates.

Although Adelphi flourishes today, it very nearly imploded, and the blame goes to many. The lessons learned pertain universally to all of higher education:

1. Because trustees have the legal and fiduciary responsibly for a university, they must not only be conversant with the mission of the institution but understand, endorse and support it.

2. If dramatic change to mission is undertaken it must be done in an open and collegial way. The understanding, if not the assent, of the faculty is critical if a substantive academic change is to be successful.

3. Institutions must clearly understand and be comfortable with the educational philosophy of a presidential candidate before an appointment is made.

Engagement within Pennsylvania

One of my most challenging statewide chairmanships was with the Pennsylvania Association of Colleges and Universities (PACU) in the early nineties when the organization, which had been formed as a cooperative venture between public and private sectors of higher education, was deteriorating from lack of trust among its members.

The organization of higher education in Pennsylvania is cumbersome with a structure historically representative of political accommodation rather than pedagogical interests. Many contend that, given a blank sheet of paper, no one would design what exists in Pennsylvania! For example, the overlapping offerings of the public sector are numerous and costly but, given the antecedents of the sector's growth, I question whether there shall ever be the political will to make changes.

Penn State, Temple, Pittsburgh and Lincoln Universities receive annual funding from the commonwealth. Penn State University (PSU) is the flagship institution with over 45,000 students on its main campus and 40,000 on its 23 branch campuses. Since 1990, when it joined the Big Ten Conference, it has changed to fit the conference model: a main campus with undergraduate honors programs, specialized degrees and graduate research programs. Many feel the corporate redesign was an attempt by Penn State to have the main campus seen as a more academically elite campus by pushing lesser students onto the branch campuses. Its simultaneous program growth on the branch campuses, including the introduction of graduate programs under Penn State credentialing, has also created animosity among many educators and politicians who consider it duplicative and unnecessary.

Other publicly funded institutions serving the same population include the community colleges, which are funded by both state and local taxes, and the schools within the State System of Higher Education (SSHE). Organized in 1981 from what was once a collective of teacher's colleges, SSHE receives a substantial part of its budget from the state and now has over 100,000 students.

Only the independent sector competes for students without direct state aid. Its state assistance comes through financial aid programs for students; good for the students, good for the taxpayers. The 94 privates comprise the larger percentage of colleges and universities in the Commonwealth of Pennsylvania. The ratio in a majority of the other states favors the publics.

Pennsylvania's general assembly years ago made a conscious effort to have the publics and privates work together in compiling funding requests. While this approach made it easier for the legislature to deal with higher education, particularly private higher education, it did nothing to promote equity between sectors.

PACU for many years was the organization that attempted to rein in the dreams of both sectors and have them function cooperatively. The effort was reasonably successful until the mutual trust began to dissipate in an increasingly difficult funding climate. State appropriations to higher education as a percentage of state budget were declining, leading to deleterious reactions within PACU. First, the public sector decried the privates' access to student aid programs such as PHEAA and AIG. Then Penn State countered by operating like a private, introducing increased tuition and fund-raising initiatives. This change in operational style increasingly concerned the independent sector. The sense of cooperative trust within and between sectors became strained and PACU became increasingly ineffective. The effort to keep it alive grew more and more difficult.

Independent Colleges and Universities: an Association

As chairman in 1991, I found myself in the midst of a sea change in relationships and realized the long-term viability of the organization was in question. As part of the leadership of the independent sector, I and others concluded it was time for the privates to become more aggressive. We were a vibrant sector of higher education, enrolling 50 percent of the undergraduate students and awarding 61 percent of the graduate and professional degrees, but were without our own representative organization. It was time for a change!

Once the independent sector elected to establish the Association of Independent Colleges and Universities of Pennsylvania (AICUP) we were fortunate to have an officer at the National Endowment of the Humanities express interest in becoming our CEO. Brian Mitchell was a savvy New Englander who understood the need for the private sector to become a political player. As a member of the committee I heartily endorsed the decision to hire him in October 1990 for his credentials were perfect: a Ph.D. historian with faculty experience and, of supreme importance, a fellow Bostonian!

Under Brian Mitchell's leadership, AICUP became a political force in Harrisburg. Never timid, Brian was so articulate and intelligent that he was able to press issues frequently besting the leadership of the public sector. He brought energy, vision and an ability to build consensus among his colleagues that set the tone for the independent sector as it exists today. He subsequently went on to become president of Washington and Jefferson College and is now the president of Bucknell University.

During his term at W&J, Mitchell returned to an AICUP annual meeting to introduce me as the recipient of the Michellini Award with sentiments that I still treasure:

> President Bruce has four qualities that I greatly admire.

He can pick talent and nurture it. . . . Bob also enjoys the idiosyncratic life of a college president more than anyone else I have met. He showed me that being a college president could be fun if you approached it in the right way. . . . President Bruce has a clear vision of who he is, what his talents are and makes no apologies for them. . . . Bob once gave me a great piece of advice: 'you don't always have to be the smartest guy in the room, and if you are, don't tell them right away.' Further, Bob Bruce is an amazing teacher, an incredible consensus builder who can conceptualize a project and see it through to completion. And finally, Bob is a loyal friend – painfully frank sometimes . . . and someone you could always count on to lead. He is the very definition of the guy you want next to you in the foxhole.

The Challenge to Tax Exemption (for Some)

In the 1990's, several municipalities attempted to generate revenue by challenging the tax-exempt status of colleges and universities. A well documented case, Washington and Jefferson College v. the City of Washington, was settled in favor of the college by the state supreme court. However, while the case was pending, Philadelphia, Pittsburgh and other municipalities nationwide joined the bandwagon by attempting to tax the services they provided.

I was appointed to a Pennsylvania committee comprised of statewide representatives of both municipalities and nonprofits that was convened in Harrisburg. We were asked to identify ways in which municipalities could be reimbursed for services without the necessity of redefining the tax-exempt status of nonprofits. A curiosity of the dialogue was the selective nature of the challenges to tax emption. The politicians failed to include churches, scouting troops, and all the other organizations that could raise the ire of taxpayers, also declaring that public sector colleges and universities, although engaged in exactly the same "unrelated business activities" as the independents, were exempt because they were public entities. It could not have been more obvious that the discussion was directed principally at private educational institutions and health systems – organizations that were perceived to have the deepest pockets and the least grassroots support.

Because the implications were substantial, many nonprofits were opposed to entering into any agreement requiring payment to a unit of government. However without an agreement, the cost of litigation would have been enormous, particularly in defending business activities engaged in by most nonprofits, and seen by the cities as unrelated to the primary mission. The final accord called for the not-for-profit to retain their tax exemptions in exchange for voluntary contributions to the host municipalities for services such as fire and police protection. To avoid any implication of taxation, the language was carefully crafted to read "voluntary contribution" instead of "payment in lieu of taxes," but the result was exactly the same.

The MAC: Crisis on My Watch

I offer one final example of the types of organizations with which presidents become involved, and yet another substantiation that a term as chairman of the board for any of them usually includes at least one crisis.

In 1993-94 during my chairmanship of the Middle Atlantic States Collegiate Athletic Association (MAC), ten member institutions withdrew to begin a new conference. The withdrawal of nearly half the original twenty-six members left a scheduling and organizational vacuum. We were able to hold the group together and successfully restructure the remaining sixteen schools into two conferences under the umbrella of the MAC. Since the conference had an automatic bid to the NCAA Division III football championship playoffs, appropriate alignment was crucial. The assignment of teams to either the new Commonwealth Conference or the new Freedom Conference was accomplished through the goodwill of the presidents who chose between the two based on conference and institutional needs; as much as possible, the distribution of institutions was based upon geographic location and historic relationships. Widener's assignment was decided when the president of Wilkes, Christopher Breisith, volunteered to move to the Freedom Conference provided Widener would schedule Wilkes each year in football because our geographic location was important to Wilkes for recruiting in the Philadelphia region. As a result, Albright, Elizabethtown, Juniata, Lebanon Valley, Messiah, Moravian, Susquehanna and Widener became the Commonwealth Conference while the Freedom included Delaware Valley, Drew, F.D.U.-Madison, King's, Lycoming, Scranton, Upsala, and Wilkes. To make the scheduling work I committed Widener to playing all of its games within the MAC each year, thus allowing other institutions to play one or two games outside of the conference—games significant to them for geographic reasons related to recruiting or because of historical rivalries. As a result of the reorganization, the MAC remained among the strongest in Division III.

Don't Hesitate

Among the most rewarding benefits of involvement with national, state and local organizations are the many personal friendships one develops while working for a common cause. In my case, the diversity of the independent sector from the very small to the very large, from the religious to the sectarian, ensured a unique and rich mix of colleagues. But whatever opportunities for political and social engagement are open to a president, he or she should follow the advice we invariably give to new students: The more you give, the more you (and your institution) get out of it!

Chapter 14

Commencement

A ritual at colleges and universities across the world is the celebration of graduation and the ceremony of commencement. Accompanying the conferral of diplomas is the address by a keynote speaker who for his or her willingness to impart the wisdom of the seasoned is awarded an honorary degree in recognition of intellectual, political or social accomplishments. The selection of a commencement speaker can be a minefield. Students always want a celebrity. Faculty like a scholar of unique achievement (oft times obscure except within a particular discipline) and the trustees usually favor a well-known business or political leader.

Devising a plan to deliver someone acceptable to at least one group involves tactics and strategy appropriate for a war room; the delivery of a "name" is even more complicated, often takes years, and can become a comic opera if the person succeeds in disgracing him- or herself between the school's initial invitation and the big day. Some larger universities pay a speaker's fee that guarantees the level of orator most people would like to hear. The speaker then also creates the basis for a major press event that in the minds of some is more important to a successful commencement than the number and quality of the graduates. It is a wonder that the majority of institutions – those with no money to spend on high profile speakers and so just cover expenses and award a degree *honoris causa* – are able to attract someone willing to give up a weekend in late May or early June to speak for twenty minutes to a sometimes inattentive audience of nearly minted bachelors, masters and doctoral candidates.

Without money for speaker compensation, the pool of interesting candidates shrinks dramatically. The focus more often than not centers on elected officials and business leaders, although successful alumni and parents of the graduates can be good choices, particularly among those who have become corporate or civic leaders.

The majority of speakers are sensitive to the special nature of the day for the graduates and their families. They appropriately share optimism, extol service to others and congratulate and celebrate the collegiate achievements of the untested future leaders sitting before them.

Widener had a broad range of talent and speakers (capable and less so) on the commencement platform during my years there. One the audience greatly appreciated was the Nobel Laureate economist from MIT, Paul Samuelson. His relationship with the University dated to the first of its Nobel Laureate Lecture Series, instituted with his address in the 1980s. Samuelson responded to my invitation by saying he didn't give commencement addresses because each time he would have to reach a new level of quality. However, he did accept honorary degrees and would give brief, appropriate thanks. Samuelson's accomplishments were such that I agreed.

In return for his honorary degree, he spoke eloquently for *five minutes*, thus drawing delighted applause from all assembled in the spring heat. Within his gracious remarks he asked the graduates to rise and face the stadium where families, spouses and friends were seated, and then to "now applaud those who made, through their financial support and love, this day possible." It was a special moment.

That moment also provided a line I used at many subsequent ceremonies for it accomplished two things. First, it made families and spouses feel special and second, it gave the students an opportunity to let off some energy before beginning the more serious portion of the ceremony.

Effective speech writing is an art. There are those who seem to have been born for the podium but for most, writing a speech is hard work, and the toughest one of all is the one that is to last twelve to fifteen minutes. I am sure that most people are unaware of the preparation time it takes for a twelve-minute speech. The speaker must have a strong beginning in which to set the stage for the heart of the message and then a strong conclusion that leaves the audience with something meaningful. Speaking for 45 to 60 minutes is relatively simple for there is time to develop several themes, use analogies and keep the audience entertained with stories as the message unfolds.

College presidents and others who speak frequently in public are always seeking themes and phrasing upon which to build. For me, finding a theme was the critical point in developing a speech. My desk had many files with notes on napkins, excerpts from other speakers, newspaper clippings and even "welcome to church" cards that had come in handy when the minister said something provocative in his sermon!

The Good and the Wearisome: Commencement Speakers

There are superb commencement speakers and there are the extraordinarily undistinguished. If you want to test someone's impact, ask at the next social gathering you attend if they remember who their commencement speaker was. The collective amnesia will startle you!

Supreme Court Associate Justice Sandra Day O'Conner delivered a wonderful speech at Widener in 1991 on the opportunities available for graduates, especially women. She related that when she graduated third in her 1952 class from Stanford University Law School, she was unable to find a job within the all-male bastion of major law firms.[1] She therefore opened an office over a shopping center in Phoenix, Arizona, where, she explained to the graduates, she took any and all cases that came through the door.

In 1981, she became the first woman appointed to the U.S. Supreme Court and a role model to several generations of women. Her importance to the judicial system stemmed from her centrist ideology as she cast the swing vote between her more liberal and conservative colleagues. The author of numerous important decisions, O'Connor became one of the most powerful women in America.

As I watched the rapt attention the graduating students gave to her remarks, I realized that the inequality and lack of inclusiveness she had encountered thirty years before were mere historical facts to these young women. Their world and the workplace they were entering were so substantially different from Justice O'Connor's early career that they took for granted the hard-won and extraordinary progress in the lives of American women, much of it due to the speaker before them.

Justice O'Connor came to the University through the efforts of Board Chairman Fitz Dixon who had met her two summers before in Maine. The evening before her address, Fitz and Edie Dixon hosted a dinner in her honor. When asked by one of the trustees in attendance how long she planned to speak, she said thirty minutes. To this someone suggested that thirty minutes might be too long. Early the next

---

[1] William H. Rehnquist was number one in the same class. I always wondered who was two and what happened to him or her.

morning, Fitz found Justice O'Connor at a desk. "I am," explained this sensitive woman, "reworking my remarks to shorten them."

Conversely, some speakers ignore time constraints with presumed impunity. The most infamous in this category was Faith Ryan Whittelsey, a Delaware County attorney who had been appointed ambassador to Switzerland by President Reagan. When I called Whittelsey in Switzerland to discuss her remarks, I suggested that fifteen to eighteen minutes would be appropriate. Commencement day was beautiful but unusually warm. As always, families began to fill the stadium in which the ceremony would be held long before the opening procession began. Thus, many would have been sitting in the sun at least an hour before Ambassador Whittelsey stood to deliver a very political speech of minimal interest to those awaiting a diploma. After twenty-five minutes, she said something akin to "as I near the conclusion of my remarks," which was greeted with hearty applause. She then proceeded to speak for another fifteen minutes! As she neared the forty-two minute mark, the chairman of the board uttered sotto voce, "it took one hundred sixty years to have a woman speaker here and after this it will be another one hundred sixty before the next one." His *voce* was not quite as *sotto* as he meant it to be; a female colleague sitting behind him smacked him with her program.

As the ambassador concluded her remarks to polite applause, a male baccalaureate candidate in the second row stood up and yelled "more, more!" As I hid my smile behind my program I thought of how much I love college students!

The Recycled Speech
Ron Brown, the first secretary of commerce and chairman of the Democratic National Committee in the Clinton administration, was commencement speaker at the School of Law in 1991, four years before his tragic death in an airplane crash in Bosnia. The occasion was a joyous one, for Secretary Brown's son was in the class of young lawyers graduating that afternoon.

His remarks were appropriately crafted although somewhat general in nature. As I watched him turn the pages of his speech I realized that each time he mentioned Widener by name, there was a deletion in his text. It was obvious he had given the same speech at another university or law school and had simply substituted Widener where appropriate. Well, why not?

My wife often suggested, as she observed me laboring over an address, "why not recycle one of your earlier speeches? I am sure the faculty won't remember and it is a different audience of students." I must confess that in the latter years of my presidency I did just that but always rewrote the opening and closing remarks. One can be original and creative just so many times.

The Controversial Dr. Watson

One of the most fascinating commencement speakers at Widener also became a cause célèbre among faculty. Dr. James D. Watson, who shared with Francis Crick the 1962 Nobel Prize in Physiology or Medicine for the discovery of the double-helix structure of DNA, became our 2001 commencement speaker thanks to then Chairman of the Board Leslie C. Quick, Jr. In response to my appeal for a scientist as speaker, Les had asked "how about Jim Watson?" "Watson of DNA?" I had asked, not knowing they had become friends as a result of Quick's support of Watson's work at Cold Spring Harbor Laboratory, NY.

When I knew the invitation had been accepted, I re-read Watson's controversial 1968 book *The Double Helix*.[2] Victor K. McElheny in his book *Watson and DNA* quotes *New York Times* reporter Nan Robertson's comment, "the book was fresh, arrogant, catty, bratty, and funny." (McElheny 2003, 143) After meeting the man, I thought it described Watson's approach to life: brash, honest, self-satisfied with his obvious genius and somewhat naïve about people.

At first the faculty approved the choice of Watson but within months it became embroiled in a controversy centered on Watson's October 2000 speech at Berkeley, an address perceived by some as anti-feminist and by others as having racial overtones. As the concerns spread across the internet, the faculty of the Center for Social Work Education, a unit of Widener's School of Human Service Professions, voted to protest Watson's appearance by leaving the ceremony before he

---

[2] At the time it was written, Harvard President Nathan Pusey instructed the Harvard University Press not to publish the book because it would be "to take sides in scientific dispute," an outrageous decision made even more astonishing by the fact that Watson was then a member of the Harvard faculty. The book is still in print today and has sold over a million copies.

received his honorary degree and returning when he finished his address. I met with the academic deans to discuss faculty concerns and the history of the invitation to Watson. They expressed support for his appearance at Widener, one saying, "Bob, the man is a giant in his field, is the faculty crazy?" Through the dean of SHSP, I then requested a meeting with the Social Work faculty, a rare invitation from a university president to a department faculty. I told them I was sensitive to their views but also to the best interests of a university whose president and trustees had invited a guest to speak. When the gathered faculty demonstrated to my satisfaction that they had done minimal research on either the alleged insensitivities at Berkeley, or other Watson controversies (and there were several), I said the meeting had a dual agenda: I wanted to understand why they were urging a boycott and they had to understand my position on the purpose of the ceremony and acceptable commencement behavior.

Following a collegial discussion in which the faculty expressed the need to make a visible statement against what they believed to be Watson's antagonism to the core values of their academic discipline (feminism, racial equality, etc.), I reminded them that they were contractually obligated to attend commencement unless specifically given permission not to do so. Then, in deference to their strongly held beliefs, I gave them that permission. I continued on, however, to say that if they attended then left before Watson's remarks, they would do so with decorum. Further, that if they attempted to return when his remarks were finished (as many planned to do), the campus security and the city police on duty would prevent their re-entry to the ceremony. They were stunned.

Most voted not to attend, a minority would attend then leave under the stipulated conditions. Most important, all understood that I felt commencement to be a celebration to honor the graduates and their families, not a forum for faculty to express views, whether political or social. There are other venues for that. An interesting sidebar to the controversy was that the Social Work dean announced she would attend and stay throughout as was, she felt, her obligation to the students. I acknowledged her wisdom then, and told her privately that had she decided otherwise, she would have been dismissed as dean; I firmly believe that as an administrator she had an obligation to enforce University policy and to support the decisions of the trustees, president and provost. Too many deans miss, or perhaps choose not to embrace, their dual responsibilities as both *us* and *them*.

The resolution of the fracas in Social Work did not end the controversy about Dr. Watson. Days before commencement, a computer science professor known for his espousal of liberal causes, took it upon himself to email Dr. Watson suggesting he reconsider his decision to attend the commencement at Widener. When I heard of this, my reaction was less than presidential.

Calmed down, I called Watson who assured me he had every intention of being in attendance and would fax me a copy of his remarks before speaking. He then exhibited his extraordinary self-confidence by suggesting that he arrive on campus early to have dinner with the faculty who had questioned his work and speech at Berkley. "I would enjoy having a dialogue with them," he said. I was bowled over: it was a brilliant idea! Despite their antagonism to Watson's Berkley address, invited faculty readily accepted and others called to request invitations. A professor of chemistry who had been one of the most outspoken against Watson was among the callers. When I asked why she wanted to have dinner with him, she replied with quintessential faculty logic, "How many times do you have the chance to dine with a Nobel Laureate?" After the event, I was told the dinner was most civil and that some faculty appeared to be in awe of their tablemate.

Jim Watson's visit to campus was particularly special since he was honoring a commitment he had made to Les Quick, who had died of cancer in March. He had been fond of Les and spoke warmly about him in his remarks.

As we waited for the academic procession to move from in front of Old Main to the campus green, I chatted with Dr. Watson about *Dr. Folkman's War* a book about the work of Dr. Judah Folkman at Harvard on angiogenesis, an approach to the treatment of cancer that involves cutting off the blood supply to cancer cells. Watson, who is deeply engaged in cancer research at Cold Stream, had been quoted as saying on the book jacket: "Judah Folkman's answer . . . has much too long been thought of as too simple to ever work. Now, however, a broad set of antiangiogenic agents based on Judah's ideas are coming on line. . . Our country's 'war against cancer' at last has found its general." To me, Watson said with a twinkle in his eye, "Judah Folkman will be remembered as the second most important Jew in history next to Jesus!" Later, he opined that with the exciting research in cancer, he thought there would be "a cure during your lifetime." (Cooke 2001)

The theme of this extraordinary individual's commencement address, ten rules for graduates, was presented in an appreciatively humorous (and non-controversial) dialogue that lasted exactly the right amount of time!

At the traditional luncheon served in tribute to the honorary degree recipients, Dr. Watson joined my family and Board Chairman David Oskin and his wife JoEllen at our table. While discussing the progress being made with various diseases, particularly cancer, Jim became deeply engaged in conversation with our daughter Kim regarding the genetics of Batten Disease, a rare neurological disorder that afflicted Kim's daughter, Betsy. The disease is so rare that the vast majority of scientists and medical professionals have never heard of it, but Watson not only knew of this ultimately terminal genetic condition, he discussed its pathology with Kim in a caring and intellectual way.

After lunch, he commented to me how impressed he was with Kim's knowledge and her approach to dealing with the terrible disease. This is an area, he stated, where gene therapy will eventually provide treatment and a cure.

Widener's First Lady Honored

For me, the real joy of the 2001 commencement was the recognition given to my wife. Judy received the honorary degree Doctor of Humane Letters in appreciation for her service to Widener over two decades. By recognizing her publicly, the Board of Trustees acknowledged the tremendous impact she had had upon the University. As I presented her with her degree I announced to the delight of the crowd that for the first time in my many years as a university president I was going to kiss an honorary degree recipient! In her response Judy was her usual sincere and gracious self. I proudly noted she received as much applause as did her co-recipient, the Nobel Prize winner James Watson, led of course by our children, Kim and Scott, and our grandchildren. Afterward, the grandchildren said they would call her "Dr. Mame" in the future. She said to me: "What was I doing on the same platform with Jim Watson?"

Justice William Rehnquist

William H. Rehnquist made two visits to Widener's School of Law. In 1982 as an associate justice of the U.S. Supreme Court he delivered the commencement address. In 1998 as chief justice he visited the Law

School to speak on his book *All the Laws But One,* a study of civil liberties in a time of war (Rehnquist 1998). Law professor Geoffrey Moulton, who had clerked for Rehnquist at the Supreme Court, extended both invitations. The honor of being selected to clerk on the Court is carried throughout the lives of those selected, and like most, Jeff had stayed in touch with his justice.

When Rehnquist accepted the second invitation, he suggested to Jeff that it would be nice to play some tennis, and also to attend the University's football game the next day. He preferred watching small college football to the big-time programs. Jeff's choices for a tennis foursome included Law Dean Arthur Frakt, an avid tennis player with a wry sense of humor. When Art asked, "do we have to let him win?" Jeff's response was most diplomatic. He said that the chief justice was very competitive and when the clerks played with him he seemed to always be on the winning side!

On Saturday, Judy and I hosted a luncheon for Chief Justice Rehnquist prior to a football game with Lycoming College. Among the guests were trustees, Widener Law professors, prominent lawyers, our children and several of our grandchildren (who thought meeting the chief justice would be cool!).

When Rehnquist walked into the room, he spied the children, Katie, Andy, and Courtney, and went right to them leaving everyone else waiting to be introduced until he could chat with the kids. As a grandfather, I suspect that he found them more interesting than lawyers or executives!

Sitting next to the chief justice during the game, I realized he knew football and was very interested in the players. The game was a thriller so it was with regret that midway through the fourth quarter with Widener in command, Rehnquist left with Jeff to catch his train back to Washington. "Let me know how it ends," he said.

I wrote on Monday, thanking him for visiting and congratulating him on the success of his book. I also suggested that had he stayed perhaps Lycoming would not have recovered an on-side kick in the final minutes to make an extraordinary comeback and win the game, fifteen to thirteen.

The Valedictorian

A long standing academic tradition is to have the undergraduate student with the highest grade point average, the valedictorian, speak at commencement. In theory it is a wonderful tradition; in practice it can be fraught with peril.

Occasionally, the most academically gifted undergraduate is an introvert, terrified at the mere thought of speaking before 6,000 people. At those times you hold your breath and smile through your own anxiety.

Once in a while, students attempt to use commencement as a forum to present political or social views. This was de rigueur during the late 1960s and early 70s, as was the hope to shock rather than inspire. At Bard College in the early 70s, I sat uncomfortably on the platform as a very gifted young woman punctuated her remarks with four-letter words. Indeed, that was the same year that the police arrived earlier in the proceedings and evacuated the tent because of a bomb threat. Although assuming it was a hoax – which it was – we all trooped out to make way for police and dogs. Enroute, a parent came up to me and said in a bemused way, "President Bruce, perhaps we should put the kids under the tent and see if it will go off!" The 60s and early 70s were a special time.

The tradition of the valedictory speech works best at a four-year liberal arts college. It begins to get problematic when a sizable number of graduate students are in attendance because the undergraduate message often loses its punch to the more mature.

One of the best speeches by a valedictorian I heard in my career was delivered at Widener in 1994 by Brian Taylor, a *summa cum laude* in Government and Politics with a GPA of 4.0. A very talented young man whose father had been a Widener football coach for twenty years, Brian had completed his baccalaureate studies in two and one-half years. Evoking the usual valedictorian themes, Brian spoke with sincerity:

> As we look ahead this morning with great trepidation to the world ahead, we must bear in mind exactly what it is that we want out of life. Riches may measure success, but riches come in many forms. The most valuable riches are those that bring happiness, and they should certainly be our goal in life. Looking at our faculty, I see a group of extraordinarily rich people – rich in both heart and soul. Such is a wealth that never depreciates and provides unlimited happiness to oneself and more importantly, to others. So let us

allow that definition of rich to be the Widener faculty's final lesson to us all, and let us utilize our great abilities, honed during our years here, to achieve a similarly brilliant treasure of happiness. . . .

As we enter the real world we are being overwhelmed with pessimism toward both our generation and its prospects for success. We have been labeled Generation X, for some feel that we are not even worthy of a name. But I say we can and will prove these soothsayers to be dead wrong. You see, the world into which we are about to enter is permeated by claims of victim hood and excuses for failure rather than self-assertion and opportunities to succeed. It is up to us to put in the work and change things around. Now you may feel as though you don't know enough yet and that you aren't ready, but this is quite natural. Actually, understanding the limitations of your knowledge is a sure sign of an education. This is the great irony of college, you enter as a teenager who thinks he knows everything, and you leave as an adult who feels he knows nothing. . . .

Commencement as a Metaphor

Planning for a commencement on a university campus is somewhat analogous to the military planning to take over a small country. Meetings begin early in winter with a university-wide committee consisting of representatives from virtually every component of the university. Chairing this entourage at Widener for many years was Thomas Carnwath, assistant to the president, who took the annual rituals to the level of an art form.

Thousands of chairs were set up on the campus lawns both in Chester and Wilmington. Simultaneously the Schwartz Center in Chester was set with its maximum of 3,200 chairs, plus platform, and wired with closed circuit television for feeds to the basketball court. Students were issued as many tickets as they wanted for an outdoor ceremony but only two for inside the Schwartz Center, creating vocal family hassles that sometimes became a matter for the security personnel. The decision to move the morning ceremony inside or stay outside had to be made at 6 AM when I met Tom, the provost and Director of Maintenance Dick Eusden on the campus. While looking at the dawn sky, asking "what do you think guys?" I was always reminded of the wonderful Norman Rockwell painting of a group of baseball umpires standing on a field looking at the sky while raindrops fell.

Through some magic or good dumb luck, we seldom made the wrong call in twenty years.

The Law School always seemed blessed. Though the chaplain often kidded that he was "in sales, not management," even when it rained all morning, by 1 PM the weather would clear and the ceremony could be held outside. However, on the very few times it did rain, moving the law ceremony to the Schwartz Center on the Main Campus was truly chaotic. There was an element of despair when the students had to travel to a campus they did not know in Chester, Pa., even though the campuses were only twenty minutes from one another.

Even on the most beautiful days, our multiple campuses made the coordination of logistics significantly more difficult. Everything that went into staging one event was magnified threefold and timing – the hardest facet of all to control – was absolutely critical because two of the three ceremonies (Chester and Wilmington) were held on the same day. The morning event was always followed by the luncheon for the honorary degree recipients. The four o'clock Law School ceremony in Delaware was always preceded by a photo session. Since many of the trustees and I attended all of these, usually having to change clothes before lunch and again before driving down Interstate-95 for the second ceremony, the clock became a slave master.

Carnwath, the major domo of the Main Campus commencement and the ringmaster of the whole circus, could be seen rushing about, walkie-talkie in his ear, sporting a straw boater with Widener's colors of blue and gold around the brim. Since Tom is 6' 1" and large he was easy to spot!

The Harrisburg Campus ceremony was held on Sunday morning in a beautiful art deco auditorium owned by the Commonwealth of Pennsylvania and located next to the state capitol. It was a theatrical setting that reminded one of Disney World. By the time I arrived home Sunday afternoon, I had traveled over 200 miles among the three campuses and shaken hands with more than 1,600 graduates.

Despite its growth over the years, Widener retained its tradition of awarding each degree individually. The trick to a timely flow was to keep the line of students moving rapidly; five on the ramp at all times, constant movement past the president to a camera, then off the platform. A system of faculty marshals in headphones helped make it all work. The lineup by school was checked time and again prior to the procession. The students' names were rechecked as they approached the ramp leading onto the stage. In case someone was out of order or the appropriate diploma was not in place, each graduate was greeted at the top of the ramp by the provost who shook the student's hand and held on until the name was called by the graduate's dean. The registrar was responsible for getting the correct degree into the hands of the president in the same three seconds that any corrections to the roll call were recorded on the master list by an assistant provost and handed to the dean who was even then reading the next name. I, in a robotic swing of my arm, never looking back to where the registrar sat with boxes of diplomas, had a scroll placed in one hand while shaking the student's hand with the other, said congratulations and turned to the next recipient. Elapsed time per graduate: twelve seconds! It was an extraordinary exercise of eye, ear and hand coordination by everyone involved – all in front of 6,000 people.

The degrees were awarded by the school or college with the names announced by the appropriate dean. The School of Engineering was always an adventure since many of the students, especially graduate students, hailed from India, Thailand or China. The dean, a native of Maryland via a long stint in West Virginia, tried valiantly but many students were not sure they had graduated when they heard their names read, and quite a few friends cheered too late.

The dean of nursing, who normally spoke relatively fast, would often get on a roll with names spewing out of her mouth so quickly the parade across the platform looked as it someone had pushed a fast-forward button. I would turn to her and say, "Marge, exhale," and on we'd go.

I always asked out of politeness if the commencement speaker wished to shake hands with the students. Veterans of the game declined, a few stood for a brief time. But Tom Ridge, then Governor of Pennsylvania, stood and shook the hand of every graduate and clearly enjoyed every moment. Tall and charming, Ridge was attractive to the point that one female master's candidate said to me as she took her diploma, "I always thought you were good-looking but he is better looking than you!"

Despite the controlled chaos on the platform, the parents and students loved the personal presentation of each graduate. Even with the growth in the number of doctoral students to 60-plus, each of whom had to each be hooded (20 seconds per student), the entire Main Campus ceremony graduated nearly 1,000 men and women, incorporated speeches by the valedictorian and honorary degree recipients, and ended in under two hours and fifteen minutes.[3]

Two of the many special ceremonies that led up to commencement day were the School of Nursing's Nightingale service, and the ROTC commissioning ceremony. Nightingale signaled the passage from student to nurse, marked by the first wearing of the traditional white uniform and cap. A beautiful ceremony that began with a procession to the strains of the Pachelbel's Canon in D, it was concluded by the lighting of individual candles and the nurses' recitation of the Nightingale pledge.

The ceremony in which ROTC graduates were commissioned as second lieutenants in the U.S. Army was also held the day before commencement. For many years, relatives or friends pinned the bars on the new officers in the courtyard of Independence Hall in Philadelphia. It was very special to have the hall where the founding fathers issued the Declaration of Independence and wrote the Constitution as a backdrop, and to have tourists and passersby become extended members of the Widener community, if only for a few moments.

Commencement day is a joyous occasion for students and parents, a day of celebration of achievement on which faculty, too, can bask in intellects broadened by their skill. At Widener, it is a day of pride for all employed at the University including administrative personnel, departmental secretaries, and a maintenance staff who shared the pleasure of being integral and genuinely important to the enterprise. The sense of community comes together in the metaphor that is commencement.

---

[3] The football coach often joked that he could use Tom Carnwath who, following commencement each year, repeatedly viewed the videotape of the event many times, assessing the timing of each segment of the ceremony and the performance of the academic deans.

Chapter 15

Friends and Colleagues: Board of Trustees

Boards of directors, or trustees, are the designated legal entity with the responsibility for and jurisdiction over the affairs of a university. Widener's Board Bylaws state: "Except as otherwise provided by law or these Bylaws, all powers, business and affairs of the Corporation shall be exercised and managed by or under the authority and direction of the Board. . . . The Board shall elect the President of the Corporation, who shall conduct the affairs of the Corporation within the guidelines designated by the Board." (Widener 2001, sec. III, 3)

The definition of the authority of the president reads: "The President shall be the chief executive officer of the Corporation, and a voting member of all Committees of the Board. The President shall discharge all duties pertaining to this office, and shall have overall responsibility, subject to the Board, for the operation of the Corporation, to include but not be limited to instructional programs, faculty, finance and budget, planning, marketing, public relations, and development. The President shall be responsible for the actions of all other persons to whom the execution of Corporation policy may be delegated." (Widener 2001, sec. XIV, 11)

The language pertaining to the responsibilities of directors is quite similar among all for-profit or not-for-profit boards. It is the relationship among the CEO, the board, and its chair that distinguishes the organizational structure. Widener Board Chairman Fitz Eugene Dixon, Jr. used to say that a board has three basic functions: "to hire the president, to set policies and assist in their implementation, and if it doesn't work, to fire the president!"

That may succinctly define the relationship between the board and the president, but there are two conditions that can make or break a presidency. First, board chairs bring to the task their unique skills and experiences and the leadership style is invariably a reflection of what made them successful in their business and personal lives. The rapport between a president and trustees, particularly the board chair, is the key element in creating a productive working relationship. Without a trusting and candid working environment the implementation of long range plans can be arduous, and the day-to-day management of the university uncomfortable. The psychology of working with a board chair depends on finding the best approaches and means of communication for the particular personality. It is an acquired skill that is crucial to the success of a president.

The second condition is to know and be comfortable with how far you will go in compromising to reach consensus. The line may or may not be articulated, but the board should know that you have thresholds you will not cross.

Board Composition

The mandate to public corporate boards is simple: enhance shareholder value in a competitive and ethical manner. Nonprofit boards are largely reflective of organizational interests and the definition of "shareholder value" is more nuanced and less definitive than simply an adherence to financial outcomes. In most cases board members are individuals who have an interest in the mission of the organization or are representative of the community in which the organization resides. The composition of a social service board will usually be notably different from that of a museum or orchestra.

Boards in private education are most often a combination of business and industry leaders, alumni, parents or past parents, and academic leaders. A Dixon dictum for potential board members was to seek someone with "time, talent and treasure," meaning a willingness to attend meetings, do committee work, develop an appreciation of the university's structure, and provide financial support.

To establish a balanced board, first create the profile of an ideal board then recruit individuals with the requisite skills; not easy, but this responsibility should be shared by the chairman, board members, and CEO. The critical components for board membership are some combination of professional skills, particularly financial acumen, political and corporate contacts, academic reputation, entrepreneurial thinking combined with sound business judgment, integrity, commitment, and access to wealth. So, too, are gender and racial background, but forcing membership to fill a politically correct profile is inappropriate and does not in the long run enhance the effectiveness of a board.

Why They Join

Successful individuals join boards to share expertise, to learn, and in the case of university trustees, to be a part of an enterprise that is doing important things for society. It is quintessentially American to have people volunteer and concomitantly feel privileged to be asked to do so.

There is an inclination in most organizations to spend much of a board meeting on financial matters. It is a natural instinct since such a large part of any operation is driven by the ability to finance the business of the organization. Numbers are not abstract; they do not require epistemological knowledge to understand, nor do they ever fail to inform a discussion with a rationale for decision making. In short, numbers provide a comfort level for many board members.

However, many trustees join university boards to experience something different. They look forward to hearing from the provost and deans about academic issues and student-related themes and concerns. To that end, Widener's chief academic officer, in concert with the chair of the board's Academic Committee, reported regularly at board meetings. Periodically special presentations by faculty and program deans were also scheduled.

On one occasion, the head of ROTC (Reserve Officer Training Corps), a U.S. Army lieutenant colonel, was invited to discuss the role of ROTC on campus and more globally in the construct of today's military. The conversation was far reaching, triggered by many board members who had experienced ROTC as undergraduates and later served in the military.

Other presentations by faculty explaining the nature of their research and how it interfaced with their teaching and work with students never failed to produce applause and subsequent discussion on how impressed the board members were with the depth of the University and the intellectual capacity of its faculty.

The Trustees' Obligation

The success of private sector institutions rests on many factors but key among them is financial stability. Directors should understand their responsibility to donate at a level that helps maintain a position of financial constancy. The ability of the members to give from personal resources or to provide appropriate introductions to others with wealth is invaluable.

I recall a visit to MBNA with Widener Trustee and Sun Company

Senior Vice President and General Counsel Don Walsh. A contemporary of MBNA's CEO Charles Cawley at Georgetown University and a member of the same men's chorus, Don had made the appointment through his personal connections. The corporate headquarters, located in the City of Wilmington near our Delaware Campus, employed a number of Widener graduates as well as current students in part-time positions, which made the rationale for asking for an MBNA gift to Widener easier; a request for corporate support is substantially improved if a quid pro quo exists. However, without Don Walsh, the opportunity to have a conversation with the CEO would have been improbable. Ultimately, the meeting was delightful with Walsh and Cawley reminiscing about Georgetown, several Jesuit professors, and class contemporaries. [1]

The other senior MBNA executives at the meeting were well informed about how many Widener graduates and students worked for them and the role the University played in the state of Delaware. The staffs of both teams had set the table well.

At an appropriate point I began to make the case for support, something all presidents are expected to do at anytime, anywhere. Their CEO interrupted me to say that they were prepared to make a $1 million contribution over three years to support financial aid for students. They also would provide summer internships for Law School students and scholarship-based summer positions for undergraduates as sales representatives. The condition of the gift was that it support minority students from Delaware, preferably from the Wilmington area.

The commitment was a win-win. The University would steer good students who might stay with the company upon graduation for summer placements at MBNA. MBNA would also be meeting one of its corporate goals of social responsibility to minority students in the city and state while Widener would increase its ability to recruit and assist needy students.

On the return to Widener's campus, an elated Don asked, "is it always that easy?" Laughingly I told him, "No!" This gift was from a corporation that had done its homework. The decision makers knew the

---

[1] MBNA was a bank holding company prior to being acquired by Bank of America in 2006. Founded in 1982, its name was an acronym for Maryland Bank, National Association. After 1991, it was the world's largest independent credit card issuer, specializing in affinity cards.

importance of the firm's relationship with the University and its own corporate policies regarding support of community based institutions and of minorities. Each of these issues was further enhanced by the many supportive documents provided by the Widener Development Office. Most critical to the process was Don Walsh. The visit came about as a result of his acquaintance with the CEO and his willingness to use that relationship to "open the door."

Networks are invaluable assets trustees bring to a board. There are many stories about board members who have not only identified new avenues of financial support but have made introductions for speakers, honorary degree recipients and political contacts who can assist with sensitive legislative issues. The ability to seek assistance from trustees who are personal friends of, or substantial contributors to, political figures is a valuable resource that can produce major benefits for a private university.

In today's society, those joining a board must understand, as Fitz Dixon use to say, "Board members need to give, get, or get off!" Not all board members are comfortable in asking for money but most are willing to provide entree for the CEO or fundraising staff. The same applies to their use of political contacts.

I was astonished at how many of my presidential colleagues felt it unseemly to become politically engaged and even more concerned if their boards were asked to wield political influence. To me, that was ignoring a major asset.

Employee/Board Communication

The Widener board assigns to the president the exclusive right to convey communications from any employee, a useful policy for eliminating splinter groups or the irate from directly approaching board members. However, it also presupposes the president's ability to fairly apprise both sides about an issue and to present an appropriately balanced case to the board. All parties must feel comfortable that issues are being presented fairly and factually. This comfort level can be enhanced by inviting staff and faculty members to participate occasionally in board committee discussions. The formal and informal conversations that occur in committee settings provide trustees with a broadened perspective. Alternatively, trustees should be encouraged to attend campus functions. For example Dixon, as chairman, knew all senior staff members, deans, and many faculty from attendance at meetings and events.

From these contacts and from time spent casually speaking with students and staff, he fully understood the campus environment.

Faculty and staff must feel that their concerns are being heard at the local level and carried forward to the appropriate vice president who will, if the issue is not resolved in the structural process, see that it is given a fair hearing by the CEO and if necessary, by the board. I know of no methodology or structure other than a shared responsibility that can guarantee a positive outcome to communication concerns. It is imperative, however, that the CEO and faculty work together with mutual respect and trust. Without them, the system may engender frustration, anger and faculty demoralization.

Among Fitz Dixon's many strengths as a board chair, one of the most important was his ability to make clear to board members that it is the CEO's role, not theirs, to manage the daily life of the University. Micro-management by board members, even with good intentions, is counter productive at best and destructive at worst. Trustees, especially those who are alumni and have special knowledge and relationships with faculty, coaches, et al. must be conscious of the line between setting policy and managing policy. The same is true, of course, for all non-profit boards, although much depends on the culture of the organization and the historical relationship of the board to the institution. One often finds in health systems or hospital boards a blurring of lines since physicians sit on the governing boards with other members who are often their patients.

When I first became a member and then chairman of a large medical center, I was astonished to receive calls about policy directly from physicians and staff. My response was always: "Have you discussed this with the CEO? If not, I would urge you to do so." After becoming chairman, I worked hard at having all employees and physicians understand that it was the CEO who should be the recipient of inquiries about policy, not individual members of the board. One would be naïve to think communications between individuals will not occur, but the construct for proper forwarding of information pertinent to organizational decisions should be clearly understood.

The line between a board member's interest versus his or her micro-management should be carefully monitored. During my presidency, an uncomfortable situation developed in the School of Business. The dean had established the position of executive in residence to expose students to distinguished, retired businesspersons who would offer informal mentoring and teach a seminar or course on leadership. One year, board members filled the position with the result that some faculty, being the intelligent people they are, saw an opportunity to influence a conveniently available trustee regarding campus policy.

Unlike executives in residence who had no emotional ties to the University, the board members spent much more time on campus than necessary, even dining regularly with faculty. Within months, they were querying me about merit salary policies. Their opinions could only have derived from conversations with several professors who disagreed with the administration's position. The irony of the situation was that, like many very successful people who are used to assuming they are right, the trustees were blind to the possibility of their own manipulation.

After some months of listening to the two trustees' growing dissatisfaction and their gratuitous concern that I did not understand the issues of the moment, I had several very candid conversations with each of them ending with strongly suggesting they retreat from their close relationships with faculty. The conversations were held with the knowledge and support of the chairman.

I am convinced that the underlying reason for both men's loss of effectiveness as trustees was their loss of objectivity. They overstepped both the conventions and expectations of board membership.

The dean of business who also felt pressured by the faculty/trustee relationships stated that he would never again recommend a trustee for the executive in residence position. I shared with him that such a recommendation would never again be approved! One evening, after both trustees had left the board, Fitz Dixon smiled and said to me, "in all the time you have been president your instincts and decision making have been correct, except in approving two trustees to be executives in residence." He was right.

Fitz Eugene Dixon, Jr., Exemplary Board Chairman

Fitz Dixon was a board chairman with substance. He understood his role and had the financial and political clout to make things happen. The heir to the Widener family fortune, he was a native Philadelphian who had spent his adult life involved with organizations in and around the city as a board member and director. He brought reputation and gravitas to the position and was loyal to the institutions he directed and used his wealth wisely. His special disposition toward Widener stemmed from the school's adoption of his family name during the transition from PMC Colleges.

Dixon was the quintessential fan of both collegiate and professional sports. The difference between Fitz and others was that he could afford to *own* teams. At various times he was owner or part-owner of nearly all Philadelphia's professional teams, the Phillies, Eagles, Wings, Flyers. In 1976 he became the owner of the Philadelphia 76ers – later winners of the 1983 National Basketball Association championship. When asked "why basketball?" the man who admitted to knowing very little about the sport was quoted in *Sports Illustrated* as saying with a laugh, "I guess I bought the basketball team because I hate soccer and this was all that was left" (SI 1978). With humor, Fitz admitted that one of his favorite stories was told by Pat Williams, then the Sixers' general manager. On informing the team management that Julius Erving was available to them, Fitz responded, "Who is Julius Erving?" Williams said, "The Babe Ruth of basketball." Fitz may have forgotten the reply for shortly afterward at a luncheon, he announced that he had just purchased a player for $6 million called Dr. J adding, "I hope he's good."

As chairman, Dixon had as passionate an interest in the Widener athletic programs as in his professional teams. He followed the Pioneers faithfully, getting to know many of the student athletes personally. He rarely missed a home football game and often accompanied me to away games. I readily admit that the informal conversations enroute to games were extremely helpful in developing an understanding of each other's thinking and, thus, a meeting of the minds on policy issues for the University. The first meeting of the minds – on a subject far less momentous than policy – occurred at an NCAA football playoff game in Ithaca; it was a story he told fondly for many years.

It was 1975, my first year at Widener, when Judy and I joined a small group traveling to the playoff on the Dixons' airplane. When we arrived, no one had saved us seats so we all sat on the five-yard line, obviously not good enough for the visiting board chairman. I accompanied him to the fifty-yard line and engaged a security guard in conversation while I motioned for Fitz to start up the stairs toward the press box. As Fitz neared his goal, the guard said, "you might as well go up too since your chairman is already there." It was freezing that afternoon. At the end of the first quarter, Fitz complained of the cold so I produced from layers of clothing a bottle of cognac that had been purchased at lunch but left on the table and said, "here, warm up." He laughed with the rejoinder, "You are presidential material!"

Fitz was a consensus builder. He was not without strong opinions, which he expected to be heard and heeded, but he willingly listened to me on the potential positives and negatives of an initiative before deciding his position. Once he reached a decision, he would direct discussion to conclude the issue as he thought best for the University.

One of my favorite recollections of Fitz Dixon was a comment he made to me regarding the success of a racehorse owned by Jim Hirschmann '82BS and Tony Britton '82BSB, two young men with whom Fitz had become acquainted during their collegiate years at Widener. In 1993, for $13,500, they bought a two-year-old mare named TwoNinetyJones who earned close to $400,000 in winnings and is now a broodmare in Kentucky.[2] After the horse won a handicap for three-year-olds at Santa Anita, Fitz (owner of seventy-plus thoroughbreds, member of the family that had founded Hialeah racetrack, and long-time chair of the Pennsylvania Racing Commission) said in appreciation: "I spend millions on horses and those kids are doing better than I am with *one* damn horse!"

During the critical transitional years from PMC to Widener, Dixon was of incalculable value as chairman. His social status and political involvement made it possible for him to attract individuals to the board with intelligence, talent and financial depth. Virgil Kauffman, Joseph Boettner, George Strawbridge Jr., John Ware, Andy Pew, and Nick Trainer were fascinating and accomplished individuals. All came aboard at Fitz's invitation and were instrumental in the survival and success of the institution.

A Few Remarkable Men

Veteran trustee Virgil Kauffman, legendary in the field of aerial photography and photogrammetry, was an early pioneer in flying with over a million miles in the pilot's seat during his career. Credited with developing aerial mapping techniques used during World War II by the Allied bombing command, and the use of the aerial magnetometer to locate oil deposits in the Middle East, he had been with Aero Service from 1924 until retiring as its president in 1961. The Society of Exploration Geophysicists's highest award is the Kauffman Medal.

Kauffman didn't stop contributing to scientific achievement on re-

---

[2] The curious name is for the breeder Jack Jones, who quipped when he golfed "this one will go 290 yards!"

tirement. It was he who realized that for 200 years expeditions had been searching in the wrong place for the salvage from Capt. James Cook's HMS *Endeavour*. He headed the 1969 expedition sponsored by the Philadelphia Academy of Natural Sciences that located the cannons and iron jettisoned by Cook to lighten his load after the ship ran aground off the Great Barrier Reef of Australia.

Judy and I accompanied Virgil to a meeting in New York the year he was president of the Explorers Club, an international organization with membership open only to individuals recognized as having achieved a pioneering feat. At the reception, we overheard Kauffman say to the U.S. astronauts who had landed on the moon, "I bet you miss the days when you flew the aircraft rather than a computer." As the astronauts were first and foremost all military pilots, he had found an immediate source of conversation. When I last saw him, Virgil was in his late eighties and failing in health, but still alert and gracious. Les Quick and I sat in front of the fire at his farm as he regaled us with stories of his extraordinary adventures, including flying under the George Washington Bridge on a dare. "You couldn't get away with it today," he smiled, "but I would *love* to do it all over again!"

Among other trustees with interesting vocations or avocations were George Strawbridge, Nick Trainer, John Ware and Eric Chung. George W. Strawbridge, Jr. was a member of the families that founded Campbell Soup Company and the retailers Strawbridge and Clothier. Holder of a Ph.D. from the University of Pennsylvania, George was an academician in Latin American Studies as well as a very astute businessman and director of several banks. He was instrumental in the consolidation and growth of numerous major financial institutions. In addition, Strawbridge owned Augustin Stables and was president of both the Thoroughbred Owners and Breeders Association and the National Steeplechase Association. His keen interest in sports led him to become a partner in the Buffalo Sabres National Hockey League franchise and an owner of the Tampa Bay Rowdies, a professional soccer team.

Alumnus and trustee Nick Trainer '64BS was president of Sartomer, a chemical company that was a U.S. subsidiary of the French energy giant, TOTAL S.A. During most of his years on the Widener board, Nick traveled to Paris several times a month. "I often wonder," he would say, "if my French counterparts really understand what I do on weekends." Nick was a corporate president who was also a football official for the NCAA Big East; the résumé for his second career includes officiating at the Rose Bowl.

John Ware, the distinguished two-time congressman, telephoned after my selection as president to congratulate me, saying, "now I plan to remain on the board. I wasn't going to if they'd selected the other fellow." As chairman of the American Water Company, at that time the largest privately held water company in the United States, he was most welcome to stay!

The Board of Trustees was also fortunate to have Eric Chung, one of America's foremost architects, join the membership after he had been commissioned to design several campus buildings. Eric's service as a trustee coincided with my administration's development of the first official campus footprint. He was enormously helpful in guiding the design of much of the campus planning and structures that fulfilled the vision.

For an institution undergoing a name change and repositioning in the marketplace, having the presence of non-alumni trustees who lent their reputations to the process was invaluable. Non-graduates Jack Schmutz and Don Walsh, general counsels and senior vice presidents of the Dupont Company and Sun Company respectively, brought depth and commitment to the board. Additionally, Connie Girard-diCarlo, the first woman president of a division of Aramark, served for many years as the chair of the Academic Committee. She was insightful in her questioning and unabashed in asking the unstated, difficult question. Peter Mattoon, managing partner of Ballard, Spahr, Andrews and Ingersoll, was also invaluable to the board. Larry Buck, long-time provost and an accomplished scholar often remarked to me that Peter Mattoon was one of the most intelligent and perceptive individuals he had ever met. Peter's questions about academic issues, always intellectually probing, simultaneously intrigued and exasperated the provost; their relationship over many years was a splendid one.

All of these trustees and many others served with pleasure under Fitz Eugene Dixon, Jr., a model board chairman. He passed away in August, 2006 at the age of 82.

A Change of Chairman

My second board chair, Leslie C. Quick, Jr.'50BS was an extraordinarily gifted person who had attended Pennsylvania Military College as a WWII veteran, and was fond of telling the story of how he came to enroll. Like so many others seeking to attend college on the G.I. Bill in late 1945 and 1946, he had found that colleges, unable to meet the extraordinary demand for admission, were turning veterans away. But when a friend told him PMC in Chester, Pennsylvania was still admitting veterans, this New Yorker "jumped on the train to Chester and was interviewed and admitted by Clarence Moll, then the admissions dean."

Out of such a serendipitous happenstance began a lifelong relationship between the man and the institution. Les joined the Board of Trustees in 1980 and served as chairman from 1985 to 1987 when Dixon elected to step down as chair and Quick was invited to accept the helm. From the perspective of my role as CEO it was a seamless transition. Fitz remained on the board as chairman emeritus so we kept his counsel and Les brought a different style to the position of board chairman.[3]

When Les took his company public on the New York Stock Exchange in the early 1980s, I was invited to serve as one of the outside directors of Quick & Reilly. In typical Quick style, the three outside directors were me, his attorney, and a friend of many years who had assisted him during the lean times. The remaining directors were family members and company colleagues.

As the individual who had created the discount brokerage business and thereby changed the investment industry, Les was a combination of risk taker and fiscal conservative. He had one of the keenest financial minds I have ever encountered. His ability to read financial data and balance sheets occasionally gave our financial vice presidents, David Eckard and later Joe Baker, heartburn. They both knew to expect that after Les was told the philosophic and academic rationale for a project, he would look at them and say, "show me the numbers."

It was always important to point out any controversial issues about a project from the earliest conversations with Les. Additionally, he was an entrepreneurial CEO accustomed to making the final decisions, but needed to be kept on point regarding agreed-upon positions. One example occurred during salary considerations. Les personally advocated

---

[3] Les Quick returned as chairman of the Board of Trustees from 1998 to 2001.

that all salary increases be based on merit but understood that it was unrealistic for colleges. Over the years, Widener had established a combination of across-the-board adjustments supplemented by merit increases. Each of the schools developed its own criteria for awarding the merit pool; the standards were fair and difficult for many faculty to achieve. Before the Executive Committee meeting on the issue, Les and David Oskin, the vice chair of the board, had agreed that the administration's recommendations were acceptable, including the percentage that would be assigned to the merit pool (which had already been approved by faculty leadership in negotiations). But when two trustees spoke against the recommendations in committee, Les interjected "Let's go all merit!" It took another thirty minutes to pull the discussion back from the brink of what would have been a critical loss of faith with the faculty who had accepted a compromise in their position on salaries. "What happened?" asked Oskin after the meeting. My response: "That's Les; he sometimes gets caught up in the moment."

Often, however, Quick maintained a stoic face in board meetings and pressed home his point despite obvious objection. During an Executive Committee debate of the pros and cons of stretching financially to add additional space to a new 50,000 sq.ft. facility, Academic Center North, Les suggested I leave the room. As president, I was a voting member of the committee and did not hide my disgruntlement. Later, when I voiced my displeasure, he said with a twinkle in his eye: "I understand. But if you had stayed in the meeting you'd have convinced them to spend the additional several million dollars without any real discussion." It was a lesson of significance to our mutual understanding of what was acceptable as we worked together as CEO and chairman. As it happened, the funding for the additional footage was approved with his enthusiastic consent.

Les was a generous person. He felt strongly that his money should serve as a catalyst to encourage others to make donations, thus many of his contributions were donated as challenge gifts. His was the lead gift for the last major building completed during my administration, the Leslie C. Quick, Jr. School of Business. The existence of that facility is testimony to Les's strong views. It was first mentioned at a luncheon meeting in New York City after I had presented various aspects of a capital campaign then being planned. "What would a new building for the School of Business cost?" he asked. Since that was not on the priority list, no numbers existed. Off the top of my head, I said "$7 million." "I'll give you half if you match it," he said.[4]

This exchange was telling. Les Quick was interested in business and knew the need was there so he decided to become the catalyst to implement a shift in priorities. He was never abashed about expressing his opinion although most of the time as chairman he tried to stifle his individual views and allow the process to go forward.

Les was fun. As a member of his corporate board, I had the pleasure of traveling to meetings at some very special places. Once at Pebble Beach we paused during a golf game on the ninth hole for a sandwich. When a seagull plucked the sandwich from Les's hand and flew off, Les took the cart and drove down the fairway swinging a five iron at the bird. When he returned to where I was bent over laughing, his comment was, "he got away. I hope he likes tuna fish!"

Les Quick died of cancer in March, 2001 at the age of 75. He had celebrated his fiftieth class reunion six months earlier.

A Second Alumnus Steps Up

The willingness of the board under the leadership of both Dixon and Quick to allow management to be entrepreneurial, to take risks based on careful analysis, enabled Widener to define its status in the marketplace. Personally, I had achieved much of what I'd set out to do and, thus, several months before Les's untimely death had announced my plans to retire at the end of the academic year. Les had agreed to remain board chair until my successor was chosen, then intended to step aside for Board Vice Chair David Oskin '64BA, who would succeed him.

Judy and I had enjoyed an immediate rapport with David Oskin and his wife JoEllen upon first meeting them. We reconnected at the 1992 Homecoming when they came to campus to meet the freshman who had been selected as the first recipient of the Steven Ross Oskin Scholarship. Named for a son who had died at age seven from eye cancer, the scholarship was and is designated for an African-American engineering or management student who demonstrates all-around excellence in high school. Although David traveled extensively around

---

[4] If only I had known that the final cost would be close to $10 million, I would have asked for more! As a result of this conversation, we simply expanded the capital goal.

the world as executive vice president of International Paper Company, he became intrigued with the progress made by his alma mater and in 1997 accepted my invitation to join the Board of Trustees, soon becoming an active and valuable member. The rapport between us that had begun in 1992 had become a warm friendship between families that continues beyond my retirement.

At the time of Les's death, Oskin graciously stepped into the chairmanship and made a Herculean effort to manage his schedule in order to provide the leadership and continuity that was needed by the University and the Board of Trustees. My only regret is that I did not have the opportunity to serve under David's leadership for more than a brief period, although he jokingly reminds me that soon after I recruited him to succeed Les as chairman, I announced my retirement!

David Oskin is a worthy successor to two excellent board chairmen. Widener is indebted for his commitment.

New Priority: Alumni as Trustees

Over time, an increase in the percentage of alumni serving on the board became a priority. Fortunately, a significant number of military graduates had moved beyond the anguish of seeing PMC disappear, understanding the decision had been necessary if the legacy of Pennsylvania Military College were to survive. Further, they began to take pride in the achievements of their new academic home. As Widener grew in name recognition, and its reputation as a creative, innovative, entrepreneurial university widened, more alumni and outside supporters were willing to be part of the journey. Nothing breeds success like success.

I envisioned that the future of Widener would become the responsibility of a combination of successful alumni and external directors. Given that the first Widener alumni were only beginning to attain positions of substance, the University reached out to graduates, both military and civilian, of the 1960s. The addition of these alumni to the board was significant not only for their contributions but also for their visibility as graduates.

This group of alumni trustees, David W. Oskin '64BA, Nicholas P. Trainer '64BS, Russell J. Bragg '57BS, Phillip G. Lewis, MD '72BS, Thomas H. Bown II '67BS, John D. Dishaw '63BA, Joseph R. Rosetti '55BS, and Peter B. Zacharkiw '72 BS '77ME (the first Widener graduate to be appointed), became great supporters and spokesmen for Widener.

Added to the mix were the skills of graduates of the Law School, including Michael G. DeFino '75JD and graduate-school alumni such as Karol Wasylyshyn '82PsyD, and Paul S. Beiderman '79MBA.

It was a point of real pride to me when James W. Hirschmann III '82BS became a member of the board. Jim, who had been a co-captain of the 1981 national championship football team, has been extraordinarily successful in business since his graduation. He is the president and CEO of Western Asset Management, Legg Mason's global fixed income asset manager and the largest of its subsidiaries. To see a graduate of the University who was "one of mine" become a part of the leadership of the University was special.

In 2000, Gen. John H. Tilelli, Jr. '63BS (U.S. Army, Ret.) was elected to the board. His membership was in many ways the final link between the distinguished history of PMC and Widener University. He was, in fact, the highest ranking officer ever to graduate from PMC; how fitting he should lead again at his alma mater.

When I retired, I had achieved my objective to have 50 percent of the board be graduates of the University. Indeed, two of them had ascended to the position of board chairman.

The willingness of America's citizens to support charitable causes rather than to have them rely exclusively on the government is one of the unique characteristics of our nation. The tradition, which had its roots in the founding of the nation, exists nowhere else in the world. We are extremely fortunate that people with time, talent and treasure are willing to lead through service on boards of trustees.

Chapter 16

The Private Side of the Presidency

A cynic once commented that being a university president means you "live in a big house and beg for a living." While the dynamics of the job are a bit subtler than that, there is an element of truth to the statement: Fundraising is a major focus of your year and a majority of presidential positions come with the expectation that you will live in the sizeable president's house. In both these obligations, the job is not unlike being in the clergy. So, too, is the impact on the personal life of the manse's residents. While the house is your family's private domicile, it is also public space to be used in pursuit of university goals. Since residency in the house is a condition of employment with most institutions and is usually tax-exempt, on the surface it appears to be a very nice aspect of the position.

It can be, or not. Our personal experience was a good one, primarily because my wife and I went into the presidency with a shared understanding of "our job." Since a president's responsibilities are so difficult to compartmentalize, we made the decision to share the experience as much as possible, a tacit acknowledgment that coping would be much easier for both of us if we knew what the other was juggling. The decision also lent added value to the institution as, over the years, Judy became one of my most trusted advisors. Being familiar with the trustees, faculty and staff enabled her to be a valuable sounding board. She understood the issues and discussed them knowingly. Her observations, unlike those of many others, were as neutral as one could get; as they say in the South, "she didn't have a dog in the fight."

The president's home at Widener University is the Billie Kirkbride House, a three-storey stone Colonial named for the wife of former trustee Dr. Chalmer Kirkbride who donated the home in the 1950s with the stipulation it become the living quarters for the first family. Complete with a brass plaque and pillared portico at the front entrance, the house is located two miles from the Main Campus in a lovely residential neighborhood. The location offers a prized degree of separation from the campus that is unique, for most presidential homes are found in the midst of the school's grounds.

The dilemma of living on a campus is illustrated by those of my colleagues who left home on weekends rather than create friction about noise between students and Campus Security. Weekend departure was most noticeably a habit for those housed near a fraternity or dormitory complex. At one point during the expansion of the Main Campus in Chester the University purchased a lovely Georgian home on the western edge of the campus. The property, located at the end of fraternity row, became the Widener Museum of Art, and later a sorority house. At the time of purchase the chairman of the board said to Judy, "this would make a splendid president's home," to which she, remembering the tales of other presidential spouses about being in such a location responded, "I guess you will have to find another president and wife."

Judy and I were the second couple to occupy the Billie Kirkbride House. While living there, we were always conscious that the home was not ours. If the grandeur weren't enough, the allotment of an operating budget for the property, and the provision of a small staff to help run it, were reminders that the property belonged to the institution. Additionally, every major physical change had to be approved by the board and be framed in an idiom appropriate to preserve the architectural character of the property.

We added a large terrace for entertaining with access through new French doors from the Music Room, and updated and expanded the kitchen to provide both personal dining and improved catering facilities. We also identified a library on the main floor as a private retreat and redecorated the entire house, using many of my wife's antiques. When we entertained the Kirkbrides for dinner, Billie Kirkbride, a rather patrician woman with distinct ideas of what constituted appropriate décor in a home, asked Judy if she could look around. She climbed to the third floor and proceeded to spend what seemed like twenty minutes or so going through all thirteen rooms. When she returned to the table she looked at Judy and pronounced with a nod of her head, "I like what you have done with it."

The Last "Team for Hire"

Judy and I often remarked how fortunate we were that our two children, Kim and Scott, were in college when I assumed the presidency of

Widener. The demands on both Judy and me would have severely challenged us to find appropriate time to raise a family and fulfill our obligations without shortchanging the needs of either the university or the children. It could have been done, but not with the sort of graceful ease so many visitors expect in a president's home, and perhaps not with the children at the top of the priority list.

In the 1980s boards of trustees at the majority of U.S. colleges and universities were still seeking the traditional presidential couple, one that, as Judy liked to say, "came as a package, only one didn't get paid." Our generation is arguably the last in which such an expectation was considered the norm. The president's wife was expected to attend numerous on-campus events, be eagerly involved in selected activities — usually with one or another of the institution's cultural programs or with the sorority system — and entertain faculty, trustees, major donors, and student groups at home on a regular basis. There was, of course, no compensation for such labor and dedication. When the then president of our neighboring institution, Swarthmore College, advertised for an assistant to the president for social activities, Judy half seriously said to Fitz Dixon that she was going to apply and get on someone's payroll!

In reality, Dixon and the Widener trustees were very sensitive to Judy's role and appreciative of the many contributions she made to the life of the University. They did not believe she should be a salaried staff person, nor did she. Both parties felt that the nuances of turning her role into employment would be decidedly inappropriate. Instead, the board established an annuity through TIAA in recognition of her service. It was, I believe, one of the first ever for a presidential spouse.

Today, many CEO wives – like those in every area of commerce – are engaged in their own careers and do not involve themselves on a daily basis with university activities. In addition, there are an increasing number of female presidents whose husbands do not have the will or the skills to perform the tradition spousal role. Thus, younger couples usually are not disposed to be considered a team for hire and, wisely, boards of directors no longer expect it. Judy and other presidential spouses with whom she became friends used to joke that they were "the last of the dinosaurs."

Although societal traditions may have changed, it was extraordinarily helpful to me to know that my wife was responsible for management of our social schedule, and hospitality in our home. For example, if long meetings kept me in the office, I always knew that she would carry on greeting dinner guests at the front entrance. I knew she and the staff would have everything in order and presented with grace and style. On the occasions when I was delayed returning from meetings in Harrisburg or Philadelphia, Judy would entertain guests during cocktails until I arrived. On average, she managed 40 events annually at the Billie Kirkbride House ranging from formal dinners for several, or for dozens, to faculty receptions, student dinners, and alumni and fundraising events for hundreds.

To a certain extent the president lives in the metaphorical "glass house." Each member of the family is always highly visible, whether at home or in public – which are often the same thing. It is important to be very mindful that you are the public face of the university. What you do and say can reflect positively or negatively on the institution. A president's family must carefully select who will or will not be confidants.

Despite the inconveniences, Judy and I enjoyed living in the president's house. Both of our children lived there with us for short periods of time as young adults. Kim stayed the first summer and fall after graduating from St. Lawrence University because she was serving as press secretary for the Republican candidate who was challenging the popular Bob Edgar for the Seventh Congressional District. Because of the size and location of the house, she and her eager young colleagues would end the day there strategizing over beer and sandwiches. It was wonderful to see them so engaged and optimistic, although their candidate was a decided underdog and ultimately lost the campaign.[1] When Kim moved on to Boston, her brother Scott and his wife Gigi, both graduates of Colgate University, came to stay until their new townhouse was ready. Scott was then completing his masters in tax at NYU while working for a big eight accounting firm and Gigi was teaching at a private girl's school. In addition, both Kim and Scott had their wedding receptions in our garden. What a luxury to have space for our children while they were getting settled! When grandchildren came along, the large home was wonderful for holidays such as Christmas

---

[1] I met then Vice President George W. H. Bush at a meeting for college presidents in Philadelphia during Kim's foray into politics. During our conversation, I mentioned her involvement with the campaign. Later, he attended a fundraiser for her candidate where he walked straight up to me and said "hello, Bob, this must be Kim" and happily posed with her for a photograph. Talk about good staff work!

sleepovers and family Easter egg hunts. The children learned to swim in the pool, and elementary-school swim parties at "Mame and Grand-dad's" house became de rigueur for Scott and Gigi's children. When we retired and had left the house, one of the grandchildren asked at a family gathering, "Where are we going to have Christmas this year?" She made us all realize that we'd been in the Billie Kirkbride House since long before her birth.

The Disadvantages and Subtle Changes

Before assuming the presidency Judy and I were members of the community. We knew the area, the workings of the University, the staff and faculty. Our children graduated from the local schools. We were established members of a church. All of this was an advantage that allowed me to begin work immediately on the major transformations needed at the University. But once I assumed office, we were very conscious of the disadvantages: the subtle and sometimes not so subtle shift in relationships with individuals we had known for some years. To many, we were no longer Judy and Bob, but had morphed into President and Mrs. Bruce of Widener University. Friends no longer just dropped in as they once had, they waited to be invited. At social gatherings what we said and consumed became a topic of conversation.

I recall one gathering at a faculty member's home after I had become president-elect when Judy said to me at 10:30 PM, "it's time to leave." When we were in the car I said, "the party was getting good, why did we leave?" She responded, "it will be a better party now we have left." Intrigued, I later asked a good friend and faculty member about Judy's comment. "Bob," he said, "get used to it! You are now the president with a lot of power. You are their boss so they're not going to be as comfortable around you as they once were." Looking back, I can count on one hand the number of times we were thereafter invited to staff or faculty social events at someone's home.

On the other hand, close personal friendships can be difficult to form since most of the president's time is spent on the job or at activities on campus. Judy and I committed ourselves to attending and supporting all aspects of the University's activities including athletic contests, lectures, student and faculty presentations, and community gatherings. Added to the events held at our home, and family commitments, there was little time for close casual friendships. It all goes with the territory.

The ripple effect of a presidency can be surprisingly broad. Judy was once in the jury pool for a case that involved fraud by public officials, a case about which I was knowledgeable because of my position in the community. She informed one of the lawyers who ignored her but the next morning the prosecutor apologized and dismissed her. He explained that the after reviewing the potential jurors, the judge had said, "Mrs. Bruce is Bob Bruce's wife. She can't sit on this case because he knows the facts and details, and I'm sure she does as well."

As we became friendly with other presidential colleagues, we found a commonality regarding the issues we faced, but also learned that we were fortunate to be housed near two cities in which we had access to numerous social and cultural activities. Colleagues located in small towns were much more restricted and truly lived in the proverbial "fish bowl." I joined several city clubs, including the Union League in Philadelphia and two dining clubs in Wilmington, Delaware where we enjoyed dinner at least once a week. We avoided becoming involved in club activities, preferring the anonymity of dining alone or with family without many people knowing who we were. Whenever we preferred to be nearer home and dined in the village of Media, a restaurant mecca near the University, we would hear the next day what we ate and drank and the measure of our demeanor as perceived from across the room.

It is important to create personal space where you are not Mr. & Mrs. President. After several years we purchased a home in Castine, a small village on the coast of Maine that became our retreat. Since we had both graduated from Colby College and loved the coast of Maine, we had always said we would own a home there someday; as president, this was the perfect time and place to recapture the casual life we'd once loved. I recall playing football at Maine Maritime Academy in Castine during my freshman year at Colby and thinking it was a beautiful town that would be fun to live in someday. Additionally during the summers of my presidency we vacationed with Fitz and Edie Dixon in Winter Harbor, Maine, and would invariably visit Castine as it grew to feel ever more comfortable for us.

The house in Castine became Judy's "physical and spiritual home." For many years she spent much of each summer in Maine and I flew back and forth from Philadelphia. In the later years of my presidency, we used to joke that I "dragged her down the turnpike" each September!

Pickets on the Sidewalk

One of the special relationships we developed was with Arlene Toler the housekeeper at the Billie Kirkbride House. Arlene was with us for eighteen of our twenty years and was key to the successful management of the residence. She was an intelligent, tough-minded lady whose experience in single handedly raising a large family was readily adapted to firm-handed management of tradesmen and repairmen. She assisted Judy in countless ways and became close to our children and grandchildren. When introducing her to friends, I would often say that this was her house, we just lived in it.

Arlene was resourceful in many ways. During a labor strike at the University, picketers carrying signs blocked the driveway to the house. When Judy commented about the difficulty to come in driving Arlene to the bus stop at the end of the day, she laughed and said: "Don't worry, I know how to get out through the back fence into the neighbors' yard. They will never see me leave."

One lasting lesson learned from the strike was that housekeepers and others employed primarily at the president's residence should be salaried and exempt, and thus beyond membership in a union.

Picketing was uncommon at our home but those sidewalk demonstrations that occurred were memorable. On one occasion pro-life advocates picketed because I was on the Board of Directors of Crozer Medical Center, a teaching hospital that abided by the Rowe v. Wade decision and offered abortions to those who requested it. I recall having a conversation that afternoon with one of the demonstrators in which I requested his home address so I could exercise my right to picket his home. He declined to give it.

An interesting follow up to the incident was the telephone call from the local police chief advising me that the picketers' counsel had brought to his attention that the police could not disperse demonstrators, as they had done that afternoon because, while the sidewalks were owned and maintained by the residents, they were considered public property!

Parking, for the Evening or the Night

Living in a quasi-public residence is most interesting because of the many guests and personalities who pass through the property. Rarely are they difficult; the vast majority are gracious, interesting and often unique. Some stay for the night. One of our favorite stories is of economist and Nobel Laureate Theodore Schultz who stayed with us following his lecture at the University.

Prior to going to bed, Judy asked Schultz if he were a breakfast eater and what time he preferred to dine. He said yes and early. The next morning Judy arrived downstairs at 6:45 AM to find Dr. Schultz sitting at the table, dressed in tie and jacket, and probably hungry. He smiled and said, "I guess I forgot to tell you I grew up on a farm and we were up each day by 5 AM.

Parking at the president's house to attend a social occasion, especially one to which 100-plus have been invited, is always problematic. In a quiet residential neighborhood like ours, the president can only hope the neighbors are understanding, as were ours, and try to include them in as many functions as possible.

The Billie Kirkbride House was fortunate to have use of the Wallingford Presbyterian Church parking lots directly across the street from the house. By happenstance, The Rev. Dr. David Drain, pastor of the church, became a friend. I asked him to serve as the head chaplain at Widener, which he did very ably for many years. He was fond of saying I had asked him to be chaplain in order to assure the use of the church's parking lot. Though it wasn't true, and we laughed at the remark, I cannot imagine the dilemma we would have had if not for the availability of church parking. My sympathies go to those who must reside in a president's house without angelic neighbors!

Parting Thoughts

The decision of when to "exit stage left," in theater parlance, is very subjective. At the core of the decision, as Judy often said, is to "do it while people will be genuinely sorry you are leaving."

Retirement should be approached in an intellectual, unemotional and deliberate manner, just as any decision making in life. It is the natural progression from phase one (growing up, maturing and being educated) and phase two (career, marriage and children), to phase three: retirement. Psychologically, the first two life phases are looked upon as ones with unlimited expectations while phase three is too often seen as one of closure, of having to face mortality as the only future expectation! For many, life moves from an active to passive voice; losing one's work, the *raison d'etre* for many to get up each morning, is seen as a form of expiration. Having been through it, I believe retirement should be viewed as an exciting and meaningful adventure; something that requires the same level of engagement and energy as the other two.

Too often, individuals who have allowed their personalities to be defined by their work and the trappings of power are those who have the most difficult time transitioning into retirement. The prospects of unstructured days vacant of professional demands and the social interactions of the job can be daunting. To that point, one of my favorite stories relating to loss of position is told by a friend, a former four-star general, who said he knew he was retired when he got into the back seat of his car one morning and there was no driver!

In my experience, a first step is to assess where you are in both your professional and personal life. Objectively reviewing the goals you had set, both long- and short-term, allows you at the appropriate time to say, "I've done it; I have accomplished in my professional world what I had hoped to achieve."

But the personal assessment is equally significant. If you achieved professional success by consciously or subconsciously short-changing your personal relationships with spouse and family (which regretably most successful professionals do), a major consideration is where you want your priorities in the future. In my case, my wife, Judy had subjugated personal preferences for the needs of my career. After more than 40 years of supporting me it was time for me to reciprocate!

If you can answer "no" to the question: "Do I have anything more to prove to myself or to contribute to my profession?" the decision then, about whether to exit gracefully is self evident. Your legacy is intact, so let someone else build on what has been accomplished.

During my tenure I had, with the able assistance of the faculty and administrative staff, taken the University to a new level of academic quality, financial stability and public recognition. I had professionally achieved a position of leadership in higher education regionally and nationally. I could and did respond "no" to what I consider the critical self-directed question asked above, thus the decision was transparent.

So, as the world and the University celebrated the new millennium of the 21st century, Judy and I concluded it was our time for transition. The last "team for hire" was out the door.

At the time of that decision the profile of Widener in academic 2000-01 was as follows: Widener University, founded in 1821, is compromised of eight schools and colleges that offer liberal arts and sciences, professional and pre-professional curricula. A private, non profit university charted in both Pennsylvania and Delaware offers programs of study leading to associate's, bachelor's, master's and doctoral degrees.

The University's schools include the College of Arts and Sciences, School of Business Administration, School of Engineering, School of Hospitality Management, School of Human Service Professions, School of Law, School of Nursing, and University College.

The University has a 40-acre suburban campus in Wilmington, Delaware that houses the School of Law, a branch of University College and graduate offerings from the School of Business Administration. The Harrisburg campus, opened in the fall of 1989, houses a branch of the School of Law and master's level nursing courses. All other undergraduate, graduate and other academic programs are offered on the 110-acre main campus in Chester, Pa.

The transformation of Widener to a notable regional university was complete. The promise of 1981 had been fulfilled. It was time for new and different challenges.

References

···

Academy for Educational Development (AED). 1975. Meeting the challenges and opportunities for the 1980s: A report prepared for the president and trustees of Widener College. New York: AED, 1 Dec.

American Association of University Professors (AAUP). 2006. 1940 statement of principles on academic freedom and tenure in *Policy Documents and Reports.* 10th ed. Washington D.C.: AAUP.———2006. 1966 statement on government of colleges and universities in *Policy Documents and Reports.* 10th ed. Washington D.C.: AAUP.

Bennis, Warren G. 1976. *The Unconscious Conspiracy.* 4th printing. New York, AMACOM

Bruce, Robert J. 1985. Challenges and responsibilities of law school boards of visitors. Paper presented at the Midyear Meeting of the American Bar Association Section on Legal Education and Admissions to the Bar. Detroit.
———1987. A case study: Widener University's acquisition and merger of two institutions. Proceedings of the National Conference at Wingspread 19-21 June 1987. Racine, Wisc.: Johnson Foundation.

Carlson, A. J. 1938. *Bulletin of American Association of University Professors.* Winter 1938. Washington, D.C.: AAUP.

Cohen, M.D. and J.G. March, Carnegie Commission on Higher Education. 1986. *Leadership and Ambiguity: The American College President.* 2nd ed. Boston: Harvard Business School Press. (1978. New York: Harper & Row)

Cooke, Robert. 2001. *Dr. Folkman's War: Angiogenesis and the Struggle to Defeat Cancer.* New York: Random House

Coyne, Jerry A., 2003. review of *Watson & DNA,* by Victor K. McElheny. *New York Times Sunday Book Review,* 15 June.

Finucane, Bob. 1984. The man in chair one at Widener University. *The Delaware County Daily Times.* Chester, Pa., 2 Sept

Kerr, Clark. 1966. *Uses of the University.* New York: Harper & Row

Knaus, William A., M.D. 1981. *Inside Russian Medicine.* New York: Everest House

Monaghan, Peter. 1984. *Chronicle of Higher Education* XXIX:13, 24. Washington, D.C.

McElheny, Victor K. 2003. *Watson & DNA: Making a Scientific Revolution.* Cambridge, Mass.: Perseus. 8:143. Quotation first published in *The New York Times,* 26 Dec. 1980, A24

Matthews, Anne. 1997. *Bright College Years: Inside the American Campus Today.* New York: Simon and Shuster.

National Collegiate Athletic Association (NCAA). 1988. *Convention Proceedings, Jan. 10-14.* Nashville: NCAA

Porter, Oscar. 1989. *Undergraduate Completion and Persistence at Four-Year Colleges and Universities.* Washington DC: National Institute of Independent Colleges and Universities

Rehnquist, William H. 1998. *All the Laws but One: Civil Liberties in Wartime.* New York: Random House

Robert, Gen. Henry M. 1990. *Robert's Rules of Order Revised.* 75th Anniversary ed., Chicago: Scott, Foresman and Co.

n.a. *Sports Illustrated* 1978. That Fitz, he's a honey. New York: Time Warner. 8 Nov.

Watson, James D. 1980. *The Double Helix: A Personal Account of the Discovery of the Structure of DNA*. New York and London. W.W. Norton & Co. Originally published 1968. New York: Atheneum Books.

Widener University. University Council. 1987. *Widener University Faculty Handbook*. rev. 1994, '96, '99, '01, '02', '04. Chester: Widener University ———. Board of Trustees. 1992. *Bylaws of Widener University, Inc*. Amended May 10, 2001. Chester: Widener University.

Index

G

H

T